I0866671

MICHIGAN PAPYRI XX
A TRANSPORTATION ARCHIVE FROM FOURTH-CENTURY OXYRHYNCHUS

American Studies In

Papyrology

Series Editor

James G. Keenan

Number 49
P. MICH. XX

A TRANSPORTATION ARCHIVE FROM FOURTH CENTURY OXYRHYNCHUS

edited by
P.J. Sijpesteijn † & Klaas A. Worp
with the assistance of
Traianos Gagos † & Arthur Verhoogt

A TRANSPORTATION ARCHIVE FROM FOURTH-CENTURY OXYRHYNCHUS

(P. Mich. XX)

edited by

P.J. Sijpesteijn † & Klaas A. Worp

with the assistance of

Traianos Gagos † & Arthur Verhoogt

DURHAM, NORTH CAROLINA 2011

P. MICH. XX

A TRANSPORTATION ARCHIVE FROM FOURTH CENTURY OXYRHYNCHUS

edited by
P.J. Sijpesteijn † & Klaas A. Worp
with the assistance of
Traianos Gagos † & Arthur Verhoogt

The American Society of Papyrologists

Library of Congress Cataloging-in-Publication Data:

A transportation archive from fourth-century Oxyrhynchus : (P. Mich. XX) / edited by P.J. Sijpesteijn & Klaas A. Worp ; with the assistance of Traianos Gagos & Arthur Verhoogt.

p. cm. -- (American studies in papyrology ; no. 49)

Includes bibliographical references and index.

ISBN 978-0-9799758-3-7 (cloth : alk. paper)

1. Oxyrhynchus papyri. 2. Manuscripts, Greek (Papyri)--Egypt--Bahnasa. 3. Greek literature--Manuscripts. I. Sijpesteijn, P. J. II. Worp, K. A. (Klaas Anthony) III. Gagos, Traianos. IV. Verhoogt, A. M. F. W. (Arthur M. F. W.)

PA3315.O83T73 2011

487'.4--dc23

2011019686

PREFACE

The genesis of the twentieth volume of Michigan papyri is unusually long and slightly complicated.

Already over various years in the early 1990s my teacher, the late Pieter Johannes Sijpesteijn, worked during his almost annual visits to the Michigan papyrus collection on the texts presented in this volume. In the course of his work he prepared a paper "What Happened to Tax-Grain upon Arrival at Alexandria?" (*Chron.d'Eg.*, 69 [1994] 132-37) in which he offered a first glimpse into the contents of a collection of texts from fourth-century Oxyrhynchus that in course of time had become dispersed over papyrus collections in Ann Arbor (University of Michigan), Florence (Biblioteca Medicea-Laurenziana), Heidelberg (Ruprechts-Karls-Universität), Milano (Università del Sacro Cuore) and St. Louis, MO (Washington University). In his paper, he discussed in particular a technical term (κριθολογία) occurring in some texts.

The subject of tax-grain was also discussed in a paper "Skipper's Receipt for Grain Delivered" (*ZPE* 113 [1996] 169-70). In this paper, Sijpesteijn presented a first edition of a Greek papyrus from the Michigan collection that featured certain similarities with the much larger archive he was still working on, but that otherwise was not directly related to the archive.

Shortly before his sudden death (in May 1996), Sijpesteijn gave me a folder containing various transcripts (partly handwritten, partly typed up), photos and draft notes, inviting me to act as a (co-)editor of this material. I contacted my colleagues in Ann Arbor, in particular Traianos Gagos, who immediately and generously gave me permission to take over from Piet as editor of these texts. Later on, Gagos kindly confirmed this permission in writing, see his paper "The University of Michigan Papyrus Collection", in: I. Andorlini a.o. (eds.), *Atti del Congresso XXII Internazionale di Papirologia (Firenze 23-29 agosto 1998)*, vol. I (Florence 2001) 529.

In the years after Piet's death I re-read his transcripts with a group of students in the Classics Department of the University of Amsterdam. During these sessions the conclusion became obvious that, even though Piet had already done a great deal of work on these texts, many papyri in this dossier still needed a considerable amount of further critical work. And indeed, it has taken quite some time to find sufficient opportunity for accomplishing this, a task that became only more complicated through the publication in 2001 of a substantial number of Oxyrhynchus papyri that were directly related to this archive (see *P.Oxy*. LXVII 4606-4613). Finally, a personal medical problem (May 2008) and — far worse — the sudden death of Traianos Gagos (April 2010) caused only further delay.

For facilitating his own efforts, the present editor owes many thanks to a number of colleagues. In particular, I wish to thank:

—Traianos Gagos (†) and Arthur Verhoogt (Ann Arbor, MI) for a great variety of services ranging from bringing individual papyrus fragments together into much larger, far more meaningful entities, by checking various suspect readings in individual Michigan texts, to giving a number of suggestions for further raising the quality of this edition; Ms. Ulrike Lau-Lamb for doing an outstanding job in restoring with meticulous care various Michigan papyri before they were newly photographed); and Mr. Randal Stegmeyer for making available his expertise not only in photographing papyri but also in digitally combining adjacent individual fragments and in transmitting these files over the Atlantic Ocean.

— Roger S. Bagnall (NYC) for giving me permission to publish a papyrus [**802**] belonging to the collection of Columbia University.

— Nick Gonis (first Oxford, now London) for giving me his 'nihil obstat' to reprint in this volume a number of related papyri from Oxyrhynchus (for these, see Appendix A).

— Carla Balconi (Milan) for making excellent digital photos of P.Med. inv. 27 (= *SB* XIV 12099) and inv. 165 (= *SB* XIV 11615) available to me, in order that they could be joined with adjacent fragments kept in Ann Arbor (see **806** and **812**).

— Ms. (now Dr.) Jacqueline Klooster and Mr. (now Dr. Drs.) Matthias Haentjes who as young students in Amsterdam demonstrated remarkable interest and care while checking readings on Sijpesteijn's photos of the papyri.

— The series editors of the American Society of Papyrologists and the anonymous referee of this volume for detecting a number of imperfections in the typescript and for making various valuable suggestions before Camera Ready Copy could be produced.

— Mr. Evert J. Smies for his invaluable help in overcoming various pitfalls produced by computers and computer software.

This volume is dedicated to the memory of two exceptional scholars whose contributions to the noble discipline of Papyrology will always be remembered.

Leiden, April 2011 K.A. Worp

TO THE MEMORY OF

PIETER JOHANNES SIJPESTEIJN

&

TRAIANOS GAGOS

A FOURTH-CENTURY ARCHIVE FROM OXYRHYNCHUS:

TABLE OF CONTENTS

III: TEXTS 41

(Numbers preceded below by an * indicate revised [partial] republications of texts first published elsewhere)

A FOURTH-CENTURY ARCHIVE FROM OXYRHYNCHUS

§ 1: GENERAL BACKGROUND

According to Aurelius Victor (*Epitome* 1.6) an amount of approximately 6,000,000 artabas (= ca 180,000 metric tons) of grain (*frumentum*) was brought from Egypt to Rome every year during the reign of the emperor Augustus. Flavius Josephus (*Bell.Jud.* II 386) states that the amount of wheat (σῖτος, πυρός) produced by Egypt sufficed to feed the city for four months.[1] These millions of artabas were brought from all over the country to Alexandria or Pelusium to be stored in the local granaries[2] from where the wheat was transported to the

---

[1]) Countless studies have been written about the corn supply of Rome. The reader is referred to the following three studies which are very relevant for the subject and offer a wealth of further literature: E. Tengström, *Food for the People. Studies of the Corn-Supply of Rome during the Late Empire*, Stockholm 1974; G. Rickmann, *The Corn Supply of Ancient Rome*, Oxford 1980; P.Herz, *Studien zur römischen Wirtschaftsgesetzgebung. Die Lebensmittelversorgung*, Stuttgart 1988 (= Historia Einzelschriften, 55). See also below, fn. 4.

[2]) In the texts published in this archive the Greek technical term mostly used is θησαυρός; for this, cf. G. Husson, *OIKIA. Le vocabulaire de la maison privée en Egypte d'après les papyrus grecs* (Paris 1983), 91-3. In **811**.22 and in **820**.3 the transliterated Latin term ὅρριον is used (cf. S. Daris, *Il lessico latino nel greco d'Egitto* [Barcelona 1991 ²] 79; cf. also H. Cadell in *Akten XIII. Papyrologenkongress* [München 1974], 63). These θησαυροί are mostly styled δημόσιοι (= 'public'), less often θεῖοι (= 'imperial'). On these granaries in general, see A. Calderini, *ΘΗΣΑΥΡΟΙ. Ricerche di topografia e di storia della*

imperial capital Rome. Later, when Constantinople became capital of the Eastern part of the *Imperium Romanum* (330ᴾ), Egyptian wheat was transported to that city; the amount had now grown to ca. 8,000,000 artabas (= ca. 240,000 metric tons) every year.[3]

The collection and transport of the tax grain[4] consisted of

pubblica amministrazione nell'Egitto greco-romano, Milano 1924 (= Stud.Scuol.Pap., IV.3).

In Alexandria, granaries are found in the district of Neapolis (cf. A. Calderini - S. Daris, *Dizionario Geografico* III 323; *Supplemento* I 202, II 130, III 79) and in the Hermaion-district (cf. *Dizionario Geografico* I 112; *Supplemento* I 21), but there were also granaries in Alexandria's neighborhood, e.g. in Chaireou (cf. *Dizionario Geografico*, V 106; *Supplemento* I 249, II 236, III 161, IV 141).

[3]) For general background information, cf. A.J.B. Sirks, *Food for Rome. The Legal Structure of the Transportation and Processing of Supplies for the Imperial Distributions in Rome and Constantinople*, Amsterdam 1992 (= Stud.Amst. 31).

For the amount of 8,000,000 artabas = ca. 240,000 metric tonnes *per annum* (mentioned in Justinian's famous 13th edict [539ᴾ], chapt. 8), cf. B. Palme, "The imperial presence: Government and army", in: R.S. Bagnall, *Egypt in the Byzantine World, 300-700* (Cambridge 2007), Chapt. XII, p. 244 fn. 2. For the equivalence of 1 artaba = ca. 30 kg, see R.S. Bagnall, *Egypt in Late Antiquity*, (Princeton 1993), 332.

[4]) The best surveys of the collection and transportation of tax grain are still M. Rostowzew, 'Kornerhebung und Korntransport im griechisch-römischen Ägypten', *Archiv* 3 (1906) 201-224; E. Börner, *Der staatliche Korntransport im griechisch-römischen Ägypten*, Diss. Hamburg 1939; N. Hohlwein, 'Le blé d'Égypte', *EtPap* 4 (1938) 33-120; J. Schwartz, 'Le Nil et le ravitaillement de Rome', *BIFAO* 47 (1948) 179-200; *O.Oslo* 17-21. In *P.Petaus* 53.4-18 (184-85ᴾ) the obligations of liturgists serving for the collection and transportation of tax grain are given as follows: 'εἰς τὸ παραφυλάξαι τὰ ἀπὸ τῶν ἀγρῶν ἀναφερόμενα γενήματα καὶ ἐπαναγκάζειν εἰς τὰς ἅλω παραφέρεσθαι καὶ ἐπιτηρ[ε]ῖν αὐτὰ ἐπὶ τῶν ἀλώνων ὄντα ἕως ἂν τὰ ὀφιλόμενα τῷ ταμείῳ μετρηθῇ, καὶ πρόνοιαν ποιεῖσθαι τοῦ κρι[θ]ο[λ]ογηθῆναι τὸν πυρὸν καὶ ἐπὶ τῆς λικ[μ]ήσεως καὶ τῆς ἰσπράξεως τοῦ πυροῦ, καὶ ἐπισφραφίζειν τοὺς θησαυροὺς καὶ ἐπίγειν τὰς ἐμβολὰς

two steps, i.e. firstly from the fields to the threshing floors in the countryside and from there to the nearest granaries situated at a navigable waterway,[5] and secondly from these granaries to Alexandria and Pelusium respectively, to be transported from there (mainly) overseas.

Most of the texts presented here concern the second phase of this process (cf. fn. 5), i.e. from the moment the tax grain was loaded into boats for transportation (naturally by waterways and the Nile) to Alexandria / Pelusium until the moment the *Praefectus annonae Alexandriae* notified the responsible officials by letter that they had fulfilled their duties correctly.[6] The officials in this archive oversaw the trans-

καὶ ἐπακολ[ο]υθεῖν τῇ καταγωγῇ --- ἐπὶ τῷ αὐτοὺς καὶ τῆς ἰρήνης πρόνοιαν ποιεῖσθαι ---' = "für die Aufgabe, das Einbringen des Korns von den Feldern zu überwachen, seinen Transport zu den Tennen zu veranlassen, es auf den Tennen zu überwachen bis die dem Fiskus zukommenden Anteile abgemessen sind, dafür zu sorgen, daß der Weizen von der Gerste gereinigt wird, für die Worfelung und das Eintreiben des Getreides verantwortlich zu sein die Speicherräume zu versiegeln, die Verladung zu betreiben und den Transport zu begleiten -- mit der Aufgabe, daß sie auch für Ruhe und Ordnung sorgen---". Several heavily mutilated texts regarding the transport of grain from the *chora* to Alexandria and from there to Rome have been published as *SB* VI 9087-9098 and XII 11082. Very interesting is of course the inscription on a vase containing a grain sample (δεῖγμα), see *SB* VI 9233.

[5]) To the 'land'- phase of the collection and transportation of tax grain belong **803** (see the introduction to this text), **807** and **819**, all three declarations to perform the κριθολογία (cf. also *P.Petaus* 53 cited in the previous footnote), i.e. to clean the wheat from barley and, by extension, from all kinds of dirt. For this activity, cf. P.J. Sijpesteijn in *CdE* 69 (1994) 132-37; Ph. Mayerson in *BASP* 41 (2004) 127-37, in particular 133-35.

[6]) For the Ptolemaic period, cf. *P.Erasm.* II. Several more texts from this period

portation of tax grain from Oxyrhynchus and the nome territory around it towards Alexandria / Pelusium. The officials who are mainly involved in this transport were the town councillors of Oxyrhynchus (cf. hereafter, § 2);[7] they bear the title ἐπιμεληταὶ σίτου / κριθῶν Ἀλεξανδρείας / Πηλουσίου (*curatores frumenti Alexandriae / Pelusii*) and work under the supervision of the highest official of the nome, the *strategus / exactor* (στρατηγός / ἐξάκτωρ).[8]

have been published subsequently, e.g. *P.Heid.* VI 369-370. For the Roman and Byzantine periods in general, cf. A.J.M. Meyer-Termeer, *Die Haftung der Schiffer im griechisch-römischen Recht*, Zutphen 1978 (= Stud.Amst., 13). See in particular her list of ναυλωτικαὶ συγγραφαί, pp. 90-103, where P.Mich. inv. 422 (listed on p. 98) = **815**, P.Cair.inv. 10544 (listed on p. 98) = *SB* XIV 11551, resp. P.Cair.inv. 10517 (listed on p. 100) = *SB* XIV 11550; for *P.Wisc.* II 65 (also listed on p. 100), cf. below, *Appendix B*, text # 7. Apparently, since 1978 no more 4th-century ναυλωτικαὶ συγγραφαί have been published (a search in the HGV for 'Inhalt = Schiffer' did not produce any significant result); cf. also the remarks on this subject in *P.Köln* X 416 introd.; simple 4th-century skipper's receipts are found in, e.g., *P.Oxy.* XLVIII 3395 and LXII 4346 (Oxy., 371^p, resp. 380^p; issued to private persons for 35, respectively 148 art.); *CPR* VIII 34 and 35 (both Hermop. IV^p; idem for 98 and 54 1/3rd art.); *P.NYU* II 48 (prov.unknown, IV^p; idem for 8 art.). *P.Neph.* 47 (Prov. unknown, IV^p; for 40 art.). A 5th-century ναυλωτικὴ συγγραφή is found in *SB* XVIII 13948 (Memphites, 407^p).

[7]) The town councillors (βουλευταί) were responsible for the collection of the taxes not only in the metropolis but also for the whole nome. Cf. A.K. Bowman, *The Town councils of Roman Egypt* (Toronto 1971) Chapt. IV: "The business of the boule".

[8]) For the role of the strategus in government grain collection, see N. Hohlwein, *Le stratège du nome* (Bruxelles 1969; = Pap.Brux. 9) 124ff.; for him as a liaison-officer between higher officials and the local town council (βουλή), cf. A.K. Bowman, *op.cit.* [fn. 7], 79-81. For relevant documentation, cf. (e.g.), *P.Oxy.* LIX 3975 (165/6^p) and 3980 (300-302^p). **802** and **805** (= *P.Wash.Univ.* II 82;

When an amount of grain was ready for transport downstream, the councillors of Oxyrhynchus tried to find a ship which still had capacity for the cargo and a boatman who was willing to undertake its transport. The boatman (κυβερνήτης) himself had to find a surety[9] for the undertaking[10] and he

367^{p}) contain, like *P.Oxy*. LXVII 4606 and 4608-4613 (see *Appendix A*), an undertaking of transportation addressed by the town councillors / *curatores frumenti* to the strategus of the Oxyrhynchite nome; in all these cases, the strategus was mentioned by name.

P.Turner 45 = **816** (374^{p}) is a letter of the *Praefectus annonae Alexandriae* to the *exactor* of the Oxyrhynchite nome to notify him that two shipments of wheat from his nome were brought to Alexandria and were duly entered in the records there. The much similar texts *P.Oxy*. XXIV 2408 (379^{p}), *SB* XVI 12580 = *ChLA* XII 519 (prov. unknown, late IV) and *SB* XXVI 16261 (Herakleop., 432^{p}), were also addressed to an *exactor*, while in *P.Ryl.* IV 652 = *SB* XXVI 16262 (Hermop., bef. 374^{p}?), the addressee is lost but has been restored as an *exactor*. In these letters of the *Praefectus annonae Alexandriae* the individual names of the *exactores* were not given, cf. the editor's note to *P.Turner* 45.2.

In *SB* XVIII 13948.9-10 (407^{p}; Memphite nome) and *SB* XIV 11548 (343^{p}; Hermopolite nome) a boatman, respectively a surety, promise that the receipts (ἄποχα γράμματα) issued in Alexandria / Pelusium for the grain will be handed over to the office of the strategus (στρατηγικὴ τάξις), although the declarations are directed to a στατιωνάριος, respectively a *curator frumenti* (ἐπιμελητὴς σίτου). In **806** (see the introduction to this text) two assistants of the exactor's office (βοηθοὶ ἐξακτορίας) promise something to the town councillors of Oxyrhynchus who function as ἐπιμεληταὶ κριθῶν (*curatores hordei*).

Though these texts do not directly illustrate the meaning of the expression στρατηγὸς ἤτοι ἐξάκτωρ found in a number of fourth century texts (see for these P.J. Sijpesteijn in *ZPE* 90 [1992] 241-50, esp. 243 + fn. 23, and 249, and J.D. Thomas in *CdE* 70 [1995] 230-39) it may be assumed that they represent two sides of the same coin. In other words, the highest levels of government in Alexandria used the term *exactor* in correspondence with a lower nome level, whereas at the nome level itself the traditional term *strategus* was used.

[9]) The fact that the surety is often either the owner of the boat with which the

concluded with the councillors a contract which can be analyzed into the following elements:[11]

1. Date by (post-)consulate, month and day.

2. Addressees: several town councillors (βουλευταί) of Oxyrhynchus who are also *epimeletae* of wheat or barley (ἐπιμεληταὶ σίτου / κριθῶν), i.e. collectors of tax grain which has to be transported to Alexandria / Pelusium.

boatman transports the tax-grain or a member of the curial class proves that it was not always easy to find a surety (cf. *P.Vindob.Sijp*., p. 17-8). With the exception of **809** - **810** (two copies of the same transaction) where two sureties appear (one represented by his son), the other cases (cf. **800**.7, **804**.14, **808**.5, **811**.6, **813**.6, **814**.5 and **815**.4) show only one surety at work. For the number of sureties who could be involved, see *P.Münch.* III 99 introd.

[10]) None of the bills of loading published in this archive mentions a remuneration (ναῦλον) of the boatman. Neither are other small payments like the σακκοφορικόν, κούμουλα etc. (cf. A.J.M. Meyer-Termeer, *op.cit.* [fn. 6], 12-15) mentioned.

[11]) A completely different form of contract is found in *P.Oxy*. XLVIII 3395 (27.vii.371[p]; cf. *P.Oxy*. XLIX 3481 [10.ix.442[p]]), a boatman's receipt for 35 artabas of wheat plus associated charges issued by a κυβερνήτης to Papnouthis and Dorotheus (cf. *P.Oxy*. XLVIII 3384 -3429, XLIX 3480). The editor assumes that the grain was received as taxes from them while acting in an official capacity and was passed on for shipment downstream, since tax receipts for individual tax payments should be issued by tax collectors rather than by boatmen. *P.Oxy*. XLVIII 3393 (8.vi.365[p]) shows Papnouthis and Dorotheos employed by the *politeuomenos* Eulogios for assisting in the collection of taxes from Terythis, a village in the 4th pagus of the Oxyrhynchite nome; according to the editor, this Eulogios was perhaps a *praepositus pagi*. One cannot exclude the possibility that around 365[p] Papnouthis and Dorotheos both served either 'Eulogios son of Eulogios' or 'Eulogios son of Ptolemaios' who were both not only town councillors (cf. below, § 2, ## 11, 12) but also ἐπιμεληταὶ σίτου Ἀλεξ-ανδρείας (*curatores frumenti Alexandriae*). In *P.Oxy*. XLVIII 3395 they may have acted as assistants of the same Eulogios or another person in his capacity of ἐπιμελητὴς σίτου (it is true, however, that in the documents the term πολιτευόμενος is never linked to the term ἐπιμελητής, cf. K.A. Worp in *ZPE* 115 [1997] 217).

3. Author: a boatman (κυβερνήτης) of a privately or state owned ship, together with his surety (ἐγγυητής).
4. Declaration of both the boatman and the surety that they have sworn an oath:

a. the boatman declaring (a) that he has received and loaded into his ship a certain number of artabas of wheat / barley in perfect condition, (b) that he will transport this cargo to Alexandria / Pelusium and deliver the wheat / barley into the granaries and that he will bring back the receipts in the name of the town councillors / *epimeletae* of wheat / barley;

b. the surety declaring that the boatman will perform all things he has sworn to do, or else that he himself (= the surety) will fulfill all obligations of the boatman.

5. Subscription of the surety (written by himself).
6. Subscription of the boatman (sometimes written by another party, because the boatman himself was illiterate).
7. Subscription by a public notary.[12]

In **809** and **813**[13] a second column of text is preserved in

---

[12]) Signatures are preserved in **808 - 810**, **813 - 814**. Such undertakings are represented in this archive by **803** (cf. the introduction), **805**, **808 - 810**, **813 - 815**.

[13]) Texts **809 - 810** concern the same cargo of 1,015 artabas of wheat. Parts of both texts, i.e. P.Mich. inv. 4027.A and 4027.B arrived in the papyrus collection of the University of Michigan in a rolled-up state and were unrolled only in October 1992. In the third and fourth centuries a κυβερνήτης gave a receipt for the loading of the grain with Alexandria as its destination not only to the authorities immediately responsible for this, but also two copies of the same receipt to the strategus (cf. A.J.M. Meyer-Termeer, *op.cit.* [fn.6], 6 and n. 63). It may be assumed that **809** and **810** were the two copies sent to the strategus. All

which the place(s) and / or the persons from which / whom the tax grain was collected are listed.[14] The councillors / *epimeletae* of wheat / barley informed the *strategus* / *exactor* in at least two ways about the total amount of wheat / barley collected, viz.:

(a) they informed him how large the total amount of wheat or barley collected and shipped by them was (cf. **805**, introd.) and

(b) they sent them lists of the ships in which they had loaded the tax grain downstream and gave the number of artabas transported by each ship (cf. **820**, introd.).

We think that **804** shows what happened when a boatman did not completely fulfill his obligations. Aurelius Silvanus son of Paul had been a surety for Horos and had

copies were signed by the boatman and his surety in their own handwriting. The state in which these two texts reached the Michigan collection does not necessarily prove that they were never unrolled and read in antiquity (that would illustrate the interest in this kind of transactions shown by the strategus or his office!); it proves that the two copies intended for the strategus stayed (at least in this case) together.

Likewise, **813** and **814**, written by different hands on Epeiph 16 = 10.vii, seem to concern the *same* cargo of [-]11 artabas of barley. If this assumption is correct, we are dealing again with two copies of a series of identical declarations which obviously were not all written by the same scribe.

[14]) Several fragments collected under P.Mich. inv. 4028 contain remnants of such second columns; cf. **817**, **821** - **826**. The first editor of *SB* XVIII 13948 did not recognize this phenomenon when he was working on his text (it also features a second column). He wrote in the *ed.princ*. (*ZPE* 62 [1986] 141) that 'it is hardly likely that here (i.e. in this second column) the persons are listed from whom the boatman took grain aboard.' In fact, however, this is exactly what *is* listed in the second column. For a similar listing of grain collected in a cargo contract, cf. (e.g.) *SB* XIV 11551.11ff.

guaranteed that Horos would transport 873 art. of wheat to Alexandria. Since Horos delivered only 300 artabas, Silvanus now declares (with Aurelius Achilleus son of Eulogios as his surety) that *he* himself will transport the remaining 573 art. to Alexandria and will perform all the obligations that Horus should have performed.

§ 2: *BOULEUTAI* AND *POLITEUOMENOI*

In the texts of this archive which cover a period of 20 years (354^{p} [**800**] - 374^{p} [**816**]), several town councillors (βουλευταί) of Oxyrhynchus are mentioned. Some of these are listed already in the Appendix of Oxyrhynchite town councillors by A.K. Bowman, *The Town Councils of Roman Egypt* (Toronto 1971) 131-47, but a substantial number of new names appears here for the first time. For the period 350 - 375^{p}, Bowman listed only 14 individual councillors of Oxyrhynchus, of which 13 were culled from *P.Oxy*. XVII 2110 (in this text, however, not all councillors participated in the discussions of the town council). Even in view of the new, additional material it remains, of course, a fact that to date only a small fraction of all members of the town council of Oxyrhynchus is known.

1	Aur. Agathinos s. Didymos	**803**.3, **807**.4, **808**.2, **809**.2, **810**.2, **811**.1
2	Aur. Ammonios s. Apion	**802**.5; *Appendix A*, *P.Oxy*. LXVII 4608.3, 4612.5, 4613.4n. (cf.

		below, # 30)
3	Aur. Apoll[	**800**.4
4	Aur. Asklep[i-	**804**.2
5	Aur. Bernicianus[15]	**800**.7-8 (ἔναρχος πρύτανις)
6	Aur. Di[	**818**.3
7	Aur. Diogenes s. Diogenes	**800**.3
8	Aur. Dionysios	**805**.4
9	Aur. Dioskoros s. Eulogios[16]	**807**.3, **808**.2, **809**.2, **810**.2, **811**.2
10	Aur. Dioskourides alias Julianus s. Julianus alias Dioskourides	*Appendix A, P.Oxy.* LXVII 4606.3
11	Aur. Dorotheos s. Arsinoos	*Appendix A, P.Oxy.* LXVII 4608.4, 4609.4
12	Aur. Dorotheos s. Thonios s. Pasion	**800**.4
13	Aur. Eulogios s. Eulogios	**800**.3
14	Aur. Eulogios s. Ptolemaios[17]	**806**.4
15	Aur. Gennadius s. Julianus	**802**.4 (ἀπὸ λογισ-

---

[15]) An Aurelius Berenicianus ἄρξας βουλευτής occurs in *P.Oxy*. XVIII 2187.8,18,30,31 (304^{p}), a strategus Aurelius Bernicianus in *SB* XVI 12543 (327^{p}; for the name cf. *BL* 9.286); were these people perhaps the grandfather or father of the president of the town council Aurelius Bernicianus mentioned in this archive? As regards the name Βερ(ε)ν(ε)ικιανός itself, it seems most likely that this derives from the Latin name Veronicianus (cf. already *PLRE* II 225 s.n. Beronicianus).

[16]) Cf. *P.Köln* III 139.1 (387^{p}).

[17]) The same person occurs as a gymnasiarch in *P.Oxy*. XVII 2110.35 (370^{p}), cf. P.J. Sijpesteijn, *Nouvelle Liste des gymnasiarques des métropoles de l'Egypte romaine* (Zutphen 1986), # 625. See also the discussion of the date of *P.Michael*. 33 by R.S. Bagnall in *CdE* 66 (1991) 284-287.

		τῶν); *Appendix A, P.Oxy.* LXVII 4610.4 (ἀπὸ λογιστῶν), 4613.3
16	Aur. Hesychios s. Julianus	**805**.3, **813**.2, **814**.2, **816**.5-6
17	Aur. Hierax s. Serenus	**807**.5, **808**.2, **809**.2, **810**.2, **811**.2, **813**.3; cf. *Appendix A, P.Oxy.* LXVII 4610.5 (restored, w/o patronymic)?
18	Aur. Horion s. Ptolemaios[18]	**813**.2, **814**.2, **816**.5
19	Aur. Jeremias s. Achillion	**803**.3 (cf. below, # 30)
20	Aur. Ju[lianus?	*Appendix A, P.Oxy.* LXVII 4606.3 (cf also below p. 17, # 5)
21	Aur. Petros s. Agathinos	**803**.3, **807**.3, **808**.2, **809**.2, **810**.2, **811**.2; cf. *Appendix A, P.Oxy.* LXVII 4608, 4609
22	Aur. Sa[	**818**.5
23	Aur. Sarapion s. Herm[	*P.Oxy.* LXVII 4607.2
24	Aur. Sarapion, s. Ploutarchos	**801**.2, **802**.5, **803**.4, **804**.3, **806**.4, **807**.4,

---

18) A Ptolemaios son of Horion occurs in *P.Oxy.* I 67.3,13 (338^{p}). In the present archive one might be dealing with the son of that man.

		808.2, **809**.2, **810**.2, **811**.2, **813**.2, **814**.2, **815**.2, **816**.24; cf. *Appendix A*, *P.Oxy.* LXVII 4606.4, 4608.4, 4609.3-4, 4612.5, 4613.4
25	Aur. Serenus (?) s. Eusebios	**802**.4 (cf. below, # 28)
26	Aur. Theon s. [Ammon]ios	**806**.4[19] (cf. below, # 29)
27	Aur. Timagenes s. Serenus	**802**.4; **807**.5, **809**.3, **810**.3, **811**.3; cf. *Appendix A*, *P.Oxy.* LXVII 4612.4n., 4613.4
28	Aur. N.N. s. Eusebios	**815**.1 (cf. above, # 25)
29	Aur. N.N. s. of]nios	**805**.3 (cf. above, # 26)
30	Aur. N.N. s. of]on	**803**.4 (cf. above, ## 2, 19)
31	Aur. N.N.	**818**.5

In addition, the following Oxyrhynchite πολιτευόμενοι are mentioned, predominantly as ship owners:

1	(Aur.) A]etius[20]	**820**.15

----

[19]) A Theon son of Ammonios occurs as a town councillor in *P.Oxy.* XVII 2110.i.3 (370^{p})

[20]) Cf. the introduction to *P.Wash.Univ.* II 83; cf. also *P.Oxy.* I 67 (= *M.Chr.*

2	Aur. Diogenes s. Diogenes	**808**.5-6, 13, 17; cf. the same (?) man in **815**.3,4, 15 (styled ex-*logistes*[21] in l. 4) and the town councillor of this same name in **800**.3 (= # 7 in the preceding list)
3	(Aur.) Eulogios s. Ploution	**811**.7
4	Aur. Gerontios s. Posidonios	**809**.18-19 (cf. ll. 5-6), **810**.20 (cf. l. 6)
5	(Aur.) Julianus[22]	**820**.14
6	(Aur.) Ptoleminos s. Eulogios[23]	**813**.6,7,19, **814**.4,6,16, **820**.11,17 (in both ll. w/o a patronymic)
7	(Aur.) Theogonios	**803**.6
8	(Aur.) N.N. son of (?) Athanasios	**820**.13

56).2, 8, 17 (338p), where an Aurelius Aetius ἄρξας προπολιτευόμενος occurs.

[21]) For the office of *logistes* (*curator civitatis*) in Egypt, cf. the documentation provided by P.J. Sijpesteijn - K.A. Worp, "Three London Papyri", in: M. Capasso, G. Messeri Savorelli, R. Pintaudi, *Miscellanea Papyrologica* (Florence 1990; = Pap.Flor. 19) II 507-520, in particular 518-520. Apparently, a (former) *logistes* of Oxyrhynchus named Aur. Diogenes is not yet known.

[22]) There is a ship owner Julianus mentioned in *P.Oxy.* XLII 3078.3.

[23]) Is this the same person as the ship owner 'Ptoleminos *exactor*' mentioned in *App. B, P.Heid.* IV 313.12?

§ 3: *EPIMELETAI*

For the *epimeletai* in general, cf. N. Lewis, *The Compulsory Public Services of Roman Egypt* (Florence 1997²), 25-6. Four texts (**803** and **807**, and *P.Oxy.* LXVII 4609 and 4612 [cf. below *App. A*, ## 3, 6]) mention *epimeletai* of wheat (ἐπιμελητὴς σίτου; *curator frumenti*),[24] seven texts (**806**, **808**, **813**, **814**, and *P.Oxy.* LXVII 4608, 4610 and 4613 [cf. *App. A*, ## 2, 4, 7]) mention *epimeletai* of barley (Gk. ἐπιμελητὴς κριθῆς) of Alexandria or Pelusium. In **802**, **805**, **809** - **810** and **815** the title '*epimeletai* of wheat of Alexandria' has been partly supplemented, because elsewhere in these texts the term 'wheat' ('σῖτος' or 'πυρός') is mentioned.[25] In **800**.4 σίτου (wheat) rather than κριθῶν (barley) is restored on the basis of the masculine participle καθεστηκότος in l. 12.

Outside this archive, the *epimeletai* of wheat (sometimes specified by the toponym Ἀλεξανδρείας *vel sim.*) are also mentioned in *P.Charite* 21.1 (-), *P.Flor.* I 75.4 (Ἀλεξ.), *P.Lond.* V

----

[24]) For the meaning of the additional element Ἀλεξανδρείας, see H. Cadell in *Atti XVII Congresso Internazionale di Papirologia*, III (Naples 1984) 1218 n. 15.

[25]) Cf. H. Cadell, 'Papyrologica: à propos de πυρός et de σῖτος', *CdE* 48 (1973) 329-38, who observes a 'disparition prèsque complète du mot πυρός après 340, et, parallelement, diffusion rapide de σῖτος au sens restreint de 'blé' dès le début du IVe siècle'. To be sure, the texts stored in the *DDBDP* feature a number of post-340 attestations of πυρός. Within this context it should be noted that in the titulature of the officials in this archive use is made of σίτου, while πυρός and σῖτος are still used indiscriminately in the body of some texts (cf. *App. A, P.Oxy.* LXVII 4606 [361ᵖ].8n.; **803**.10 [366ᵖ], **809**.9, **810**.9 [both 372ᵖ]); cf. also R.S. Bagnall in *P.Col.* VII 145 introd.

1823.1 (-), *W.Chr.* 434 = *P.Münch.* III 99.2 (Ἀλεξ.), *P.NYU* I 11a. 202f. (ἀποστελλομένου ἐν Ἀλεξανδρείᾳ), *P.Stras.* VII 654.4 (-), *SB* XII 11023.5 (λαμπροτάτης Ἀλεξ.), XIV 11548.3f. (-), 12154.1f. (Ἀλεξ.?), and 12217.1f. (καταφερομένου ἐπὶ τὴν λαμπροτάτην Ἀλεξάνδρειαν).[26]

The *epimeletai* of barley (κριθῆς / κριθῶν)[27] are mentioned outside this archive also in *P.Charite* 15.24, *P.NYU* I 5.58f., 64f. (both add ἀρτοποιίας = "for baking"), *P.Oxy.* XLIII 3115^{v}.1, LX 4072.5 ([ἀποστελλομένης] ἐν Ἀλεξανδρείᾳ), *P.Panop.Beatty* 1.392, *P.Sakaon* 15.2,31, *SB* XII 11133.4-5, and *M.Chr.* 95.9; cf. also *P.Cair.Isid.* 9.281.

Finally, *P.Oxy.* XXXVI 2766.5 mentions an ἐπιμελητὴς σιτοκρίθου ἀνακομιζομένου ἐπὶ τὴν Μικρὰν Ὄασιν ("*epimeletes* of wheat and barley to be sent to the Oasis Parva").

All of these *epimeletai* occur in documents dating from the reign of the emperor Diocletian onwards and they come from the Oxyrhynchite, Hermopolite, Arsinoite and Panopolite nomes.

In **808**.3 one finds *epimeletai* of barley of Pelusium (ἐπιμεληταὶ κριθῶν Πηλουσίου), in *App. A, P.Oxy.* LXVII 4606.5 *epimeletai* of wheat of Pelusium (ἐπιμεληταὶ σίτου Πηλουσίου).

----

[26]) In *PUG* II 69.1 the editor supplements ἐπιμελητοῦ σ[ίτου Ἀλεξ-ανδρείας ?], cf. also l. 9. This text has a curious character, cf. *P.Wash.Univ.* II 82, p. 101, fn. 10.

[27]) In the titulature of the ἐπιμεληταί there is always singular σίτου versus either κριθῆς (sg.) or κριθῶν (pl.). We do not have an explanation to offer for this.

Pelusium[28] was the point of entry and exit from Egypt via Palestine and Syria. The fact that the grain from the Oxyrhynchite nome was transported to granaries in Pelusium highlights the fact that this grain was intended primarily for Constantinople (as could be expected at this time) and was transported by ship from Pelusium to the capital of the Eastern Roman Empire.

The main obligation of these *epimeletai* was to look after the collection and transport of commodities for which they were *epimeletai* from their place of office to Alexandria[29] and Pelusium. N. Lewis (*op.cit.* [p. 24], 27) states that they belonged to the bouleutic class, though the first editor of *P.Turner* 45 (now = **816**) apparently had some doubts about this assumption (cf. his note to l. 6). In our texts the *epimeletai* were in most cases *disertis verbis* styled '*bouleutai* of the illustrious town of Oxyrhynchus' (βουλευταὶ τῆς (λαμπρᾶς καὶ λαμπροτάτης) Ὀξυρυγχιτῶν πόλεως). We assume, therefore, that even when the *epimeletai* are not styled *bouleutai*, they nevertheless held this office and were chosen by the town council from among its members.

The following listing shows how many *bouleutai* / *epimeletai* are mentioned within each text:

---

[28]) This toponym is mentioned also in **812**.2 and **820**.3 (in both texts the context is unclear). In general, cf. A. Calderini- S. Daris, *Dizionario Geografico* IV 120; *Supplemento* I 227, III 125; *P.Oxy*. LXVII, p. 191; S. Timm, *Das christlich-Koptische Ägypten*, II (1984) 926, s.n. al-Farama.

[29]) Cf. **811**.21, where the destination of the grain is εἰς Νεάπολιν τῆς λαμπροτάτης Ἀλεξανδρείας.

6 persons	**807, 809 - 811**
5 persons	**802, 803, 808;** *App. A, P.Oxy.* LXVII 4608, 4609, 4613
more than 4 persons	**800;** *App. A, P.Oxy.* LXVII 4610, 4612
4 persons	**813, 814**
more than 3 persons	**805, 815;** *App. A, P.Oxy.* LXVII 4606
3 persons + colleagues	**806**
more than 2 persons	**804**
2 persons + colleagues	**816**
unknown	*App. A, P.Oxy.* LXVII 4611

No text features more than six *epimeletai* and this may have been the maximum number of *epimeletai* responsible for the handling of the tax grain. Apparently, the documents were not always directed to the complete commission of *bouleutai* / *epimeletai*, i.e. not all responsible *epimeletai* were mentioned by name; cf. **808** (3.ix.372[p]), featuring 5 men, versus **809** (6.xi.372[p], i.e. only three days later) featuring 6 men. It is, therefore, impossible to tell how many colleagues (κοινωνοί) are involved in **806** and **816**; here, only three and two persons respectively are mentioned by name, while the other members of the board of *epimeletai* are summarized under the term 'colleagues'.

From **806**.5 it appears that the *epimeletai* served in principle for a period of one indiction year; this is in conformity with the practice in other texts like *W.Chr.* 433.4-5 and 434.2-3.

§ 4: *POLYKOPITAI* AND *KYBEPNETAI*

A *polykopites* (πωλυκωπίτης) is a 'sailor who serves on a πολύκωπον (πλοῖον)', i. e. on a rather small Nile ship equipped with at least two sets of oars[30] attested in a substantial number of texts from the 3rd - 6th century A.D.[31] Next to the two sailors Paymis and Paabeus in **816** (cf. ll. 16 and 26), the term *polykopites* in **809**.17,19-20, **810**.18, 21, *P.Cair.Masp.* I 67058.vii.11, II 67136.16, 23, III 67287.i.16; *P.Lond.* V 1712.6,27; *P.Vindob.Bosw.* 13.i.6,12; *SB* XII 10926.5, and XIV 11593.30, and in C. Zuckerman, *Registre fiscal*, l. 655.

In **809**.4,13 and **810**.4,14 Jacob son of Jason is styled *kybernetes* (κυβερνήτης), i.e. a boatman on a ship with a number of oars (πλοίου πολυκώπου); he and his ship return in **811**.10, but the principal person in that papyrus is a certain Aur. Horion son of Heraklas who acts as a *katastates* (καταστάτης), i.e. in a function or office that is not yet fully understood. Other *kybernetai* referred to in this archive occur in **800**.6 (Aur. Apphous son of Tithoes), **802**.13 (Germanus), **803**.6 (Aur. Olympios son of Pinouthios), **804**.20 (Aur. Silvanus son of Paulos who had

---

[30]) Cf. *SB* XII 12010.6: twenty sailors serve on five *polykopa*, hence there were four sailors for each πολύκωπον.

[31]) Cf. E. Wipszycka in *CdE* 35 (1960) 219; L. Casson, *Ships and Seamanship in the Ancient World* (Princeton 1971 [repr. Baltimore 1995]) 334; for the ship type see also the literature cited in *P.Turner* 45 [= **816**].6n. In general, for transport on the Nile from the Ramesside to the Graeco-Roman periods, see S. Vinson, *The Nile Boatmen at work* (Mainz 1998; = Münchner Ägyptologische Studien, 48).

taken over the obligations of a boatman Aur. Horos son of Horos), **807**.7 (Aur. Elias son of Thonios), **808**.4 (Aur. Serenus son of Leon), **813**.5 and **814**.4 (Aur. Isidoros son of Horion), **815**.3 (Aur. Paësis son of Horos). These boatmen all originate from the Oxyrhynchite nome. The role of the boatman Jacob son of Jason is exceptional, as he originally came from the Panopolite nome,[32] but is living now in Babylon[33] while serving on an imperial boat belonging to the 'unit of Memphis' (ἀριθμὸς Μέμφεως).[34] On the other hand, *P.Oxy.* XXIV 2415[35] presents the names of various nomes from which boatmen came to the Oxyrhynchite nome. Finally, there is a certain Psoeis from the village of Papa in the Herakleopolite nome who may have a boatman (cf. the restoration of the function in **812**.3).

----

32) Cf. the 'nauta ex civitate Panopolitarum' in *P.Lond.* V 1825 + *BL* 6.65, 8.194.
33) For this toponym, cf. A. Calderini - S. Daris, *Dizionario Geografico* II 17f.; *Supplemento* I 75, II 33, III 25.
34) This word (cf. Lat. 'numerus') can have the meaning of 'unit of troops' (not necessarily military personnel). Apparently (cf. *CPR* VIII 34.2, 35.4), flotillas of imperial *polykopa* were stationed in Memphis, an important harbor, from where ships could be dispatched in order to collect and to transport grain and other commodities to Alexandria and other destinations, as the occasion arose.
35) Cf. below, *Appendix B* # 2 (early IV^{p}, cf. N. Gonis in *ZPE* 143 [2003] 165).

§ 5: IMPERIAL OATH FORMULAS

In the Michigan texts one often finds an imperial oath formula (see index 4).[36] **800**.9-10 (354^p) features for the first time in the papyri published to date a formula σεβάσμιος θεῖος ὅρκος τῶν δεσποτῶν ἡμῶν Κωνσταντίου Αὐγούστου καὶ Κωνσταντίου τοῦ ἐπιφανεστάτου Καίσαρος, i.e. mentioning by name the rulers of that year (Constantius II and Constantius Gallus, cf. *CSBE*^{2} Appendix G, p. 276). In **803** (366^p), **804**, **805** (both 367^p), **815** (365^p) and **819** (365-367^p) one finds an oath formula mentioning the emperors Valentinianus and Valens, but without Gratianus[37] and without the article τῶν before the element *αἰωνίων* Αὐγούστων ('eternal Augusti').[38] In **807 - 811**, **813 - 814** (all from 372-373^p) the emperor Gratianus is included in the oath formula (cf. *CSBE*^{2}, Appendix G, p. 278).

In the introduction to *P.Wash.Univ.* II 82 (= **805**) the editors offered a list of 4th-cent. loading receipts arranged by the names of the issuer and the addressee.[39] They found that

---

[36]) On imperial oath formulas in general cf. E. Seidl, *Der Eid im römisch-ägyptischen Provinzialrecht*, II (Münich 1935; = Münch.Beitr. z.Papyrus-forschung & Antiken Rechtsgeschichte, 24). On oath formulas found in papyri from Byzantine Egypt see *CSBE*^{2}, Appendix G.

[37]) Flavius Gratianus (*PLRE* I 401) became an Augustus only on 24.viii.367 at the age of 8 years; therefore, **804**, **805**, and **819** need to be dated before that date.

[38]) The article τῶν is left out in the oath formula in **807**.12-15. It remains to be seen whether the article should be supplemented in *P.Oxy.* XLVI 3308 at the beginning of line 11; in *P.Lips.* I 47.8 the supplement <τῶν> in the formula does not seem necessary.

[39]) Although deriving from a later date and another origin, *SB* XVIII 13948 (Memphite, 14.ix.407) is interesting in this respect; cf. also *P.Wash.Univ.* II, pp.

when an issuer's name follows after the name of the addressee, the latter is presumably the higher-ranking party within the terms of the transaction; under these circumstances, an imperial oath occurs within the body of the receipt without exception. The texts in the present archive confirm this finding.

§ 6: TOPOGRAPHICAL INDICATIONS

In **801** (359^{p}), *Appendix A, P.Oxy.* LXVII 4606 (361^{p}), **806** (369^{p}), **813** and **814** (both 373^{p}) the metropolis of the Oxyrhynchite nome is referred to as ἡ λαμπρὰ καὶ λαμπροτάτη Ὀξυρυγχιτῶν πόλις.[40] This is normal; D. Hagedorn has proved[41] that starting by the end of the third century A.D. this titulature is in very frequent use; for the fourth century he found only two serious deviations.[42]

In *Appendix A, P.Oxy.* LXVII 4610, 4612 (both 363^{p}) and in **803** (366^{p}), **804** (367^{p}), **807**, **808** - **10** (all from 372^{p}) however, the metropolis is referred to as ἡ Ὀξυρυγχιτῶν πόλις without any epithet at all. In *Appendix A, P.Oxy.* LXVII 4608, 4609, 4613, and in **800**, **811** and **815** this seems to be the most

101-03.

40) We are dealing only with the first occurrence of the name of this metropolis within a given text. When it appears for the second or *n*th time in the same text, the rules as developed by D. Hagedorn (cf. the next footnote) are not always strictly applied.

41) In *ZPE* 12 (1973) 277-92; cf. also E.M. Grocholl in *ZPE* 85 (1981) 268-70.

42) Cf. *loc.cit.* [fn. 41], 288 and fn. 37.

likely supplement. This archive therefore contains a substantial number of texts featuring deviations from normal 4th-century practice regarding the name of the metropolis Oxyrhynchus.

In the archive the following villages within the Oxyrhynchite nome occur (they are listed in alphabetical order):[43]

Ἀδαίου	**826**.23
Ἀκούτου	**821**.9
Ἑλικ(ῶνος) (δ πάγου)	**826**.3
Κευῶθις	*Appendix A, P.Oxy.* LXVII 4611.ii.9
Μοῦχις (ε πάγου)	**809**.35
Παλῶσις (η πάγου)	*Appendix A, P.Oxy.* LXVII 4612.6
Πινύρεως (ε πάγου)	**809**.37
Σεφώ (ζ πάγου)	*Appendix A, P.Oxy.* LXVII 4611.ii.12
Ταμπεμοῦ (ε πάγου)	**809**.31
Τεξεί (ζ πάγου)	**826**.2
Φοβώου	**811**.5

§ 7: CHRONOLOGICAL ELEMENTS

The consular formulas in the Michigan texts do not present particular problems. For the individual consulates, see

----

[43]) For these villages, cf. P. Pruneti, *I centri abitati dell'Ossirinchite* (Florence 1981) and A. Benaissa, *Rural Settlements of the Oxyrhynchite Nome. A Papyrological Survey* (Köln / Leuven 2009; *Trismegistos Online Publications* 4, Version 1.0, October2009: see the website www.trismegistos.org; ISBN: 9789490604042).

index 1 and *CSBE*[2], under years 354, 359, 364, 366, 367, 372, 373, 374.

Likewise, there are no particular problems with the indictions in the archive. In most cases (cf. index 3), individual indictions are qualified as εὐτύχης / εὐτυχοῦσα and νέα; for the expression νέα ἰνδικτίων, cf. *CSBE*[2], Ch. 5.

METHOD OF PUBLICATION

The texts in this volume are presented according to the usual papyrological practices. Punctuation, breathings and accents have been added, except in a few cases where the correct accentuation was uncertain. The following signs have their usual meanings:

( )	Resolution of an abbreviation or a symbol
[ ]	Lacuna in the papyrus
< >	Letters omitted by the scribe
⟦ ⟧	Letters written, then cancelled by a scribe
{ }	Letters erroneously written by a scribe
α̣ β̣ γ̣ δ̣	Letters seriously damaged and read with some degree of uncertainty
. . . . . .	Letters whose remains could not be read
[± 5]	Approximate number of letters in a lacuna

Fractions: d = 1/4
L or S = 1/2
> = 2/3

Papyrus texts have been cited according to the practice of J. Sosin, R.S. Bagnall et al. *Checklist of Editions of Greek, Latin, Demotic, and Coptic Papyri, Ostraca and Tablets* (Web-version: http://scriptorium.lib.duke.edu/papyrus/texts/clist.html, updated 11.ix.2008).

Journals are cited according to the practice of the same *Checklist*, and that of *L'Année Philologique*, respectively.

Transliterations of personal names of Latin origin feature, if applicable, an ending in -us; transliterations of personal names of Greek origin feature, if applicable, an ending in -os.

P.Mich. XX publication numbers (**801** - **826**) are referred to in bold type without repeating the siglum *P.Mich.* XX.

In the indices, an indication like '**811**.15/16' means that the word in question occurs in text **811**, distributed over two lines (15 and 16). An indication like '**811**.15 - 19' means that the word in question occurs in text **811** in each of lines 15, 16, 17, 18 and 19.

800: UNDERTAKING BY A BOATMAN TO DELIVER WHEAT TO ALEXANDRIA

P.Laur. IV 162 (+ Tav. CXI) 354P

H. 17.9 x W. 13.3 cm. Part of a *tomos synkollesimos* (cf. W. Clarysse, "Tomoi Synkollesimoi", in: M. Brosius [ed.], *Ancient Archives and Archival Traditions. Concepts of Record-Keeping in the Ancient World,* Oxford 2003, 344-359). At the bottom of the papyrus a *kollesis* is visible. It preserves traces of at least 6 lines of writing on a preceding document. Verso blank.

1 Ὑπατείας τῶν δεσποτῶν ἡμῶν Κωνστ[αντίου Αὐ-
γούστου τὸ ζ´ καὶ Κωνσταντίου τοῦ ἐπιφανεσ-
τάτου]
2 VACAT Καίσαρο[ς τὸ γ´, Month, Day]
3 Αὐρηλίοις Εὐλογίῳ Εὐλογίου καὶ Διο̣[γ]έ̣[ν]ε̣ι̣ Δ̣ι̣[ο-
γένους καὶ N.N. son of N.N.]
4 κ̣αὶ Δωροθέῳ Θωνίου Πασίωνος καὶ Ἀπ̣ολλ[son of
N.N. τοῖς πᾶσι βουλευταῖς τῆς]
5 V A CA T Ὀξυρυγχιτῶν πόλεως κ̣[α]ὶ ἐπ̣ι-
[μεληταῖς σίτου Ἀλεξανδρείας VACAT]
6 παρὰ Αὐρηλίου Ἀπφοῦ Τ̣ιθοῆ(τος) ἀπὸ τοῦ Ὀξυ-
ρ[υγχίτου κυβερνήτου πλοίου ± 20]
7 μετ᾽ ἐγγύου τῆς τοῦ γόμου παραδόσεως καὶ τ[οῦ ἐπε-
νεγκεῖν ἐκ πλήρους ἄποχα γράμματα Αὐρηλίου]
8 Β̣ερνικιανοῦ βου(λευτοῦ) ἐνάρχ(ου) πρυτ(άνεως) τῆς
αὐ[τῆς πόλεως. VACAT]
9 Ὁ̣μ̣ολο̣γ̣ο̣(ῦμεν) ὀμνύν̣(τες) τὸν σεβά̣σ̣[μιον θε]ῖον

ὅρκ[ον τῶν δεσποτῶν ἡμῶν Κωνσταντίου Αὐγούστου καὶ]

10 Κωνστα[ντίου το]ῦ ἐπιφανεστάτου Καίσαρ[ος, ἐγὼ μὲν ὁ κυβερνήτης παρειληφέναι καὶ ἐμβεβλῆσθαι εἰς τὸ προκείμενον πλοῖον]

11 ἀπὸ γεν[ήματος] τ̣ῆς εὐτυχοῦς ιγS νέας [ἰνδικτίονος σίτου νέου καθαροῦ ἀδόλου καὶ ἀβρόχου καὶ ἐκτὸς]

12 πά̣σης ἐτίας κα̣θ̣εστηκότος μέτρῳ̣ [δημοσίῳ̣ μετρήσει τῇ̣ κελευσθείσῃ̣ ἐπὶ τὸ αὐτὸ (ἀρτάβας) *n*,]

13 τὸ δὲ δῖγμα ἀ̣κ̣έ̣ρ̣ε̣ο̣ν βασταχὲν κ̣α̣ὶ̣ σ̣υ̣μ̣[βληθὲν πρὸς τὸν γόμον ἐφάνη ὀρθὸν καὶ αἱ ἀρτάβαι ἠ-]

14 νέχθησαν πρὸς λιτρισ̣μὸ̣ν ἑξῆ̣ς̣ ̣ ̣[

15 καὶ ἦ̣ξεν ὁ ξέστης λί(τραν) α (οὐγκίας) [γS (?), τὸν δὲ γόμον κατενέγκω ἐπὶ τὴν λαμπροτάτην]

16 Ἀλεξάνδρειαν καὶ παρα[δώσω εἰς τοὺς ἐκεῖσε δημοσίους θησαυροὺς ἀριθμῷ πλήρης]

17 καὶ τῆς παραδόσεως ἄ[ποχα γράμματα ὑποδέξασθαι ἐπ᾽ ὀνόματος ὑμῶν τῶν ἐπιμελητῶν, ἐγὼ δὲ ὁ ἐγγυητὴς ἑκουσίᾳ̣ καὶ αὐθαιρέτῳ̣]

18 γ̣νώμῃ̣ ἐ̣γ̣γ̣υ̣ᾶσθαι τ[ὸν προκείμενον κυβερνήτην παραδίδοντα τὸν γόμον κτλ.

---

1 ϋπατειας Pap. 12 l. αἰτίας 13 l. δεῖγμα ἀκέραιον βασταχθὲν

"[In the consulate of our lords Constantius Augustus for the 7th time and Constantius the most noble] Caesar [for the 3rd time, Month, Day]. To Aurelius Eulogios son of Eulogios and

Aurelius Diogenes son of Diogenes and N.N. son of N.N, and Aurelius Dorotheos son of Thonios grandson of Pasion and Aurelius Apoll--, all councillors of the city of the Oxyrhynchites and commissioners of wheat for Alexandria, from Aurelius Apphous son of Tithoës from the Oxyrhynchite nome, boatman of the --- ship, with as surety for the delivery of the cargo and the complete production of the certificates of delivery Aurelius Bernicianus, councillor, acting prytanis of the same city. We acknowledge swearing the august imperial oath of our lords Constantius Augustus and Constantius the most noble Caesar, that I the boatman have received and loaded into the above mentioned ship from the harvest of the fortunate 13th new indiction a total of *n* artabas of new, clean, unadulterated unwetted wheat, free of any fault, and measured with the public measure according to the regulation measurement. The sample, having been transported untouched and after having been compared with the cargo turned out to be correct and the artabas were then weighed --- and each *sextarius* weighed 1 lb. and 3.5 (?) oz., and (I agree) that I shall transport the cargo to the most illustrious Alexandria and I shall deliver it to the public granaries there in full and I shall receive certificates of the delivery in the name of you, the commissioners. I, the surety, (acknowledge) that I serve of my own free will as surety for t[he above mentioned boatman that he will deliver the cargo ---]."

1-2. For the consulate of 354[P] see *CSBE*[2], App. D, *s(ub) a(nno)* 354.

3-4. While an Aurelius Diogenes son of Diogenes occurs also in **808** (cf. 5-6n.; he may be mentioned also in **816**.3, 4, 15), the βουλευταί Aurelius

Eulogios son of Eulogios, Aurelius Dorotheos son of Thonios grandson of Pasion, and Aurelius Apoll-- are known only from this text. In l. 4 one finds the only town councillor whose grandfather's name is apparently given as well, although the absence of the article before the grandfather's name is slightly unusual and worthy of note. Theoretically it is conceivable that one should assume a textual lacuna in front of Πασίωνος, i.e. read '<καὶ N.N.> Πασίωνος'.

5. This is apparently the only text in the archive in which βουλευταῖς and ἐπιμεληταῖς are linked by the copula καί (l. 5).

6. On the plate one can see that there is a small horizontal stroke to the right of the eta of Τιθοη- indicating an abbreviation. It is also possible of course that one should resolve the genitive of the name as Τ̣ιθοή(ους).

7. Between the two gammas of ἐγγύου a small space has been left blank. The supplement of ἐκ πλήρους in the restoration is not quite certain, cf. **808**.5-6n.

7-8. The words Αὐρηλίου] | Βε̣ρ̣νικιανοῦ βου(λευτοῦ) ἐνάρχ(ου) πρυτ(άνεως) τῆς αὐ[τῆς πόλεως seem to have been added later by a second hand in a space originally left blank. It is not inconceivable that Aurelius Bernicianus was also the owner of the ship on which Apphous was boatman. The name Βερ(ε)ν(ε)ικιανός is most probably to be equated with Lat. 'Veronicianus'. Is the Oxyrhynchite town councillor & *prytanis* of this name in the present text identical with the Oxyrhynchite *strategus* of the same name in *SB* XVI 12543.3 (327P; cf. *BL* 9:286)?

9. The plural ὁ̣μολο̣γ̣ο̣(ῦμεν) ὀμνύ̣(τες) can be explained as a declaration of the boatman and the surety together. To be sure, the abbreviation of the two verbs at this point within a document is not common; but the first editor's note *ad loc.* does not leave much of an opportunity to read the verbs in the singular.

10. The present restoration is too long if compared with the restoration of lacunas in other lines, but some words, esp. κυβερνήτης and προκείμενον, may have been abbreviated to κυβ(ερνήτης) and προκ(είμενον).

11. The harvest of the 13th indiction (354/5) fell in the summer of 354P.

11-12. ἐκτὸς πάσης ἐτίας (l. αἰτίας) καθεστηκότος: cf. *P.Oxy.* LIX 3980.11-

12, ἐκτὸς πάσης φαυλότητος τυγχάνοντος, and the editor's note ad loc. The gender of the form καθεστηκότος shows that one is dealing here with σῖτος rather than with κριθή.

13-15. One finds here — unfortunately within a much mutilated and incomplete passage — a stipulation which does not seem to appear in any other such receipt published to date. For the interpretation of these lines (and the possible supplement of l. 13), cf. already P.J. Sijpesteijn, "What Happened to Tax-Grain upon Arrival at Alexandria?", *CdE* 69 (1994) 132-37. Apparently, the phrase seems to stand apart from the surrounding construction Ὁμ̣ολ̣ογ̣ο̣(ῦμεν) (l. 9) --- ἐγὼ μὲν --- παρειληφέναι καὶ ἐμβεβλῆσθαι (l. 10) --- (ἀρτάβας) *n*, (l. 12) --- τὸν δὲ γόμον κατενέγκω (l. 15) --- καὶ παρα[δώσω (l.16); cf. the use of the 3rd ps.pl. ἠνέχθησαν in ll. 13-14 which cannot be fitted into this construction.

15. For the restoration of the numeral γS with οὐγκίας, cf. N. Kruit - K.A. Worp in *Archiv* 45 (1999) 112 and n. 22.

For the finite verbs κατενέγκω and παραδώσω (both restored), cf. **802**.10n. For the use of the aor.subj. κατενέγκω instead of the indic.fut. κατοίσω, see B.G. Mandilaras, *The Verb in the Greek Non-Literary Papyri* (Athens 1973), §§ 375 and 541 (1); cf. also below, **808**.10n. The restoration of a compound of φέρω other than καταφέρω seems less likely, but the restoration of an alternative verb like κατάγω is also conceivable, cf. the similar phrasing in **804**.11 and see **803**.8n.

17. For the confusion between the aor. inf. ὑποδέξασθαι and the fut. inf. ὑποδέξεσθαι, cf. already S.G. Kapsomenakis, *Voruntersuchungen zu einer Grammatik der Papyri der nachchristlichen Zeit* (München 1938) 32-33.

18. For a possible continuation of this text, cf. **804**.14, **808**.13, **809**.13, **810**.13, **811**.13, **812**.16, **814**.15, **815**.12 and **816**.11.

801 : PRESCRIPT OF A TEXT OF UNKNOWN CONTENTS

P.Mich.inv. # 4028.A 1.x.359p

H. 2 x W. 13.3. cm. Margins: at the top 2.0, at the right 0.7 cm. Broken at the LH side and at the bottom. No *kollesis* visible. Verso blank. Photo: see http://wwwapp.cc.columbia.edu/ldpd/app/apis/item?mode=item&key=michigan.apis.4364.

1 [Ὑπ ατείας Φλαουίων Εὐσεβίο]υ καὶ Ὑπ ατίου τῶν λαμ(προτάτων) Φαῶφι γʹʹ.

2 [Αὐρηλίῳ Σαραπίωνι Πλ]ο̣υτάρχου βουλ(ευτῇ) τῆς λαμ(πρᾶς) καὶ λαμ(προτάτης) Ὀξ υρυγχιτῶν πό-λεως

3 [παρὰ Αὐρηλίου N.N. Πα]πνουτίου ἀπὸ τοῦ ἄνου Κυνοπολίτου χαίρειν.

4 [± 35]τις π̣ .[. .] .[.]ρ̣ον̣ . . . . . .

----

1 ὑπατιου Pap. 3 Πα]πνουτίου: -υ ex ς; l. ἄνω

"In the consulate of Flavius Eusebios and Flavius Hypatios, *viri clarissimi*, Phaophi 3. To Aurelius Sarapion son of Ploutarchos, councillor of the illustrious and most illustrious city of the Oxyrhynchites, from Aurelius N.N. son of Papnoutios from the Upper Cynopolite nome, greetings. ---"

Only three lines of the document's opening (with the

date and the names of addressee and sender) and a few letters of a fourth line (with the beginning of the body of the document) have survived. The text may be attributed to the archive because of its inventory number and because l. 2 apparently features the name of a councillor of Oxyrhynchus, '[Sarapion] son of Ploutarchos', known from many other texts belonging to this archive (see general introd., § 2).

1. For the consulate of 359ᴾ, cf. *CSBE*², App. D, *s.a.* 359; the size of the lacuna at the start of the line (cf. the beginning of l. 2) prevents us from supplementing a post-consular formula (in 360ᴾ). As 359/360ᴾ is a leap year, Phaophi 3 = 1.x.
2. For the Upper Cynopolite nome (between the Oxyrhynchite nome in the north and the Hermopolite nome in the south), cf. N. Litinas in *Archiv* 40 (1994) 143-155, 157-64 and *P.Pher.* introd., § 3 'Exkurs'.

802: UNDERTAKING BY TOWN COUNCILLORS TO DELIVER WHEAT TO ALEXANDRIA

P.Col. inv. 154 — 364ᴾ

H. 20.8 x W. 23.8 cm. The sheet of papyrus is broken at the top, at the LH and at the RH side, but the bottom margin of 6 cm is complete. The color of the ink in lines 13-14 looks different from the ink color in ll. 1-12. Photo: http://wwwapp.cc.columbia.edu/ldpd/app/apis/item?mode=item&key=columbia.apis.p943.

1 Μετὰ τὴν ὑπατε]ι̣α̣ν <Ι>ου̣λ̣ι̣α̣ν̣[οῦ αἰωνίου Αὐγούσ-

του] καὶ Φ̣λ̣(αουίου) Σ̣α̣λ̣λ̣ο̣υ̣στίου{ς}

2 VACAT τοῦ [λαμπροτά]του

3 [Γαίῳ Ἰουλίῳ Λευκαδίῳ στρατηγ]ῷ Ὀ̣ξ̣[υρ]υ̣γχίτου̣

4 [παρὰ Αὐρ(ηλίων) Γενναδίου Ἰο]υλιανοῦ ἀπὸ λογιστῶν καὶ Σ̣ε̣ρ̣ή̣ν̣ο̣υ̣ (?) Ε̣ὐ̣σ̣ε̣β̣είου (?) καὶ Τιμ[αγένους Σερήνου]

5 [καὶ Ἀμμων]ίου Ἀπίωνος καὶ Σαραπίωνος Πλουτάρχου τῶν πάντων βο̣υ̣[λευτῶν τῆς Ὀξυρυγχιτῶν πόλεως]

6 [ἐπιμελητῶν σίτου Ἀλ]ε̣ξανδρίας. Ὁμολογῶμεν ὀμνύντες τὸν σεβά̣[σμιον θεῖον ὅρκον τοῦ δεσπότου ἡμῶν]

7 [Ιουλιανοῦ αἰωνίου Αὐγο]ύστου παρηλιφέναι παρὰ τῶν ἑξῆς ἐγγεγραμμαίν[ων καὶ ἐμβεβλῆσθαι]

8 [εἰς τὸ ὑποτεταγμένον π]λοῖον ἀπὸ κανόνος τῆς εὐτυχοῦς ζ νέας ἰνδικ̣τίωνος σ̣ί̣[του νέου καθαροῦ ἀκρίθου καὶ ἀβρόχου καὶ ἐκτὸς]

9 [πάσης αἰτίας καθεστηκό]τος μέτρῳ δ̣η̣μοσίῳ μετρήσει τῇ κελευστίσῃ ἐπὶ ταὐτ[ὸ σίτου ἀρτάβας *n*]

10 [τὸν δὲ γόμον κατενέγκουμεν] ἐπὶ τὴν λαμ(προτάτην) Ἀλεξάνδριαν καὶ παραδώσωμ̣ε̣ν̣ εἰς τοὺς ἐκεῖσ[ε δημοσίους θησαυροὺς]

11 [ἀριθμῷ πλήρης καὶ ἐ]πὶ̣ τῆς τούτων παρ̣[αδ]ώσεως ἄποχα γ̣ρ̣ά̣μ̣μ̣α̣τ̣α̣ ἐ̣π̣ε̣ν̣ε̣γ̣κ̣ῖν εἰς τ̣ὸ̣ ἐ̣ν̣ [μηδενὶ μεμφθῆναι ἢ]

12 [ἔνοχοι εἴημεν τῷ (θείῳ) ὅ]ρ̣κῳ/. VACAT Ἔ̣[στ]ι̣ [δέ·]

13 (M. 2?)[εἰς πλοῖον τοῦ N.N.] ὀ̣φφ(ικιαλίου) οὗ κυ-

βερ(νήτης) Γερμανὸς τυγχάνουσα ἀπὸ τοῦ Ọ̓ξ̣(υρυγχίτου)[αἱ π(ροκειμέναι) τοῦ σίτου ἀ(ρτάβαι) *n*]

14 [οὗ ἐγγυηταὶ N.N. son of]υ̣ γεοῦχος, Γεννάδιος β/. σ̣τ̣α̣τ̣[ι]ω̣νάρ(ιος).

4 l. Εὐσεβίου? 6 l. Ἀλεξανδρείας, ὁμολογοῦμεν 7 l. παρειληφέναι, ἐγγεγραμμένων 9 l. κελευσθείσῃ 10 l. παραδώσομεν, Ἀλεξάνδρειαν 11 l. ἐπενεγκεῖν, παραδόσεως 13 l. τυγχάνων?

"After the consulate of Julianus eternal Augustus and of Flavius Sallustius *vir clarissimus*. To Gaius Julius Leukadios, strategus of the Oxyrhynchite nome, from the Aurelii Gennadios son of Julianus, ex-*logistes*, and Serenus son of Eusebios and Timagenes son of Serenus and Ammonios son of Apion and Sarapion son of Ploutarchos, all town councillors of the city of the Oxyrhynchites (and) commissioners of wheat for Alexandria. We agree, swearing the august imperial oath by our master Julianus the eternal Augustus, that we have received from the persons mentioned here below and have loaded into the ship mentioned hereunder from the land tax of the fortunate 7th new indiction of pure unadulterated wheat, unwetted and free of any fault and measured with the public measure according to the regulation measurement *n* artabas of wheat in total and that we will transport the cargo to the most illustrious Alexandria and hand it in its full number over to the public granaries and at the handing-over thereof we shall produce receipts in order to remain free from any blame, or may we be liable to the imperial

oath. As follows:
To the ship of N.N. *officialis* of which Germanos is the pilot, happening to be(?) from the Oxyrhynchite nome, the aforementioned *n* artabas, of which the sureties are ... the landlord, Gennadios the *beneficiarius* (?), *stationarius* - - - "

This text is directed by five town councillors of Oxyrhynchus to Gaius Julius Leukadios, strategus of the Oxyrhynchite nome. The senders undertake to deliver an unknown quantity of wheat to Alexandria and their undertaking is confirmed by an imperial oath formula in ll. 6-7 (cf. the general introd., § 5) and dated by a post-consular formula (cf. 1n.). For the formula in general, see the parallel documents found in **805**, *P.Oxy*. LXVII 4606, 4608, 4610, 4612, 4613 (= *App. A*, ## 1, 2, 4, 6, 7).

1-2. Julianus Aug. IV and Fl. Sallustius were the consuls of 363p, cf. *CSBE*[2], App. D, *s.a*. 363; therefore, the document was apparently written in 364p (cf. also l. 8n.). For some reason, an indication of the month and day seems to be lacking. Probably the month fell in the early part of the year 364.
3. For the role of the strategus in such documents, cf. the general introduction above, § 1 fn. 9; for the restoration of the name of the strategus Gaius Julius Leukadios, cf. J. Whitehorne, *Strategi and Royal Scribes*[2], 113.
4. The reading of Σε̣ϱ̣ήν̣ο̣υ̣ Ε̣ὐ̣σ̣ε̣β̣είου is insecure, due to mutilation of the papyrus (some fibers should be straightened); for now it seems supported only by the list of persons in *P.Oxy*. LXVII, p. 206. Cf. also **815**.1-2, where one finds Εὐσεβίου as a patronymic.
5. Or read β(ουλευτῶν)? If so, read also in l. 14 β(ουλευτής)? The present

restoration at the right of l. 5 may be too long; abbreviate Ὀξ (υρυγχιτῶν) πόλ(εως)?

6. The present restoration at the right is probably too long, but it is not obvious which word could be dropped or abbreviated.

8. Ind. 7 = 348/9, 363/4 or 378/9p. Both the first and the 3rd option seem impossible (cf. also ll. 1-2n.) The restoration at the right is probably too long; some qualifications of the wheat as restored (cf., e.g., ἀκρίθου καὶ ἀβρόχου) are only *exempli gratia*.

10-11. The same phenomenon of writing finite forms (κατενέγκω / κατενέγκουμεν and παραδώσω / παραδώσομεν, instead of infinitives is found also in the parallel passsages in **800**.15-17, **808**.10-13, **809**.10-12, **810**.10-13, **813**.13-15, **814**.10-12 and **815**.9-11. For the sequel, ἀριθμῷ πλήρης --- ἄ[ποχα γράμματα ὑποδέξασθαι, see *ibidem*. In fact, in the case of the second part there are variations between a shorter and an extended formula, viz.:

813.14-15: [καὶ τῆς τούτων παρα]/[δόσεως ἄποχα γράμματα ὑποδέξασθαι

814.11-12: καὶ τῆς τούτων π[αραδόσεως] / ἄποχα γ̣ράμ̣μ[ατα ὑποδέξασ]θ̣α̣ι̣

800.17: καὶ τῆς παραδόσεως ἄ[ποχα γράμματα ὑποδέξασθαι ἐπ᾽ ὀνόματος ὑμῶν τῶν ἐπιμελητῶν

815.10-11: καὶ τῆς] / τούτων παραδόσεως [ἄποχ]α γράμματα ἐπ᾽ [ὀνόματος ὑμῶν τῶν ἐπιμελητῶν ὑποδέξασθαι.

808.11-13: καὶ τῆς τού/[των παρ]α̣δώσεως ἄποχα γράμματα ὑποδέξασθαι ἐπ᾽ ὀνόματος ὑ̣[μῶ]ν̣ τῶν ἐπιμελ̣η̣τ̣ῶν καὶ ἐπενε̣γκῖ̣ν̣ / [καὶ ἀναδοῦ]ν̣αι ὑμῖν (likewise, **804**.12-13, **809**.11-12, **810**.12-13)

12. It is not certain that Ἔ[στ]ι̣ [δέ·] is really there, but at least it may be expected before a listing of additional information.

14. Maybe one should read here in fact β/φ/ (=β(ενε)φ(ικιάριος) (cf. *App. A* # 1 = *P.Oxy*. LXVII 4606.16). This reading, and that of σ̣τ̣α̣τ̣[ι]ωνά̣ρ(ιος) is supported only by the consideration that most probably not only town councillors and similarly placed persons, but also government officials in general could act as sureties. It is, however, true that it does not seem

normal to have more than one surety for one single cargo. Unfortunately, we did not find another solution for the question how to match the preceding nominative γεοῦχος and the qualifications coming after the name of Gennadios into the assumption of one single surety.

803: UNDERTAKING BY A BOATMAN TO DELIVER WHEAT TO ALEXANDRIA

P.Mich.inv. # 4017 25.xi.366P

H. 24.8 x W. 26.5 cm. Margins: at the top ca 1.5, at the bottom ca 7.5, at the LH side ca 2.5 cm. There is no RH margin. Photo: see http://wwwapp.cc.columbia.edu/ldpd/app/apis/item?mode=item&key=michigan.apis.4353.

1 Ὑ̣π α̣τείας Γρατ̣ι̣α̣ν̣[ο]ῦ τοῦ ἐπιφανεσ[τάτο]υ υἱοῦ τοῦ δεσπ[ότο]υ ἡμῶν Ο[ὐ]αλεντιν[ιανοῦ]
2 VACAT αἰωνίο[υ Αὐγο]ὐ̣στου καὶ Δαγαλ-λ̣[αί]φου το̣ῦ̣ λαμ(προτάτου), Ἀθὺρ κθ.
3 Αὐρηλ̣ί̣[ο]ι̣ς̣ Ἀγα]θί̣ν̣ῳ̣ Διδύμου κα̣ὶ̣ Ἰ̣ερε̣μία̣ Ἀ̣χιλλίω̣ν̣ος καὶ Πέ̣τρῳ̣
4 Ἀγαθίν[ου καὶ ± 9]ωνος καὶ Σαραπίωνι Πλουτάρχου τῶν πά̣ντων βουλευτôν τ[ῆς]
5 Ὀξυρυ[γχιτῶν πόλεως ἐπι]μελητε̂ς σίτου Ἀλεξαν-δρίας VACAT
6 παρὰ Α[ὐρηλίου (M. 2) Ὀλυμπίου] Πινουθίου κυ-βερ(νήτου) πλοίου Θεο[γ]ονίου πολειτευομ[έν]ο̣υ̣.
7 (M.1) Ὁμολο̣γ̣[ῶ ὀμνὺς τὸν σ]εβάσμιον θεῖ[ο]ν ὅρκον τῶν

δεσποτῶν ἡμῶν Οὐαλεν-
8 τινιανοῦ κ[α]ὶ [Οὐάλεντος α]ἰωνίων Αὐγούστ̣[ων ...
κατα]χθῆναι ἀπὸ τῆς Ὀξυρυγχιτῶν
9 πόλεως ἀκολο[ύθω]ς̣ [α]ἷ̣[ς] ἐ̣θέμην χιρογραφ[ίαις
<?> τῆς εὐτυ]χούσης̣ δεκάτης νέας ἰνδικτίω-
10 νος ποιροῦ νέου καθαροῦ ἀκρίθου καὶ ἀδό[λου καὶ
οὐ]χ ἕνα κόκκον κριθῶν ἔχοντος̣
11 ἀλλὰ καθαρότατον τ̣υγχ[ά]ν̣[ον]τος καὶ δ̣[ιὰ κριθο-
λογί]α̣ς τὴν εὑρητίσαν κριθὴν ἐν τοῦ̣
12 φόρτῳ̣ ἐκλελέχθη ἐπὶ τῷ αὐτὸ (ἀρτ.) χλβ, [τὸν δὲ
γόμον] παραδοῦναι εἰς τοὺς κατὰ Ἀλεξάνδ̣ρ̣-
13 ιαν θείους θησαυροὺς καὶ ἄποχα γράμματα̣ [ὑπο-
δέξασθαι π]αρὰ τῆς τάξεως τοῦ κυρίω μου
14 διασ̣η̣μ̣ο̣τ̣ά̣του αἰπάρχου τῆς ἀννώνη̣[ς· εἰ δὲ κίνησ]ίς
τις γίγνοτω πρόφ̣ασιν
15 κριθῶν ἢ ἄλλη τινος ῥ̣υ̣παρίας διὰ τὸ προεῖν̣α̣[ι
καθαρὸν] τὼν σῖτον καὶ πρὸς κόκκον ἀκρι-
16 βος ἐ̣κλ̣έγοντα καὶ ἄκριθω̣ν γενόμενον ὑποδ[έ-
δεγ]μαι δηλόνοτι ἐγὼ ⟦αὐτὸς⟧ ὑπεύ-
17 θενος ἔσωμαι τῷ̣ προσπίπτοντι δημιώμασι <καὶ>
οὐ[δὲν τὸ] σύνολον ἔσχον τινι ἐν-
18 καλῖν περὶ τούτου εἰς τὸ <ἐν> μηδενὶ μεμφθῆναι ἢ
ἔν̣οχοι εἶμεν τῷ̣ θείῳ̣ ὅρκῳ̣.
19 (M.3) Αὐρήλιος Ὀλύμπ̣ιος Πινουθίον ἐπόμασα τὸν θῖον
ὥρκον κ̣αὶ ἔ[σ]χ̣ον τὴν κριθολογίαν ὁς πρόκιτε.
20 Αὐρήλιος Θῶνις ἔγραψα ὑπὲρ αὐτοῦ βραδέα γράφον-
τος μετ᾽ ἐ[μ]ο̣ῦ ὑποσημιουμένου.
21 (M.4) Ὀλύμπιος σεσημίου̣μαι.

Verso (writing at 180° to the front, in big letters):

22 Συνκολλη σιμοι[

23 [Ἀλ]εξαν δρείας [

24 μηνὶ Νοεμβ[ρίῳ

25 At ca 4 cm from the bottom, on the left: κριθολογία.

There is one kollesis visible, at 11.5 cm from the LH side of the front.

1 There seems to be an ink trace before the upsilon of Ὑπατείας 4 l. τοῖς πᾶσι βουλευταῖς 5 l. ἐπιμεληταῖς Ἀλεξανδρείας 6 l. πολιτευομένου 9 l. χειρογραφ[ίαις 10 l. πυροῦ 11 l. καθαροτάτου, εὑρηθεῖσαν, τῷ 12-13 l. Ἀλεξάνδρειαν 13 l. κυρίου 14 l. ἐπάρχου, γένοιτο, προφάσει 15 l. ἄλλης, τὸν 15-16 l. ἀκριβῶς 16 l. ἄκριθον 16-17 l. ὑπεύθυνος ἔσομαι τῷ, ζημιώματι 17-18 l. ἐγκαλεῖν 19 l. Πινουθίου ἐπόμωσα θεῖον ὅρκον ὡς πρόκειται 21 l. σεσημείωμαι 22 l. συγκολλήσιμοι

"In the consulate of Gratianus the most noble son of our lord Valentinianus, the eternal Augustus, and of Dagalaifus the most illustrious, Hathyr 29. To the Aurelii Agathinus son of Didymus and Jeremias son of Ptollion and Petrus son of Agathinus and N.N. son of N.N. and Sarapion son of Ploutarchos, all councillors of the city of the Oxyrhynchites (and) commissioners of wheat for Alexandria, from Aurelius Olympios son of Pinouthios, boatman of the ship of Theogonios of the curial class. I acknowledge swearing the august imperial oath of our lords Valentinianus and Valens, the eternal Augusti, that [ ] has been transported downstream from the city of the Oxyrhyn-

chites in accordance with the contract which I drew up (regarding the cargo) of the fortunate new tenth indiction which I received in total 632 artabas of new, clean, barley-less, unadulterated wheat which does not contain any berry and which is absolutely clean, since any barley found in this cargo has been removed by cleaning it out and that I have deposited the cargo into the imperial granaries in Alexandria and that I have received receipts from the office of my lord, the *praefectus annonae vir perfectissimus*. If any trouble will arise on account of barley or any other kind of dirt, because the wheat was clean before and I have received it after the berries had been carefully removed and it had become without barley, naturally I am liable to the punishment befalling upon me, since I am absolutely unable to reproach anybody else about it, so as to incur no blame, otherwise may I be liable to the imperial oath.
I, Aurelius Olympios son of Pinouthios, have sworn the imperial oath and I have accepted the cleaning away of barley as written above. I, Aurelius Thonis, have written for him, since he is a slow writer and signs here below with my help.
I, Olympios, have signed it."
(Verso) "Glued together (documents), (concerning) Alexandria, in the month November. Cleaning of barley."

This is a remarkable document. In l. 19 the boatman (κυβερνήτης) Aurelius Olympios declares that he has taken upon himself the κριθολογία (cf. **807**). This statement is in accordance with his words in ll. 14ff. In ll. 8-14, however, he began by declaring that he had transported a cargo to Alexandria and delivered it into the imperial granaries for which he had received receipts from the office of the *praefectus annonae Alexandriae*. In his subscription (ll. 19ff.) Olympios does not mention the transport anymore. Apparently Olympios both transported 632 artabas of wheat to Alexandria and had taken upon himself to clean these artabas from barley. In the present text what is emphasized is the fact that he has cleaned the cargo which was also transported by him and that therefore he is also responsible for the cleaning of the cargo upon its arrival in Alexandria.

1. For the consuls of 366p, cf. *CSBE*², App. D, *s.a.* 366. In *SB* XIV 12099 there is a question about the post-consulate of Gratianus and Dagalaifus (in 367p). On the basis of the present text the lacuna in that text at the end of l. 1 should be supplemented as -- ἡμ[ῶν Οὐαλεντινιανοῦ αἰωνίου Αὐγούστου καὶ Δαγαλαίφου]. Although Dagalaifus was *magister peditum* in 364-366p in the West (cf. *PLRE* I 239), the word στρατηλάτου is apparently omitted in the consular formula (for a similar phenomenon, see *P.Lips*. I 49.22ff.).

3-4. While a Jeremias son of Ptollion and N.N. son of]ων seem to occur only here, other councillors (Aurelius Petros son of Agathinos, and Aurelius Sarapion son of Ploutarchos) occur in other texts as well (see introduction, § 2). There is a problem in the reading of the name of Aurelius Agathinos son of Didymos (for him, see *ibidem*); instead of Ἀγα]θί̣ν̣ῳ̣ one is tempted to read]θ̣ι̣σ̣..η, but there is no other councillor who is known to be a son of Didymos.

6. An Olympios son of Pinoution, originating from Oxyrhynchus, occurs in *P.Fuad. I Univ.*, Append. II 284v.4 (IVp). For the κυβερνήτης, see A.J.M. Meyer-Termeer, *Die Haftung der Schiffer*, 7f. and 10f. It is noteworthy that the place of origin of Olympios is not given. For the title πολιτευόμενος,

see now N. Gonis in *P.Worp* 26. An Oxyrhynchite *politeuomenos* named Theogonios is not yet known.

8. A restoration of the article τῶν in the oath formula before ạἰωνίων does not seem warranted, cf. introd. § 5.

[κατα]χθῆναι: κατάγω and καταγωγή are technical terms for grain transport downstream, cf. *P.Dubl*. 4.9n.; cf. above, **804**.11. In the preceding lacuna of only three letters one may restore the pronoun ἐμέ, although after an introductory ὁμολογῶ an *accus. cum inf.* construction is not necessary. Alternatively, a restoration of [κατενε]χθῆναι may also be considered; cf. also **800**.15n.

9. The present restoration seems to contain all that can be fitted into the lacuna; apparently, the scribe accidentally omitted an element like οὖ ὑπεδεξάμην γόμου (for which cf. **807**.10) between χειρογραφ[ίαις and τῆς εὐτυ]χούσης. For the term νέα ἰνδικτίων, cf. above, introd. § 7, and *CSBE*[2] Chapt. 5. The 10th indiction (366/7[P]) was the current one.

10-11. The qualifications of πυρός (for the use of this term, cf. the introduction, fn. 26) are traditional; νέος means that the wheat does not come from a previous harvest; for καθαρός = 'clean' and ἄδολος = 'unadulterated' see A.J.M. Meijer-Termeer, *op.cit.*, 113; ἄκριθος means that the wheat was free from barley. The present text shows that these qualifications were added to σῖτος / πυρός prematurely , since it was only by and after the κριθολογία of Olympios that the πυρός became ἄκριθος.

For a discussion of the term κόκκος = 'grain', cf. *CPR* XIV 1.12n. For a discussion of the term κριθολογία = 'barley picking', cf. Ph. Mayerson in *BASP* 41 (2004) 127-137.

11-12. καὶ δ̣[ιὰ κριθολογί]ας ------- ἐκλελέχθη: for the reduplication instead of the augment in the verb ἐκλελέχθη, cf. B.G. Mandilaras, *The Verb*, § 423. Maybe this phrase was intended as a remark between parentheses and one should change τὴν εὑρητῖσαν κριθήν into the nominative as the subject of ἐκλελέχθη.

12. Of course, these 632 artabas of wheat did not constitute the total of the wheat tax paid by the Oxyrhynchite nome in 366[P]. Depending on the

amount of wheat that was available and on how much empty space there was in a ship docked at the harbor a corresponding amount of wheat was loaded (cf. *SB* XVIII 13948.15-16). *SB* XIV 12208 (1st half IV^{p}) gives an impression of the total revenue of wheat (437,779 art.) to be collected from the Oxyrhynchite nome. Cf. also R.S. Bagnall, 'Agricultural Productivity and Taxation in Later Roman Egypt', *TAPA* 115 (1985) 289-308 (= idem, *Later Roman Egypt: Society, Religion, Economy and Administration* [Aldershot, 2003; = *Collected Studies Series*, 758] article XVII).

12-13. κατὰ Ἀλεξάνδρ̣ο̣ | ιαν: κατά has here the meaning of 'in', cf. E. Mayser, *Grammatik*, II.2 [Leipzig - Berlin 1934] 431f. There is an inconsistency between the introduction and the translation of *P.Turner* 45 (= **816**) on the one hand ('in the vicinity of Alexandria') and the note to ll. 4-5 on the other hand.

Most often the granaries (θησαυροί) in Alexandria are styled δημόσιοι (cf. below, index verborum s.v. θησαυρός); the adjective θεῖοι = 'imperial', i.e. 'under imperial supervision', occurs also in **816**.5.

13-14. παρὰ ----- ἀννώνη[ς: for the office of the *praefectus annonae Alexandriae*, cf. *P.Ryl*. IV 652 = *SB* XXIV 16262.3 and *P.Turner* 45 (= **816**).4. In l. 2 of the latter text (373^{p}) the λαμπρότατος ἔπαρχος ἀννώνης Ἀλεξανδρείας is called 'Flavius Claudius Patricius'. It is conceivable that the same person was *praefectus annonae* in 366^{p}, the year of the present text. For further literature concerning this office, see F.A.J. Hoogendijk in *ZPE* 112 (1996) 165f.

15. ῥυπαρία: although the adjective ῥυπαρός occurs very frequently in the papyri (cf. A. Gara, *Prosdiagraphomena e circolazione monetaria*, Milano 1976), the substantive ῥυπαρία = 'dirt, filth' appears here for the first time in the papyri. While this is a general term (i.e. any kind of filth), in the present text, mainly earth will have been meant (cf. *W.Chrest*. 432).

16. αὐτός: the word is deleted by the dash drawn through it.

17-18. εὔθενος (l. εὔθυνος) ἔσομαι τῷ προσπίπτοντι δημιώμασι (l. ζημιώματι, or even τοῖς προσπίπτουσι ζημιώμασι?): instead of εὔθενος (l. εὔθυνος) one expects the adjective ὑπεύθυνος. Hereafter, the omission of the copula καί is striking, but it may be observed that the scribe of this text omits words more often (cf. l. 9n., and l. 18, insertion of <ἐν>).

οὐ[δὲν --] -- περὶ τούτου: these words give the reason why Olympios will be responsible towards the treasury. This addition to the normal formula is unusual.

18. The plural ἔνοχοι εἶμεν is a reminiscence of the fact that Olympios as the transporter of the 632 artabas of wheat was accompanied by a guarantor.

19. ἐπόμασα (l. ἐπόμωσα): the compound ἐπόμνυμι instead of the simplex ὄμνυμι starts to appear in third century texts and is regularly used in Byzantine texts.

19-21. Obviously, Aurelius Olympios is a slow writer (βραδέως γράφων; cf. H.C. Youtie, *Scriptiunculae,* II [Amsterdam 1973] 629) and needs the help of a professional scribe. Even so, he adds his own signature in l. 21. This shows once again what importance was attached to the fact that a party to a contract signed it, one way or another, with his 'own' hand.

804: RECEIPT OF GRAIN NOT TRANSPORTED BY THE FIRST TRANSPORTER

P.Mich.inv. # 4025 367P

Rather dark papyrus broken into two fragments. Fragm. (a): H. 5.7 x W. 7.8 cm. Margins: at the top 2, at the LH side 2.5 cm; broken at the RH side and at the bottom. Fragm. (b): H. 17.2 x W. 37.5 cm. Margins: at the LH side, 2.8, at the RH side 0.8, at the bottom 2.5 cm. On the verso of (b) there is one line written along the fibers. Photo: see http://wwwapp.cc.columbia.edu/ldpd/app/apis/item?mode=item&key=michigan.apis.4361.

1 Ὑπ ατείας Λουππικ̣[ίνου κόμιτος ἱππικῆς τε καὶ πεδι-
κῆς δυνάμεως καὶ Ἰο βίνου τῶν λαμπροτάτων,
Month, Day]
2 Αὐρηλίοις Ἀσκληπ̣[ι
καὶ N.N.]
3 κ̣α̣ὶ Σαραπίωνι Πλου[τάρχου καὶ ± 12] ̣[

---

4 [τῆς ± 8 π]όλεως. Ἐ̣π̣ ι̣δὴ Ὧρ ο̣ς̣ [Ὥρ ου
± 56 ἀπὸ τῶν]
5 [ἐμβληθεισῶν] (ἀρταβῶν) ωογ τῆ̣ς ὑμ̣[τέρας ἐπιμε-
λείας ± 30 ἐν τῇ παραδόσει γενό-]
6 [μ]ενος ἐπὶ τῆς λαμπροτάτης Ἀλ̣εξανδ̣[ρείας μόνον
παρέδωκεν πυροῦ ἀρτάβας τριακοσίας ἀκο-
λούθως τῇ ἐπενε-]
7 χθείσῃ ὑπ' αὐτοῦ ἀποχῇ τῶν δημοσίω̣[ν ± 30 καὶ
λοιπάζονται ἀρτάβαι πεντακόσιαι]
8 ἑβδομήκοντα τρῖ̣ς, (ἀρτάβαι) φογ, τούτου χ[άριν ὁμο-
λογοῦμεν ὀμνύντες τὸν σεβάσμιον θεῖον ὅρκον
τῶν δεσποτῶν ἡμῶν]
9 Οὐαλεντινιανοῦ καὶ Ο[ὐά]λεντος αἰωνίων [Αὐ-
γούστων παρ]ειληφ[έναι καὶ ἐμβεβλῆσθαι εἰς τὸ
προκείμενον πλοῖον τὰς ἀρτάβας τὰς]
10 λοιπασθείσας ὑπ[ὸ τ]οῦ αὐτοῦ Ὧρ ου εἰς [± 10 ὑπ]ὲ̣ρ̣
τούτ̣[ου ± 16 ἀρτάβας πεντακοσίας ἑβδομήκοντα]
11 τ̣ρῖς {τ} ἐπὶ τῷ μὲ [ταύ]τας καταγαγεῖν ἐπ̣[ὶ τ]ὴ̣ν̣
λ̣α̣[μ]π̣ροτάτην Ἀλεξά̣ν̣δ̣ρ̣ιαν [κ]α̣ὶ παραδοῦναι
ε̣ἰ[ς τοὺς ἐκε]ῖ̣[σε ̣] ̣ δημοσ[ίους θησαυροὺς]
12 [ἀ]ριθμῷ πλήρης [κα]ὶ τῆς τούτων παραδώσεως

ἄποχα γράμματα ὑποδέξασθαι ἐπ᾽ ὀνόματος τοῦ αὐτοῦ Ὥρου καὶ ἐπ̣[ε]ν̣ε̣γκῖν

13 [κ]αὶ ἀναδοῦναι ὑμῖ̣ν· ἐγὼ δὲ ὁ ἐγγυητὴς Ἀχιλλέως ἑκουσίᾳ καὶ αὐθερέτῳ γνώμῃ ἐγγυᾶσθαι τὸν αὐτὸν Σιλβανὸν παρα-

14 [δ]οῦντα τὰς αὐτὰς τοῦ̣ σίτου ἀρτάβας πεντακοσίας ἑβ{.}δομήκοντα τρῖς καὶ ἐπιφέροντα τὴν τούτων ἀποχὴν <ἐκ> πλήρους̣

15 [ἀ]μέμπτως ἢ ἐμὲ τὸν ἐγγυητὴν ἐπάναγκες ὑποστῆναι πάντα τὰ πρὸς αὐτὸν περὶ τούτου ζητούμενα ἢ ἔνοχος εἴη

16 τ̣ῷ θείῳ ὅρκῳ. V A C A T

17 (M. 2) Αὐρήλιος Ἀχιλλεὺς Εὐλο̣γίου ἐγγυῶμαι τὸν προκίμενον κυβερνήτην Σιλβανὸν ἐπιφέροντα

18 τὴν ἀποχὴν ἐκ πλήρο̣υ̣ς ὡς πρόκιται.

19 (M. 3) Αὐρήλιος Σιλ[βανὸ]ς̣ Παύου π̣[αρ]έλαβον καὶ ἐνεβαλ̣όμ[η]ν τὰς τοῦ ποιροῦ ν̣έ̣ου καθαροῦ ἀρτάβας π̣ε̣ν̣τ̣α̣κοσίας ἑβδομή-

20 κοντα τρῖς καὶ παρα[δώσω ὡς πρό]κιται.

Verso

21 ἐπ′ [ὀνόματος]Ωρ ου Ὥρ ου διὰ Σιλβανοῦ Παυῆ (ἀρτ.) φογ.

1 l. Λουπικίνου 4 l. ἐπειδὴ 6 ὔμε- Pap. 8/11/14/20 l. τρεῖς 10 ὔπο Pap. 11 τρῖς: the sigma was written over a cancelled epsilon (the scribe started writing τρι επ-, then realized that he was committing a mistake and finished his original pi only half way); l. Ἀλεξάνδρειαν 12 l. παραδόσεως; ὔποδεξασθαι Pap.; l. ἐπενεγκεῖν 13 ὔμιν Pap.; l. Ἀχιλλεύς, αὐθαιρέτῳ 15 ἢ ἐμὲ: ἢ ἐ- ex corr., ὔποστηναι Pap.; l. εἴην 17 l.

προκείμενον 18/20 l. πρόκειται 19 l. πυροῦ.

"In the consulate of Lupicinus, *comes equitum et peditum*, and of Jovinus, *viri clarissimi*, Month, Day. To the Aurelii Asklepiades (?) son of N.N., --- and Sarapion son of Ploutarchos, and [---, all councillors of the city of the Oxyrhynchites, commissioners of wheat for Alexandria, from Aurelius Silvanus son of Paues from ---, boatman of a --- ship with as surety for the delivery of the cargo and the production of certificates of delivery Aurelius Achilleus son of Eulogios ---] of the --- city. Whereas Horos (son of N.N., boatman --- whose surety I was?), handed over from the loaded 873 artabas of your commission (of the harvest of the fortunate 11th new indiction) when he proceeded to the delivery in the most illustrious Alexandria only three hundred artabas according to the receipt (of the *epitropoi*) of the public (granaries in Alexandria) which he brought back, and (whereas) there remain five hundred seventy-three artabas, total 573 art., therefore we acknowledge swearing the august imperial oath of our lords Valentinianus and Valens, eternal Augusti, to have received and loaded into the aforementioned ship the five hundred seventy three artabas left over (to be delivered) by the same Horos ---- on condition that I shall transport these to the most illustrious Alexandria and deliver them in full in the public granaries there and receive certificates of delivery of these in the name of the same Horos which I shall bring back and shall hand over to you. And I, the surety Achilleus, (swear) that I serve of my own free will as surety for the same Silvanus that he delivers the said five hundred seventy-three artabas of wheat and that he brings the receipt in full without blame, otherwise I, the surety, shall of necessity undertake all that is being requested from him or may I be liable to the imperial oath. (M. 2) I, Aurelius Achilleus son of Eulogios, serve as surety for the aforementioned boatman Silvanus that he will bring back the receipt in full as has been written above. (M. 3) I, Aurelius Silvanus son of Paues, have received and loaded the five hundred seventy-three artabas of new clean wheat and I shall deliver them as stated above." (Verso) "To the name of Horos, son of Horos, through Silvanus son of Paues, 873 art."

The boatman Aurelius Silvanus son of Paues declares to an unknown number of councillors of Oxyrhynchus, probably in their capacity of ἐπιμεληταὶ σίτου Ἀλεξανδρείας, that he will transport 573 artabas of wheat to Alexandria. Aurelius Achilleus son of Eulogios is his surety and guarantees that Silvanus will fulfill all his duties. This looks like a usual bill of loading but for the fact that the 573 artabas of wheat loaded now by Silvanus should have been transported to Alexandria by a certain Horos as part of a cargo of 873 artabas of wheat. Apparently Horos delivered only 300 artabas to Alexandria, rather than the total amount (873 art.) entrusted to him. It may be assumed that Silvanus had been Horos' surety for this transport of the original amount and is now being held responsible for the remainder of the total cargo, i.e. for those 573 artabas of wheat that never arrived in Alexandria. It does not become apparent what happened to the 573 artabas originally also entrusted to Horos. It might well be that these were not accepted by the officials in Alexandria, since they were not of good enough quality. Within this context it should be noted that Silvanus promises to bring back a receipt in the name of Horos (l. 12) rather than in his own name or that of the commissioners to whom he will hand over the receipt (cf. **800**.17, **808**.13, **809**.12, **810**.12, **815**.11).

1. For the consulate of 367p and its post-consulate in 368 see *CSBE*[2], App. D, *s.aa.* 367, 368.

2-3. The councillor Aurelius Asklep[ios / -iades / -iodoros (?) appears only here; we cannot say with certainty to how many councillors this text was directed (cf. the general introduction, § 3). The size of the lacuna (± 65 letters) at the end of both lines makes it certain that the addressees were also styled ἐπιμεληταὶ σίτου (cf. l. 14) Ἀλεξανδρείας.

4. At least the name and the description of the boatman, Aurelius Silvanus son of Paues (cf. l. 19), and the name and description of his surety, Aurelius Achilleus son of Eulogios (cf. l. 17), must have found a place in the lacuna. Moreover, in the lacuna of approximately 56 letters after Ὡρ ος [Ὡρ ου a further description of this Horos is expected, thereafter something like οὗ ἤμην ἐγγυητής.

5. After ἐπιμελείας (or should one restore here πολιτείας [cf. **807**.8]?) a possible supplement (already incorporated into our translation) is: ἀπὸ γενήμ(ατος) τῆς εὐτυχοῦς ια νέας ἰνδικ(τίωνος).

6-7. In itself one might also restore participles like ἐπα] | χθείσῃ or παρενε] | χθείσῃ, but the verb ἐπιφέρω is the most commonly used when it comes to the production of receipts.

7. One could supplement, e.g., δημοσίω̣[ν θησαυρῶν ἐν Ἀλεξανδρείᾳ ἐπιτρόπων, κτλ.

10. Restore, perhaps, εἰς [παράδοσιν]; in the lacuna at the end, restore perhaps πυροῦ νέου καθαροῦ ἀρτάβας κτλ., cf. l. 19.

11. The scribe uses an ἐπὶ τῷ + inf. construction instead of ἐγὼ μὲν κτλ. In l. 16 he continues, however, with the usual ἐγὼ δὲ ὁ ἐγγυήτης κτλ. Similar

ἐπὶ τῷ + inf. constructions are found in **806**.9 and **811**.9.

13-14. For the form παραδοῦντα, cf. **813**.16n.

14. Αὐτός often has the same meaning as προκείμενος, cf. l. 10 (τοῦ αὐτοῦ Ὥρου) and in l. 13 (τὸν αὐτὸν Σιλβανόν).

19. The personal name Παυῆς produces here a genitive Παύου, in l. 21 a genitive Παυῆ.

805: UNDERTAKING BY TOWN COUNCILLORS TO TRANSPORT WHEAT TO ALEXANDRIA

P.Wash.Univ. II 82 367P

H. 17 x W. 6.9 cm. Coarse and dark papyrus fragment, torn vertically along several different lines of stress at intervals of approximately 2 cm. Top margin preserved, but the column of writing has been interrupted by tears at LH side, the RH side and at the bottom. On the verso traces of 10 lines of writing, badly faded, across the fibers, from an account (no obvious connection with the text on the recto). Photo: see http://library.wustl.edu/units/spec/manuscripts/papyri/wtu.inventory.231.html.

1 [Ὑπ ατείας Φλ(αουίων) Λουπικίνου καὶ] Ἰο ουε̣[ίν]ου τῶν [λαμπροτάτων]

2 [Month, Day. Τῷ δεῖνι στρατη]γῷ Ὀξ υ̣ρ̣υγχίτο[υ παρὰ Αὐρηλίων]

3 [± 30]νίου καὶ Ἡσ υχίου̣ [Ἰο υλιανοῦ καὶ N.N.]

4 [± 30] καὶ Διονυσίου ̣[± 11]

5 [± 20 τῶν πάντων β]ουλ(ευτῶν) τ̣ῆς Ὀξ υρυ[γχιτῶν πόλεως]
6 [ἐπιμελητῶν σίτου Ἀλ εξανδρείας, δι᾽ ἡ]μῶν τῶν ἑξῆς [ὑπογραφόντων.]
7 [Ὁμολογοῦμεν ὀμνύντες τὸν σεβάσ]μιο̣ν θῖον ὅρκον τῶν δ̣[εσποτῶν]
8 [ἡμῶν Οὐαλεντινιανοῦ καὶ Οὐάλε]ντος αἰωνίον Αὐγούστ̣[ων παρειλη-]
9 [φέναι παρὰ τῶν ἑξῆς ἐγγεγραμμένω]ν καὶ ἐνβε-βλῆσθαι ι̣ς̣ [τὸ ὑποτεταγμένον]
10 [πλοῖον ἀπὸ λόγου γενήματος τῆ]ς εὐτ̣υχ̣οῦς̣ ια ν̣έ̣α̣[ς ἰνδικτί-]
11 [ονος σίτου νέου καθαροῦ ἀκρίθου κα]ὶ̣ ἀβρ̣ό̣χ̣ου καὶ ἐκτὸ̣ς π[άσης αἰτίας]
12 [καθεστηκότος μέτρῳ δημοσίῳ] μ̣[ετρή]σ̣ε̣ι̣ τῇ κ̣ε̣λ̣ε̣υ̣σ̣θε[ίσῃ ἐπὶ τὸ]
13 [αὐτὸ (ἀρτάβας) *n*, τὸ δὲ] ̣σιν βα̣[σταχθὲν? ± 6]
14 [± 35] ̣ σίτου παρσ̣ι̣ν̣[± 6]
15 [± 33] ̣[̣] ̣ ̣ια καὶ αὐτ̣ο[± 6]
16 [± 35] ̣ο[± 14]
17 [τὸν δὲ γόμον κατενεγκεῖν ἐπὶ τὴν λαμπροτάτ]η̣ν Ἀλεξα[νδρείαν

- -

1 l. Ἰοβίνου 7 l. θεῖον 8 l. αἰωνίων 9 l. ἐμβεβλῆσθαι εἰς

"In the consulate of the Flavii Lupicinus and Iovinus, *viri clarissimi*, [Month, Day]. To N.N. strategus of the Oxyrhynchite nome from the Aurelii NN. son of NN. [and N.N. son of -]nios and Hesychios son of Julianus and N.N. son of N.N. and Dionysios son of N.N. [ ], all town councillors of the city of the Oxyrhynchites (and) commissioners of wheat for Alexandria, through us whose signatures appear below. We agree, swearing the august imperial oath by our masters Valentinianus and Valens, eternal Augusti, that we have received from the persons mentioned below and have loaded into the ship mentioned hereunder from the produce of the fortunate 11th new indiction of pure unadulterated wheat, unwetted and free of any fault and measured with the public measure according to the regulation measurement - - - and that we will transport the cargo to the most illustrious Alexandria - - -."

This heavily mutilated text is apparently directed by an unknown number of town councillors of Oxyrhynchus to the strategus of the Oxyrhynchite nome. Parallels for this type of document occur in **802**, *P.Oxy.* LXVII 4606, 4608, 4610, 4612, and 4613 (cf. *App. A*, ## 1, 2, 4, 6 and 7). Actually, one cannot be certain whether the commodity to be transported was indeed wheat (as restored above in ll. 6 and 11) or barley, but the use of σίτου̣ in l. 14 may be taken, despite the uncertain context, as an indication in favor of wheat.

In their introduction the first editors rightly drew attention to the imperial oath formula in ll. 7-8 (cf. the general introd., § 5) and the rarely attested consulate (cf. **804**.1n.). In ll. 12ff. the same stipulation may appear as in **800**.13ff. (see note ad loc.). In their note to l. 2 they expressed their uneasiness about the addressee's title as *strategus* which rests on the doubtful reading]γ̣ω (the alternative reading being]τ̣ω). The parallel texts in **802** and *P.Oxy*. LXVII 4606, 4608, 4610, 4612, 4613 (cf. *App. A*, ## 1, 2, 4 ,6 and 7) now prove that the strategus is indeed the addressee to be reckoned with. In itself, the declaration might also be expected to have been directed to the *exactor* of the Oxyrhynchite nome (cf. *P.Heid*. IV 313, introd.).

As to the authorship of the text it should be noted that the first editors wrote in their introduction (p. 99): "The appearance of the word ἐμβεβλῆσθαι after the imperial oath establishes this text as a receipt for lading, probably, from what remains of the subsequent lines, for lading of grain." They are right, but we are not dealing with authors who actually loaded the grain. The town councillors/commissioners of grain to be transported to Alexandria declare to the strategus that they collected grain from various persons and that they had taken care that it was loaded into a ship which transported (or would transport) it to Alexandria. We are, therefore, at the beginning of the process of the collection of government grain, i.e. before the actual transports would begin.

Notes (for other commentary, see also the *ed.princ.*)
2-5. The precise number of the senders of this document is unknown; for this question cf. the introduction to the archive, pp. 19-20.
3. Ἡσυχίου [Ἰουλιανοῦ]: assuming that the supplement is correct (no other Hesychios appears in the archive) this man also appears in **813**.2 and **814**.2 (both 373[p]) and in **816**.5-6 (374[p]).
4. Perhaps the letter before the lacuna can be read as a (much damaged) theta. If this is correct, one may consider supplying the father's name after Διονυσίου as Θ̣[έωνος. For a Dionysios son of Theon who probably was an

Oxyrhynchite town councillor, cf. **820**.6-7n.
9. In view of the total space available in the lacuna (ca 29 letters) it seems less likely to restore here [φέναι παρὰ διαφόρων ὀνομάτω]ν (cf. **806**.8-9), i.e. 24 letters, instead of [φέναι παρὰ τῶν ἑξῆς ἐγγεγραμμένω]ν (cf. **809**.8), counting 28 letters. Moreover, the latter is the usual wording within the whole formula of such documents, cf. **802**.7, **809**.8, **815**.7; remarkably enough, it is missing in **810**, the duplicate of **809**.
12. For the formula μετρήσει τῇ κελευσθείσῃ, cf. **800**.12, **802**.9, **808**.10, **809**.10, **810**.10, **813**.12, **814**.10, **815**.9, *P.Oxy*. LXVII 4606.9, 4608.8, 4610.10, and 4612.i.9 (=. *App. A*, ## 1, 2, 4, 6)); the first editors read]̣ ̣σ̣εν τῇ κε̣λ̣ε̣ύ̣σ̣ι̣ (l. κελεύσει).
13. Probably one should restore in the lacuna τὸ δὲ δεῖγμα (cf. **800**.13) followed by an adjective meaning 'untouched, undisturbed'. We cannot convince ourselves that]̣σιν βα̣[conceals a form of συ̣νβλ̣[ηθέν.
14. The first editors read ἐπαρσ̣ι̣ν̣[, but we think that the remains of their epsilon belong in fact to the preceding upsilon and that this does not have to be dotted. If one reads here παρε̣ν̣[εγκεῖν, there is the problem that this verb does not normally occur at this place within the known formulas using the verb.
16. The omicron may be preceded by either a gamma or a (damaged) tau; this may belong in fact to the τὸν δὲ γόμον phrase now restored at the beginning of l. 17.
17. The subject of κατενεγκεῖν is the ship mentioned in l. 9, or (rather?) the κυβερνήτης in command of this. The first editors read here]ν μεγα[, but the image allows us to read instead of με̣γα[the expected Ἀλεξα[which is part of a standard formula within the context of such document.

806: DECLARATION BY TOWN COUNCILLORS CONCERNING THE ADMINISTRATION OF BARLEY FOR ALEXANDRIA

P.Mich. inv. # 4020 + P.Med. inv. 27 = *SB* XIV 12099 (Milano; cf. *BL* 10:211) 24.ix.369P

P.Mich. inv. 4020 has two larger fragments and several scraps without ink. Fr. (a): H. 10.5 x W. 4.5 cm. Margin at the top 2.2 cm; broken on all other sides. Fr. (b) H. 18.2 x W. 20.3 cm. Margins: at the top 2.5, at the right 1.2, at the bottom 2 cm. There is a *kollesis* at 5.4 cm from the LH edge and another one at 18.6 from the first *kollesis*. The verso is blank.

P.Med.inv. 27 (= *SB* XIV 12099), fits exactly into the gap of ll. 1-6 of the Michigan papyrus. The Milanese part of this text is given below between half brackets (⌞----⌟). Photo: see http://wwwapp.cc.columbia.edu/ldpd/app/apis/item?mode=item&key=michigan.apis.4356.

1 Ὑ̣[πατ]είας Οὐαλεντινια̣⌞νοῦ τοῦ ἐπιφανεστάτου υἱοῦ τοῦ δεσπότου ἡμ⌟ῶν Οὐάλεντος Αὐγούστου καὶ Φλαουίου Οὐίκτορος

2 VACAT ⌞τοῦ λαμπροτάτου στρ⌟ατηλάτου Θὼθ κζ VACAT

3 [Αὐρήλ]ι̣οι Θώνιος Θωνί⌞ο̣υ καὶ Νειλάμμων Ἀμμωνίου ἀμφότεροι βοη⌟θοὶ ἐξακτορίας τῆς λαμ(πρᾶς) καὶ λαμ(προτάτης) Ὀξυρυγχιτῶν

4 [πόλε]ως Αὐρηλίοις Σ̣⌞αραπίωνι Πλουτάρχου καὶ Θέωνι̣⌟ [Αμμων?]ίου καὶ Εὐλογίῳ̣ Πτολεμαίου καὶ τοῖς κοινωνοῖς

5 [ἐπιμε]ληταῖς κριθῶ̣⸤ν Ἀλεξανδρίας τῆς ιαS´ ἰνδι⸥κ̣-
τ̣ί̣⸤ονο⸥[ς] χαί[ρ]ε̣ιν. Ἐπιδὴ Ἑρμίας ἀπὸ πραιπο-
σίτων

6 [ἀποχ]ὰ̣ς δύο ἐπή̣ν̣[εγ]κ̣ε̣ν̣ τ[ῶ]ν̣ π̣α̣ρ̣[αδοθ]έντων ὑπ᾽
αὐτοῦ ὑπὲρ τῆς αὐτῆς ιαS´´ ἰνδικτίονος κριθῶν
ἀρταβῶν

7 [χιλίω]ν̣ διακ̣[οσίω]ν̣ τεσσαράκοντα μίας, (γίν.) (ἀρτ.)
Ἀ̣σμα, μίας μὲν (ἀρτ.) (M. 2?) σια, (M.1) τῆς δὲ
ἑτέρας (ἀρτ.) (M.2?) Ἀλ, αἱ προκ(είμεναι), (M. 1)

8 [± 6]μ̣μ̣[± 7] ̣ τῇ πολειτίᾳ̣ ὑ̣πὲρ τῆς αὐτῆς ιαS
ἰνδικτίωνος καὶ τα[ύ]τας ὑπεδέξατο παρὰ διαφό-

9 [ρων ?κυβερνητῶ]ν̣, κατὰ τοῦτο ὁμολ[ογοῦμ]ε̣ν ἐπὶ
τῷ ἡμᾶς τὸ προκίμενον μέτρον τῶν κριθῶν
(ἀρταβῶν) Ἀσμα

10 [....... λογογρα]φῆσαι τῇ αὐτῇ ιαS´ ἰ̣νδικτίονει καὶ μὴ
ἐξεῖναι ἡμῖν ταύτας λογογραφεῖν τῇ ιγS´ ἰνδικ-
τίονει

11 [διὰ τὸ λογογραφῆ]ναι τῇ αὐτῇ ιαS´´ ἰνδικτίονει. Κυ-
ρία ἡ ὁμολογία ἁπλῆ γραφῖσα καὶ ἐπερ(ωτη-
θέντες) ὡμολογήσαμεν.

12 ὡς πρόκειται.

---

13 (M. 2) [Αὐρήλιος Θών]ιος ὁ προκίμενος συμφωνῖ μοι
ὡς πρόκ(ειται).

14 (M. 3) [Αὐρήλιος Νειλάμμων ὁ προκείμενος]
σ̣υμφωνῖ μοι ὡς πρόκ(ειται).

5 l. Ἀλεξανδρείας, ἐπειδή 6 l. παραδοθεισῶν 7 l. μίαν, τὴν, ἑτέραν 8 l. πολιτείᾳ; παρα: π- < α corr. 9 l. προκείμενον 10 l. ἰνδικτίονι (2x; also in 11) 11 l. γραφεῖσα 13 l. προκείμενος συμφωνεῖ (also in 14).

"In the consulate of Valentinianus, the most distinguished son of our lord Valens Augustus, and of Flavius Victor, *vir clarissimus, dux*, Thoth 27. The Aurelii Thonios son of Thonios and Neilammon son of Ammonios, both assistants of the bureau of the *exactor* of the illustrious and most illustrious city of the Oxyrhynchites, to Aurelius Sarapion son of Ploutarchos and Aurelius Theon son of Ammonios and Aurelius Eulogios son of Ptolemaios and their partners, commissioners of barley for Alexandria for the 11th indiction, greetings. Since Hermias, former *praepositus*, brought back two receipts for the one thousand two hundred forty-one artabas of barley delivered by him for the same 11th indiction, total 1,241 art. one of 211 art., and another for 1,030 art., and (since) the aforementioned (artabas) [have to be credited] to your tenure of office for the same 11th indiction and (since) he received them from different boatmen (?), therefore we acknowledge that we shall credit the aforementioned amount of 1,241 artabas of barley all to the same 11th indiction and that we are not allowed to credit it to the 13th indiction, but that we shall credit it to the 11th indiction. The agreement, written in one copy, is authoritative and on being asked the formal question we gave our assent as stated above. (M. 2) I, Aurelius Thonios, the aforementioned agree as it is stated above. (M. 3) I, Aurelius Neilammon, the aforementioned agree as it is stated above."

A certain Hermias, a former *praepositus*, delivered 1,241 artabas of barley from the crop of the 11th indiction (ἀπὸ γενήματος τῆς ια ἰνδικτίωνος) to the public granaries at Alexandria. He brought back from Alexandria two receipts, one for 211 artabas and another for 1,030 artabas. The division of the total cargo into two parts may be connected with the fact that the cargo was received from different persons (ll. 8-9). While these 1,241 artabas for barley had to be credited to the account of the 11th indiction, the present text was written in the 13th indiction (in which Hermias apparently only presented these two receipts for the barley transported by him in the 11th indiction to Alexandria). No explanation is offered as to the reason why Hermias presented receipts for barley delivered as tax and transported to Alexandria in the 11th indiction only after some 2 years of delay, and it is not clear what happened at the balance of the books of the 11th indiction and during the 12th indiction. The two assistants of the office of the *exactor* stress emphatically that the 1,241 artabas of barley have to be credited to the 11th indiction.

1-2. For the consuls of the year 369[p] the young Valentinianus Galates, son of the emperor Valens (cf. *PLRE* I 381) together with Flavius Victor (at that time *magister equitum*, cf. *PLRE* I 957-959), cf. *CSBE*[2] App. D, *s.a.* 369.
3. ἐξακτορίας: *LSJ* presents s.v. ἐξάκτωρ the following lemma: "= Lat. *exactor*, *BGU* 21 ii 17, Tz.*H*. 5.6: - hence -ορία, ἡ, *his office*, *P.Lond*. 2.378.8, *P.Gen*. 56.32". 'Office' in English can have different meanings. In *P.Lond*. II 233 (pp. 272f.) = *P.Abinn*. 58.8 and in *PSI* VI 684.10 ἐξακτορία has the meaning of 'function / office of exactor'. In the present text (and in *P.Stras*. II 197.5 and in *P.Warren* 3.4,23) the word has the meaning of 'bureau of the

exactor'. In *P.Gen.* I 56 the text is too damaged to make a decision. For the situation in Petra (Jordan), cf. *P.Petra* III 30.187n. For the role of the exactor in the collection and transport of tax-grain, cf. the general introduction, § 1.
4. Although this is not stated in the text, it seems likely that all three persons qualified as ἐπιμεληταὶ κριθῶν were also councillors of Oxyrhynchus, see the general introd., § 2 (on Oxyrhynchite town councillors) and § 3 (on the number of ἐπιμεληταί found in the archive). Aurelius Sarapion son of Ploutarchos is well documented in the archive, Aurelius Eulogios son of Ptolemaios and Aurelius Theon son of Ammonios (?) apparently do not occur elsewhere in this archive. For a town councillor Theon son of Ammonios, cf. *P.Oxy*. LX 4091.7 [352P] and XVII 2110.i.3, ii.34 [370P]; cf. also **805**.3, where one is dealing with 'N.N. son of -]νίου'; a supplement [Ἀμμω]νίου is, of course, not certain, as there are more Greek names ending in -νιος.
5,6,10,11. The scribe marked the indiction numerals ια / ιγ by either S′ or S″; for such markings, cf. H.C. Youtie, *The Textual Criticism of Documentary papyri: Prolegomena* (London 1974; = *BICS* Suppl. 33) 20 n. 2.
5. ἀπὸ πραιποσίτων: for attestations in Greek papyri of the Latin term *praepositus*, cf. S. Daris, *Il lessico Latino nel greco d'Egitto* (Barcelona 1991²) 91-2. Cf. also **821**.11n. for possibly the same (ex-) *praepositus*.
6. The gen.pl.masc. π̣α̣ρ̣[αδοθ]έντων for fem. παραδοθεισῶν (the participle goes with κριθῶν ἀρταβῶν), is interesting; perhaps a neuter word like γραμμάτων or ματίων (a subdivision of the artaba) was responsible for the scribe's gender confusion?
8. In the lacuna at the beginning of this line there was probably a statement that all of the 1,241 artabas of barley had to credited to Oxyrhynchus and its neighborhood for the 11th indiction. Given the remainder of a fairly long horizontal dash above line level, the letter before τῆ πολειτίᾳ̣ (l. πολιτείᾳ) could stem from a sigma, but we fail to understand how the original wording of the text should be reconstructed here.

For the interpretation of πολιτεία (usually meaning 'citizenship', cf. *BGU* V 1210.113, *M.Chr.* 372.10, *et alibi*) here as 'term of (civil) office', cf. *LSJ* s.v. II.2.

For the spellings ἰνδικτίων- / ἰνδικτίον- in this text (cf. ll. 5, 10, 11), cf. S.P. Goodrich, *The Indiction Cycle* (Diss. Princeton Univ. 1937) 68.

8-9. It escapes our precise understanding why it is of interest that the 1,241 artabas of barley were collected from different boatmen; we suppose that there may be a link with the fact that the total was split up into one receipt of 211 art. and another of 1,030 art.

9. The scribe uses after ὁμολ[ογοῦμ]ε̣ν an ἐπὶ τῷ + inf. construction. Similar constructions are found in **804**.11 and **811**.9.

For μέτρον, cf. P.J. Sijpesteijn in *ZPE* 62 (1986) 140-44 (= *SB* XVIII 13948), note to l. 19.

10. The supplement in the lacuna at the beginning of this line does not cover the full lacuna and is meant only *exempli gratia*. The remaining space may have been occupied by an adverbial expression.

To date, the verb λογογραφέω occurs in the papyri apparently only in *P.Prag*. II 204^{v}.15 and in *P.Beatty Panop*. 1.171, where it appears to have the meaning of 'to account for'; far more frequently attested are the nouns λογογραφία and λογογράφος (cf. N. Lewis, *The Compulsory Public Services of Roman Egypt*^{2}, s.v.). In the present papyrus the meaning of λογογραφέω seems to be that of 'to credit to'.

10-11. The two assistants betray a certain bureaucratic state of mind as they keep stating explicitly that they will credit the 1,241 artabas of barley to the 11th indiction, i.e. not to the 13th indiction, but to the 11th indiction.

807: DECLARATION BY A BOATMAN TO HAVE UNDERTAKEN THE CLEANSING OF WHEAT

P.Mich. inv. # 4026 viii-ix.372[p]

H. 27 x W. 15.5 cm. Margins: at the top 1.5, at the bottom 3.5, at the LH side 1 cm. At the RH side the writing runs for the most part to the edge, but there are lines with a margin of ca 0.25 - 1.5 cm. There is a *kollesis* at 13.7 cm from the LH side. Photo: see http://wwwapp.cc.columbia.edu/ldpd/app/apis/item?mode=item&key=michigan.apis.4362.

1 [Ὑπατ]ε̣ίας Φλ(αουίου) Μοδέστου τοῦ λαμ-π(ροτάτου) ἐπάρχου τοῦ ἱεροῦ
2 πραιτωρίου καὶ Φλ(αουίου) Ἀρινθέου τοῦ λαμ-π(ροτάτου) Θὼθ ̣ ̣
3 Αὐρηλίοις Διοσκόρῳ Εὐλογίου καὶ Π[έ]τρῳ Ἀγα-θίν<ο>υ
4 καὶ Ἀγαθίνῳ Διδύμου καὶ Σαραπίων[ι] Π̣λουτάρχου
5 καὶ Ἱέρακι Σερήνου καὶ Τιμαγένι Σερήνου τοῖς πᾶσι
6 βουλ(ευταῖς) τῆς Ὀξυρυγχιτῶν πόλεως ἐπιμεληταῖς σίτου Ἀλεξ(ανδρείας)
7 παρὰ Αὐρηλίου Ἡλία Θωνίου ἀπὸ τοῦ Ὀξυρυγχίτου
8 κυβερ(νήτου) πλοίου Θέωνος ἀννουμέρεις τάξεως
9 τοῦ λαμπ(ροτάτου) δουκός· ἀκολούθως ᾗ ἐθέμην χειρο-
10 γραφίᾳ οὗ ὑπεδεξάμην γόμου σίτου τῆς εὐτυχοῦς
11 [πρώτ]ης νέα̣ς̣ ἰ̣ν̣δ̣ι̣κ̣τ̣ί̣[ωνο]ς ἀπὸ τοῦ αὐτοῦ Ὀξυ-

ρ̣[υγχ]ίτου
12 [νομοῦ VACAT ὁμολογῶ] ὀμνὺς τὸν σεβάσ̣[μιον]
13 θεῖον ὅρ̣κ[ον τῶν δεσπ]οτῶν ἡμῶ̣ν̣
14 Οὐ[α]λεντινιανοῦ καὶ Οὐά̣λ̣εντος κ̣αὶ Γρατιανοῦ
15 αἰω̣ν̣ίων Αὐγούστων ὑποδεδέχθαι με τὴν
16 κριθολογίαν παρὰ τῶν ἐμβαλαμένων κτητόρων
17 πρὸς τό, εἰ συμβαίη —ὃ μοὶ εἴ̣οιτο— κίνησίν τινα
18 γενέσθαι < > ἢ ἄλλης τινὸς ῥυπαρίας ὑπὸ τῆς
19 μίζονος ἐξουσίας προφάσι κριθολογία<ς> τοῦ
20 αὐτοῦ γό̣μου ἐμ̣ὲ τὸν κυβερ(νήτην) ὑποστῆναι τὸ
21 περὶ τούτου ἀπο̣βησόμενον εἰς τὸ ἐμ μ̣η̣-
22 δ̣ένι μεμφθῆναι ἢ ἔνοχος εἴην τῷ θείῳ̣ ὅ̣ρκῳ̣.

---

23 (M. 2) Αὐρήλιος Ἡλ ίας̣ Θωνίου̣ ὤμασα τὼν τῖων
ὅ̣ρ̣κ̣ον
24 καὶ ἔσχον τὴν κριθολογίαν ὡς πρόκιτα̣ι̣.
25 Αὐρήλιος Θών[ιο]ς Ἀμμω̣νίου ἔγραψα ὑπὲρ αὐ-
26 τοῦ γράμμα̣[τ]α μὴ εἰδώτος.

5 l. Τιμαγένει 8 l. ἀννουμέρου 10 ϋπεδεξαμην Pap. 15 ϋποδεδεχθαι Pap. 17 l. μὴ 18 ϋπο Pap. 19 l. μείζονος, προφάσει 23 l. ὤμοσα τὸν θεῖον 24 κριθολογίαν: -ν ex -ς corr.; l. προκειται 26 l. εἰδότος

"In the consulate of Flavius Modestus the most illustrious *praefectus sacro praetorio* and Flavius Arintheus, *vir clarissimus*, Thoth -. To the Aurelii Dioskoros son of Eulogios and Petros son of Agathinos and Agathinos son of Didymos and Sarapion son of Ploutarchos and Hierax son of Serenus and Timagenes son of Serenus, all councillors of the city of the Oxyrhynchites (and) commissioners of wheat for Alexandria, from Aurelius Elias son of Thonios, from the Oxyrhynchite nome, boatman of the ship of Theon *a numeris* of the office of the most illustrious *dux*. In accordance with the contract which I drew up regarding the cargo of wheat of the fortunate first new indiction from the same Oxyrhynchite nome which I accepted, I acknowledge swearing the august imperial oath of our lords Valentinianus, Valens and Gratianus the eternal Augusti that I have taken upon me the *kritholiogia* (= removal of barley) from the landowners who have loaded it (= the cargo of wheat), so that if (which hopefully may not happen) any trouble would arise or any other kind of hindrance (?) from the higher authority because of the removal of barley of the same cargo, I, the boatman, will take upon me what will happen in connection therewith, so as to incur no blame, otherwise may I be liable to the imperial oath. (M. 2) I, Aurelius Elias son of Thonios have sworn the imperial oath and I have taken upon me the removal of the barley as written above. I, Aurelius Thonios son of Ammonios have written for him because he does not know letters."

Aurelius Elias son of Thonios declares that he has accepted the job of removing the superfluous barley (*kritholiogia*, cf. **803**.10-11n.) in a cargo of an unknown number of artabas of wheat. This declaration corresponds to another, similar document stating that Elias would transport the cargo in question (cf. ll. 9-12). It should be noted that Elias promised to remove the barley from the wheat provided by the κτήτορες (ll.

15-16). In fact, it was these taxpayers who were responsible for the clean delivery of the tax wheat.

1-2. On the consuls mentioned here, cf. *CSBE*[2] , App. D, *s.a.* 372, and the post-consulate in 373. Basically, one may distinguish two different consular formulas for this year, i.e.:
a. a short formula: 'ὑπατείας (Φλαουίου) Δομιτίου Μοδέστου καὶ Φλαουίου Ἀρινθέου τῶν λαμπροτάτων', and
b. a much longer formula: 'ὑπατείας Δομιτίου Μοδέστου τοῦ λαμπροτάτου ἐπάρχου τοῦ ἱεροῦ πραιτωρίου καὶ Φλαουίου Ἀρινθέου τοῦ λαμπροτάτου στρατηλάτου/κόμητος καὶ μαγίστρου τῆς πεδικῆς δυναμέως / παρατάξεως'.
Within each of these formulas various divergences can be observed.

Originally, the day numeral after the month of Thoth was read tentatively as δ̣ (= 4; therefore, in the year 372, Thoth 4 = 1.ix), but on balance it seems wiser not to insist upon reading it.
3-6. For these well-known town councillors and commissioners of (tax) wheat to be transported to Alexandria, see the general introduction, §§ 2 and 3.
8-9. Aurelius Elias is boatman on a ship owned by a certain Theon who is ἀννούμερος in the office of the *dux*, i.e. the military commander-in-chief of Egypt. The same shipowner (not necessarily the same boat) is referred to in *P.Oxy.* LVII 4612.12 (363[p]). For the office of an ἀννούμερος, cf. I. Cervenka-Ehrenstrasser, *Lexikon der lateinischen Lehnwörter in den griechischsprachigen dokumentarischen Texten Ägyptens*, I (Wien 1996) 75f.; only one attestation, *O.Ashm.Shelt.* 74.2 (= *SB* I 2253, # 11), appears here and the precise meaning of the term was then unknown (Shelton: "Perhaps someone technically serving in a *numerus* who has been detailed to other duties such as attendance in the court of a *praeses*"). In our view we are dealing with a person who for some reason or another is added for a certain period of time to the normal numerical strength (= '*numerus*') of an office (= 'τάξις'). Further discussion is given by J.R. Rea, 'P.Ant. I 44 revised', *Tyche* 11 (1996)

187-93, esp. 192-93.

A number of further attestations of a form ἀννουμέρις has turned up in *O.Douch*, I 6, III 257, 270, IV 356, 383, 397, *SB* XVI 12358 (= *O.Douch* III 251) and in *O.Waqfa* 11, where it is treated as a personal name.

8-9. ἀκολούθως ῇ̣ ἐθέμην χειρογραφίᾳ: ῇ̣ should be taken as the direct object of ἐθέμην and should stand in the accusative. We are dealing, of course, with an *attractio casus*, ἀκολούθως being followed regularly by the dative. Comparing **803**.8ff. one may expect the clause 'ἀκολούθως --- νομοῦ' (ll. 9-12) to follow the clause ὁμολογῶ ὀμνύς etc. in l. 12ff., rather than to precede it.

9. For the office of the *dux*, cf. I. Cervenka-Ehrenstrasser, *op.cit.*, II (2000) 256-260.

12. The word νομοῦ at the beginning is not a necessary supplement; cf., e.g., l. 7 above, where it is omitted. The 'vacat' hereafter covers a space of approximately 8 letters.

16. ἐμβαλαμένων κτητόρων: for the form of the participle (instead of the more regular ἐμβαλομένων), see B.G. Mandilaras, *The Verb*, § 317.2.

The Greek word κτήτωρ is the equivalent of the Latin term '*possessor*', cf. *P.Oxy.* LIV 3758.8n.

17. εἴοιτο: for this form, cf. B.G. Mandilaras, *op.cit.*, § 117.

17-20. The wording of this passage is garbled. A comparison with **803**.14-15, εἰ δὲ κίνησ]ίς τις γίγνοτω πρόφασιν | κριθῶν ἢ ἄλλη<ς> τινὸς ῥ̣υπαρίας shows that in the present text something like προφάσει κριθῶν has fallen out in l. 18 before ἢ ἄλλης τινὸς ῥυπαρίας. Maybe the scribe intended to repair his omission by then adding the words προφάσι --- γόμου in ll. 19-20.

18-19. τῆς μίζονος ἐξουσίας: here, the office of the *praefectus annonae Alexandriae* is meant (cf. **803**.13-14).

25-26. Judging by his handwriting the scribe Aurelius Thonios son of Ammonios is not the same person as the Aurelius Thonis who wrote **803**. Cf. also below, **811**.23n.

808: UNDERTAKING BY A BOATMAN TO DELIVER BARLEY TO PELUSIUM

P. Mich. inv. # 4019 3.ix.372^{p}

H. 28.2 x W. 39 cm. The piece of papyrus was cut off regularly at all sides. There are 7 vertical and 1 horizontal folds. Margins: at the top 1.5, at the LH side 3, at the bottom 6, underneath l. 21 4 cm. There are 3 *kolleseis*, at 2, 19 and 37 cm from the LH side. Photo: see http://wwwapp.cc.columbia.edu/ldpd/app/apis/item?mode=item&key=michigan.apis.4355.

1 Ὑπ ατείας Φλαου̣ίου Μοδέστου τοῦ λαμ(προτάτου) ἐπάρχου τοῦ ἱεροῦ πραιτωρίου κ̣α̣ὶ̣ Ἀρινθέου τ̣ο̣ῦ̣ λαμ(προτάτου) στρατηλάτου Θὼθ ς̣.

2 Αὐρηλίοις Διοσκόρου Εὐλογίου καὶ Πέτρου Ἀγαθίνου καὶ Ἀγαθίνου Διδύμου καὶ Σαραπίωνι Πλου̣τάρχου καὶ Ἱέρακι Σ̣ε̣ρήνου

3 VACAT τοῖς πᾶσι βουλευταῖς τῆς Ὀξυρυγχιτῶν πόλε̣ω̣ς ἐπιμεληταῖς κριθῶν Πηλουσίου

4 παρὰ Αὐρηλίου Σερήνου Λέωνος ἀπὸ τοῦ Ὀξυρυγχίτου κυβερνήτου πλοίου Ἰσχυρίωνος πρωτήκτωρος υ̣ἱοῦ Λ̣ι̣μ̣ε̣νίου

5 ἀπὸ πριμιπιλαρίου μετ' ἐνγύου τῆς τοῦ γόμου παραδώσεως κ̣αὶ τοῦ ἐπενεγκεῖν ἄποχα γράμματα (M. 2) Αὐρηλ̣[ίο]υ̣

6 Διογένης Διογένους πολειτευομένου. V A C A T (M. 1) Ὁμολογοῦμ̣ε̣ν

7 ὀμνύντ̣ες τὸν σεβάσμιον θεῖον ὅρκον τῶν δεσποτῶν ἡμῶν Οὐαλεντινιανοῦ καὶ Οὐάλεντος καὶ Γρ̣ατιανοῦ̣

8 [τῶν αἰ]ω̣νίων Αὐγούστων ἐγὼ μὲν ὁ κυβερνήτης παριλη̣φέναι καὶ ἐμβεβλ̣ῆσθαι εἰς τὸ προκίμενον πλοῖον ἀπὸ λόγου

9 [πρώτης νέ]α̣ς̣ ἰνδικτίωνος κριθῆς νέας καθαρᾶς ἀδόλου κα̣ὶ ἀβρόχου καὶ ἐκτὸς πάσης αἰτίας καθεστηκο̣ιείης

10 [μέτρῳ δημ]ω̣σίῳ μετρήσι τῇ κελευτίσι ἐπὶ τὸ αὐτὸ (ἀρτάβας) Αϙα//, τὸν δὲ γόμον κατενέγκουμεν ἐπὶ τὴν

11 [Πηλουσιωτ]ῶν πόλει καὶ παραδώσωμεν εἰς τοὺς ἐκεῖσε δημοσίους θησαυροὺς ἀριθμῷ πλήρης καὶ τῆς τού-

12 [των παρ]α̣δώσεως ἄποχα γράμματα ὑποδέξασθαι ἐπ᾿ ὀνόματος ὑ̣[μῶ]ν̣ τῶν ἐπιμελ̣η̣τ̣ῶν καὶ ἐπεν̣εγκῖ̣ν̣

13 [καὶ ἀναδοῦ]ν̣αι ὑμῖν, ἐγὼ δὲ ὁ ἐνγυητὴς (M. 2) Διογένης (M.1) ἑκουσί[α̣ καὶ α]ὐθερέτῳ γνώμῃ̣ [ἐγ]γ̣υᾶσθαι τὸν αὐτὸν

14 [Σερῆνον] κυβερνήτην παραδίδουντα τὸν γόμον τῶν κρ̣[ιθῶν ἐκ] π̣λήρους καὶ ἐπιφέροντα τὴν ἀ̣ποχήν·

15 [εἰ δὲ συμβαί]η̣ αὐτὸν ἐν τῇ παραδόσι γενόμενον λυπασ[θῆναι, ἐπάν]αγκές ἐμὲ τὸν ἐνγυητὴν ὑποστῆναι

16 [καὶ πληρῶσ]αι τὸ ζητούμενον πρὸς αὐτὸν μέτρον καὶ καθ[αρὰν τὴν ἀ]π̣οχὴν ἐπενεγκεῖν ἢ ἔνοχοι

εἴην τῷ θείῳ ὅρκῳ.
17 (M. 2) [Αὐρήλιος] Δ̣ιογένης ἐγγυῶμ̣α̣ι̣ τ̣ὸ̣ν̣ προ̣-
κείμενον κυ̣[βερνήτη]ν̣ Σερῆνον παραδίδουντα τὸν
γόμον
18 [τῶν κριθῶν] καὶ ἐπιφαίροντα τὴν ἀποχὴν ὡς πρό-
κι[ται.]
19 VACAT (M.3) Αὐρήλιος Σερῆνος Λέωνος παραίλαβα
κ<αὶ> ἐναιβαλόμην τ̣[ὸν γόμον κριθ]ῆς καθαρᾶς
ἀρτάβας χιλίας̣ ἐνενήκοντ̣α̣
20 μίαν καὶ παραδώσω ὡς πρόκιται. Αὐρήλιος Ἀπφοῦς
Σαρ[απίωνος ἔγ]ραψα ὑπὲρ αὐτοῦ γράματα μὴ
εἰδότος.
21 (M.4) Δι' ἐμοῦ Ἁρπά̣λ̣[ου ἐγρά(φη).]

1 ϋπατειας φλαουϊου, ϊερου Pap. 2 Αὐρ̅η̅λίοις: -οι- ex ω; l. Διοσκόρῳ, Πέτρῳ; 2nd Ἀγαθίνου l. Ἀγαθίνῳ; διδυ̅μ̅ου Pap., ϊερακι Pap. 4 ι̅σχυριωνος, ϋιου Pap. 5 μετ' Pap.; l. ἐγγύου 6 Διογένης: Δ- ex corr.? (Λ?), l. Διογένους 8 Αὐγούστων: first abbreviated as Αυγs? l. παρειληφέναι, προκείμενον 9 ϊνδικτιωνος Pap.; l. καθεστηκυίης 10 l. δημοσίῳ, μετρήσει, κελευσθείσῃ, κατενέγκομεν 11 l. πόλιν, παραδώσομεν 12 l. παρ]αδόσεως, ἐπενεγκεῖν 13 ϋμιν Pap.; l. αὐθαιρέτῳ; ἐγ]γυᾶσθαι: -θ- ex -τ- corr. 14/17 l. παραδίδοντα 15 l. παραδόσει, λοιπασ[θῆναι, ἐγγυήτην 16 καθαρὰν: θ- ex -τ- corr.; l. ἔνοχος 18 l. ἐπιφέροντα, πρόκειται 19 l. παρέλαβον καὶ ἐνεβαλόμην 20 l. πρόκειται, γράμματα

"In the consulate of Flavius Modestus the most illustrious *praefectus sacro praetorio*, and Arintheus the most illustrious commander, Thoth 6. To the Aurelii Dioskoros son of Eulogios and Petros son of Agathinos and Agathinos son of Didymos and Sarapion son of Ploutarchos and Hierax son of Serenus, all from the city of the Oxyrhynchites (and) commissioners of barley for Pelusium, from Aurelius Serenus son of Leon, from the Oxyrhynchite nome, boatman of a ship of the *protector* Ischyrion son of Limenius the ex-*primipilarius*, with as surety of the delivery of the cargo and the production of the certificates of delivery Aurelius Diogenes son of Diogenes, of the curial class. We acknowledge, swearing the august imperial oath of our lords Valentinianus and Valens and Gratianus, the eternal Augusti, that I the boatman have received and loaded into the aforementioned ship on account of the first new indiction 1,091 artabas in total of new, pure, unadulterated barley, unspoiled by water and free of any fault and measured with the public measure according to the regulation measurement and we shall transport the cargo to the city of the Pelusiotes and we shall deliver it to the public granaries there in full and (we acknowledge), that we shall receive receipts of delivery of these issued to the name of you, the commissioners, and bring them back and give them to you and that I, the surety Diogenes, serve on my own free will as guarantor for the same boatman Serenus, (to the effect) that he delivers the cargo of barley in full and that he brings back the receipt; and if it would happen that he defaults at the delivery, that I, the surety, of necessity will take upon me the amount asked from him and that I shall bring the receipt free, or else may I be liable to the imperial oath.

I, Aurelius Diogenes, serve as a surety for the above mentioned boatman Serenus that he delivers the cargo of barley and that he brings back the receipt as stated above.

I, Aurelius Serenus son of Leon, have received and loaded the cargo of one thousand ninety-one artabas of pure barley and I shall deliver it as stated above. I, Aurelius Apphous son of Sarapion, have signed for him since he does not know letters. It has been written through me, Harpalos."

3. On Pelusium in antiquity, cf. A. Calderini - S. Daris, *Supplemento al Dizionario geografico* II 163, III 125, IV 109; cf. also below, l. 10-11n. and *P.Mich*. XVIII 795 and the literature cited there. The same destination is found in *P.Oxy*.LXVII 4606.5 (= *App. A* # 1; 361[p]), though there the commodity is wheat. The question, why Pelusium (rather than Alexandria) occurs in these texts as the destination of the transport, is problematical. Given the occurrence of the toponym in the title of commissioners of barley (or wheat), it is a 'structural' element, rather than an exceptional destination caused by, e.g., a sudden surplus of activity in the harbor of Alexandria. So much seems certain that in the year 372 there was no justification for this destination to be found in special historical circumstances (cf. *P.Oxy*. LXVII, p. 191).

4-5. Ἰσχυρίωνος πρωτήκτορος υἱοῦ Λιμενίου ἀπὸ πριμιπιλαρίου: this man, a shipowner, is not known from elsewhere. Ischyrion is still a πρωτήκτωρ = *protector divini lateris* (not to be confused with the *defensor*), cf. S. Daris, *Il lessico Latino*, 96; A.H.M. Jones, *LRE*, passim [esp. 53f., 129f., 636ff., 657f.]; *PLRE* I 1121ff., II 1302ff. and III 1520ff. His father apparently was a former *primipilaris*; on this official, cf. B. Dobson, "The Significance of the Centurion and 'Primipilaris' in the Roman Army and Administration", in: D.J. Breeze - B. Dobson, *Roman Officers and Frontiers*, Stuttgart 1993 (= *Mavors. Roman Army Researches*, 10) 143-185.

Unfortunately, the ink has faded towards the right border in the first lines of this text, but their reading seems nevertheless certain.

5-6. ἄποχα γράμματα: before the ἄποχα γράμματα the words ἐκ πλήρους are lacking, both here and in **811**.6. On the basis of **813**.7, these words were restored in similar passages in **800**.7, **814**.5 and **815**.4 (the latter two are copies of the same text).

5-6. Originally a large space was left open, then the name of Aurelius Diogenes and his title was inserted subsequently in different ink; the same happened with the amount in l. 10 and the name of Diogenes in l. 13. While it is not possible to tell with certainty which hand was responsible for this, probably this is M. 2 (cf. ll. 17-18). An Aurelius Diogenes son of Diogenes, town councillor and *curator frumenti*, occurs also in **800**.3, maybe also in **815**.3,4,15, as a shipowner and surety (ἔγγυος), although in the latter text he is styled ἀπὸ λογιστῶν.

9. The absence of the qualification of the indiction as εὐτυχοῦς/εὐτυχούσης is noteworthy; cf. above, § 7, and **810**.9. In itself one may, of course, also restore [τῆς αS// νέ]ạς̣.

10. κατενεγκοῦμεν (l. κατενέγκομεν; cf. also **813**.13n.): the plural can be explained by assuming that both the boatman and the surety are involved. In itself, one may wonder whether one is dealing with a contracted form (from *ἐνεγκέω) of the future of the verb φέρω. While B.G. Mandilaras (*The Verb*, § 541, sub 1) denies the existence of such a future, F.T. Gignac states that a contracted future based on the reduplicated aorist stem ἐνεγκ- is found occasionally, including in contexts in which a formal distinction between indicative and subjunctive exists. Indeed, various compounds with an element -εγκοῦμεν (1st ps.pl.) are attested (see Gignac, *Grammar*, II 287-88).

21. The notary Harpalos, who also occurs in **809**.24, **810**.25 and **811**.26, is already known from several other Oxyrhynchite texts, cf. J.M. Diethart - K.A. Worp, *Byz.Not.*, Oxyrhynchites # 1.7 (p. 79).

809: UNDERTAKING BY A BOATMAN TO DELIVER WHEAT TO ALEXANDRIA & LIST FROM WHERE GRAIN ORIGINATED

P.Mich. inv. # 4027.A (col. I, LH) + inv. 4024 (col. I.1-24, line ends of the RH side; Col. II) 6.xi.372[p]

H. 26.3 à 26.5 x W. ca 52 cm. Margins: at the top 1.5 cm (on the left section) to 0.7 cm (on the right section), at the bottom 2 cm (on the LH side) - 4 cm (on the RH side), at the LH side: 4 cm; there is no margin at the RH side. Verso: blank. Two *kolleseis* visible, one at ca 16 cm on the RH side of 4027a and one at ca 6 cm from the RH side of inv. 4024. Photo: see http://wwwapp.cc.columbia.edu/ldpd/app/apis/item?mode=item&key=michigan.apis.----.

Col. I:

1 Ὑπατείας̣ Φλ(αουίου) Μοδέστο[υ] τ̣οῦ λαμ-π(ροτάτου) ἐπ̣ά̣ρχου τοῦ ἱεροῦ πρ̣α̣ιτωρίου καὶ [Φλ](αουίου) Ἀρινθέου̣ [τοῦ λαμπ(ροτάτου) κόμη-τος καὶ μαγίστρου τῆς πεδικῆς παρατάξεως Ἀθ]ὺρ ι̣.

2 Αὐρηλίο̣ις Διοσκό[ρ]ω̣ Εὐλογίου̣ κ̣αὶ Πέτρω̣ Ἀγα̣θίνου καὶ Ἀγα̣[θί]νω̣ Διδύμ̣[ου καὶ Σαραπίωνι Πλουτ-άρχου καὶ Ἱ]ε̣ρακι

3 Σερήνου κ̣αὶ Τιμαγένει Σ̣[ε]ρ̣ήνου το[ῖ]ς̣ πᾶσι βουλευ-τα̣ῖ̣ς τῆς Ὀξυρυγ̣χ̣ιτῶν πό̣[λεως ἐπιμεληταῖς σίτου

Ἀλεξανδρεία]ς
4 παρὰ Αὐρη[λί]ου Ἰακὼβ Ἰ̣[ά]σωνος ἀπ̣[ὸ] Πανὸς πό-
λεως οἰ̣κοῦντος ἐν [Βα]βυλῶνοι [κυβερνήτου δεσ-
ποτικοῦ πολυκώπ]ου
5 ἀπὸ ἀριθ̣μοῦ Μέμφεως̣ μετ᾽ ἐγγ̣ύου τῆς τοῦ̣ γόμου
παραδό̣σ̣εως καὶ το[ῦ ἐπενεγκεῖν ἄποχα γράμ-
ματα (M. 2) Αὐρηλί]ω(ν)
6 [Γεροντ]ί̣ο̣[υ] Π̣οσιδωνίου κ̣[α]ὶ̣ Εὐλογίο[υ Π]λου-
τίωνο̣ς̣ δ̣ι̣ Ἀμμωνίο[υ υἱοῦ.] (M. 1) ⸢Ὁμ]ο̣λογ̣[οῦμεν
ὀμνύντες τὸν σεβάσμιον θεῖ]ον ὅρκον
7 τ̣ῶ̣ν̣ δ̣ε̣σ̣π̣οτῶν̣ [ἡ]μ̣ῶν Οὐαλε[ν]τινιανοῦ κα̣[ὶ] Οὐά-
λεντος̣ καὶ Γρα̣τ̣ι̣α̣ν̣[οῦ τῶν] α̣ἰ̣ων[ίων Αὐγούστων
ἐγὼ μὲν ὁ] κυβερ(νήτης)
8 παρειληφ̣έναι παρὰ τ̣ῶ̣ν ἑξῆς ἐ̣[γ]γεγραμμένων καὶ
ἐνβε̣β̣λῆσθαι εἰς τὸ [προτεταγμέν]ο̣ν̣ π̣λ̣[οῖον ἀπὸ
λόγου τῆς εὐ]τυχοῦς
9 πρώτης νέας ἰνδι̣[κ]τ̣ίονος πυ̣ρ̣οῦ νέου κα[θ]α̣ροῦ
ἀ̣κ̣ρ̣ίθου καὶ ἀβρ[ό]χ[ου καὶ ἐκτὸς πάσ]η̣ς α̣ἰ̣τ̣ί̣[ας
καθεστηκ]ό̣τος
10 μέτρῳ̣ δ̣ημοσίῳ̣ με̣τρήσι τῇ̣ κε̣[λ]ε̣υσθίσῃ̣ ἐπὶ̣ τὸ αὐτὸ
(ἀρτάβας) (M. 2) Ἀ̣ιε (M. 1) [τὸν δ]ὲ γόμον κ̣[ατ-
ενέγκω ἐπὶ τὴν] Ἀλεξάνδρειαν
11 καὶ παραδ̣ώσωμεν̣ εἰς τοὺς ἐ̣[κ]εῖσαι δημοσί̣ους
θησαυρ[ο]ὺ̣ς ἀριθ[μῷ̣] π̣λήρης καὶ τ[ῆς τούτων
παραδόσε]ω̣ς
12 ἄποχα γρ̣α̣μματα ὑπο̣δέξασθαι [ἐ]π᾽ ὀνόματος ἡμῶν
τῶν ἐ̣πιμελητῶν̣ καὶ ἐπενεγ[κεῖν καὶ ἀναδοῦναι
ὑμῖν, ἐ]γ̣ὼ δὲ

13 ο̣ ἐ̣γγυητὴς V A C A T ἑκουσίᾳ καὶ αὐθαιρέτῳ γνώμῃ ἐγγυ̣ᾶσθαι τὸν αὐ[τὸν Αὐρήλιον Ἰα κ]ὼβ κυβερνήτην

14 παραδίδ̣ουντα τ̣ὸν γόμον τοῦ σ[ί]του ἐκ πλήρους καὶ ἐπιφέ̣ροντα τὴν ἀπ̣[ο]χήν. Εἰ δὲ̣ σ̣[υμβαίη αὐτὸν ἐν παραδόσει γ]ε̣νόμενον

15 λοιπασθῆνα̣ι ἐπάναγκ̣[ε]ς ἐμὲ τὸν ἐγγυητὴν VACAT ὑ̣ποστῆναι κ[αὶ] πληρῶσαι τ̣ὸ [ζητούμενον πρὸς αὐτὸν μ]έτρον

16 καὶ καθαρὰ̣[ν <τὴν ἀποχὴν ἐπ>ε]νεγκεῖν εἰ[ς]τ̣ὸ ἐν μηδενὶ μεμφθῆ̣ν̣αι ἢ ἔνοχ̣ο̣ς εἴην τῷ θ̣ε̣ίῳ ὅρκῳ. (M. 3) Αὐ̣[ρήλιος Εὐλόγιος Πλουτί]ω̣νος δι᾽ ἐμοῦ

17 Ἀμ μωνίου υἱοῦ ἐ̣νγυῶμαι ἅμα Γεροντί[ο]υ Ποσιδωνίου τὸν προκ̣[είμ]ενον Ἰα κὼβ̣ [πο]λ̣υκ̣ω[πίτην] παρα]δ̣ί̣δ̣ο̣ντα τὸν γόμον

)————

18 τῶν τοῦ σί̣τ̣ου ἀρταβῶ̣ν χειλίω̣ν δεκαπέντε ἐκ πλήρους καὶ ἐπιφέρ[ον]τ̣α τὴν ἀποχὴ[ν] ὡ̣ς̣ πρ[όκειται. (M. 4) Αὐρ̣ή̣[λιος] Γερόντιος Ποσι-

19 δωνίου πολ̣ιτευόμενος ἐγγυῶμαι ἅμα Εὐ̣λογίῳ Πλουτ̣ί̣ωνος δι᾽ Ἀ̣μμωνίου υἱ[οῦ τὸν] προκ[ίμενον Ἰακ]ὼβ πολυκωπί-

20 τ̣ην παραδ̣ίδουντα τ̣ὸν γόμον τῶν τοῦ σίτ̣ου ἀρταβ̣ῶ[ν χιλ]ί̣ω̣[ν δ]εκαπέντε ἐκ̣ πλήρο[υς] καὶ ἐπι̣[φέρ]οντα τὴν

21 ἀπ̣ο̣χ̣ὴ̣ν̣ [ὡς π]ρ̣ό̣κιτ̣α̣ι̣. (M. 5) Αὐρ̣ήλ[ι]ος Ἰα κὼβ Ἰάσ̣ω̣ν̣ος πα[ρ]έλαβον κ̣αὶ ἐν[εβ]αλόμ[η]ν̣ τὰς τοῦ πυ-

22 ϱοῦ νέο[υ κα]θαϱοῦ ἀκϱίθου καὶ ἀβϱόχ̣[ου] ἀϱτά̣βας
χιλ[ί]ας δ[εκ]απ^{ε}ν[τε] κ̣αὶ παϱαδώ-
23 σω ὡς π̣[ϱόκ]ε̣ι̣ται.
24 (M. 6) Δι᾽ ἐμοῦ Ἁϱπάλ̣ου ἐγ̣ϱ̣ά(φη).

Col. II:
25 (M. 7) Ἔστι δέ·
26 σίτου ὑποστάσεως (ἀϱτάβαι) Ἀι̣ε̣
27 οὕτως·
28 αS ἰν̣δικ(τίωνος)
29 πολ(ιτικά)·
30 κωμητ(ικά)·

31 ε πάγου, Ταμπεμοῦ, δι(ὰ) Νικία Παταψόιτος
32 καὶ Αὐσίου Ἐπάϱχου κ̣α̣ὶ̣ κ̣ο̣ι̣(νωνῶν) σιτολ(όγων)
(ἀϱτ.) τλζL
33 Ποσομποῦς, δι(ὰ) Γεϱοντίο̣υ̣ καὶ Εὐλογίου
34 πϱεσ(βυτέϱων) (ἀϱτ.) σξδ
35 Μούχεως, δι(ὰ) Θεοδώϱου καὶ Ἰωάννου
36 καὶ κοι(νωνῶν) σιτολ(όγων) (ἀϱτ.) ϱβ
37 Πινύϱεως (ἀϱτ.) οεL
38 οὕτως·
39 Ἰσὰκ καὶ Παῦλος καὶ Πέτϱος
40 καὶ Ὡϱιγένης (ἀϱτ.) λς β>
41 Ὧϱος καὶ Παῦλος καὶ ⟦Σ̣ο̣φ̣ί̣α̣⟧ {κ̣α̣ὶ̣} Πακ̣ῦ̣σ̣ι̣ς
42 καὶ Παῦλος καὶ Πιν̣ῦ̣χ̣ι̣ς καὶ Σοφία
(ἀϱτ.) ιδ Ld/
43 Πανοῦφις κ̣[α]ὶ Θέκλα (ἀϱτ.) β d/

44 Σιλβανὸς καὶ Ἰωάννης καὶ
45 Παπνοῦθις καὶ Ἑρμίας καὶ οἱ κοι(νωνοὶ)
(ἀρτ.) καLγ̣/
46 αἱ π(ροκείμεναι).

2 ϊερακι Pap. 4 l. Βαβυλῶνι 5 μετ' Pap., l. ἐγγύων 8 l. ἐμβεβλῆσθαι 10 l. μετρήσει, κελευσθείσῃ 11 l. παραδώσομεν 12 l. ὑμῶν 13 εγ'γυητης, εγ'γυασθαι Pap. 14, 20 l. παραδίδοντα 15 εγ'γυητης Pap. 16 μηδενί partly from correction 17 l. Γεροντίῳ 18 l. χιλίων 32 αυσιου Pap. 39 ϊσακ Pap., 1st καί: κ ex π corr. 44 ϊωαννης Pap.

"In the consulate of Flavius Modestus, the most illustrious *praefectus sacro praetorio*, and of Flavius Arintheus, the most illustrious commander, Hathyr 10. To the Aurelii Dioskoros son of Eulogios and Petros son of Agathinos and Agathinos son of Didymos and Sarapion son of Ploutarchos and Hierax son of Serenus and Timagenes son of Serenus, all councillors of the city of the Oxyrhynchites (and) commissioners of wheat for Alexandria, from Aurelius Jakob son of Jason, from Panopolis, living in Babylon, boatman of an imperial ship from the flotilla stationed in Memphis, with as surety for the delivery of the cargo and the production of the certificates of delivery the (M. 2) Aurelii Gerontios son of Posidonios and Eulogios son of Ploution, through his son Ammonios. (M. 1) We acknowledge swearing the august imperial oath of our lords Valentinianus and Valens and Gratianus the eternal Augusti that I, the boatman, have received from the people mentioned below and have loaded into the above mentioned ship from the harvest of the fortunate first new indiction in total (M. 2) 1,015 (M. 1) art.

of wheat, new, pure, without barley and unwetted and free of any fault and measured with the public measure according to the regulations and I shall transport the cargo to Alexandria and I shall deliver it to the public granaries there in full and I (acknowledge that I) shall receive certificates of delivery of these in the name of you, the commissioners, and bring them and give them to you and that I, the surety < > serve of my own free will as surety for the same boatman, Jakob, that he deliver the cargo of wheat in full and that he bring back the receipt. If it would happen that he defaults at the delivery, I the surety < > will of necessity take upon me the amount asked from him and I shall bring a clean receipt so as not to incur blame in any regard whatsoever, otherwise may I be liable to the imperial oath.

(M. 3) I, Aurelius Eulogios son of Ploution, represented through me his son Ammonius, guarantee together with Gerontios son of Posidonios that the above mentioned Jacob the *polykopites* deliver the cargo of one thousand fifteen artabas of wheat in full and that he produce the receipt as stated above.

(M. 4) I, Aurelius Gerontios son of Posidonios, belonging to the curial class, guarantee together with Eulogios son of Ploution, represented through his son Ammonios, that the above mentioned *polykopites* Jakob, deliver the cargo of one thousand fifteen artabas of wheat in full and that he produce the receipt as stated above.

(M. 5) I, Aurelius Jakob, son of Jason, have received and loaded the one thousand and fifteen artabas of wheat and I shall deliver as stated above.

(M. 6) It has been written through me, Harpalos."

Column II:
(M. 7) "That is: for the total of wheat: 1,015 art. As follows: for the 1st indiction, taxes from city-dwellers: ---; taxes from village-dwellers: of the 5th *pagus*, for Tampemu, through Nikias son of Patopsois and Ausios son of Eparchos and their associate *sitologi*: 337 1/2 art.; for Posompous, through Gerontios and Eulogios, village elders, 264 art.; for Mychis, through Theodoros and Johannes and their associate *sitologi*, 102 art.; for Pinyris, 75 1/2 art., as follows: Isaak and Paulos and Petros and Horigenes (delivered) 36 2/3 art.; Horos and Paulos and ⟦Sophia⟧ Pakysis and Paulos and Pinychis and Sophia (delivered) 14 3/4 art.; Panouphis and Thekla (delivered) 2 1/4 art.; Silvanus and Johannes and Papnouthis and Hermias and their partners (delivered) 21 1/2 1/8 art.; = the aforementioned."

809 and **810** refer to the same shipment. In both texts, the subscribing hands are identical. **809**, however, contains a second column which is now lost in **810**; on the other hand, only the ends of the first column have been preserved. For an element possibly missing here in l. 6, see **810**.6n. For duplicates of documents in general, see B. Nielsen, "A Catalog of Duplicate Papyri", *ZPE* 129 (2000) 187-214.

1. In this text and in **810** the longer version of the consular formula of Flavius Domitius Modestus and his colleague Flavius Arintheus (see **807**.1n.) is used. Instead of τῆς πεδικῆς δυνάμεως one finds τῆς πεδικῆς

παρατάξεως; for this wording, cf. the end of the consular formula in *P.Flor.* I 30 = *SB* XXII 15286.27: τ[ῆς ἱππικ]ῆς παρατάξεως (Fl. Nevitta was a *magister equitum*).

2-3. For these well-known town councillors of Oxyrhynchus and commissioners of (tax) grain to be shipped to Alexandria, cf. the general introd., §§ 2-3.

4-5. For the *polykopites* Jakob son of Jason, cf. the general introd., § 4.

5-6. μετ᾽ ἐγγύου: normally, a boatman who loaded grain into his ship and promised to transport the cargo to Alexandria was accompanied by one surety (called ἔγγυος *and* ἐγγυητής in the same text, cf. l. 13, **800**.7,17, **808**.5,13, **810**.5,13, **811**.6.16, **813**.6,15, **814**.5,12, and **815**.4,11). Jacob son of Jason has *two* sureties (cf. **802**.14), although the singular used here and in **810**.5,13 indicates that in this case, too, only one guarantor was expected. The fact that a second hand added the names of the two guarantors (cf. also **810**.5-6) and the fact that the names of these two guarantors were not filled out in **810**.13 suggests that Jacob had difficulties in finding a surety. In the end he came up with *two* persons willing to share the burden together (a fact stressed in the subscriptions of these sureties). The two guarantors may be identified with the two *presbyteroi* of the village Posompous mentioned in **809**.32-33; at the same time it is striking that Gerontios identifies himself in l. 19 as being a *politeuomenos*, i.e. he would have belonged to the curial class of Oxyrhynchus.

8. For the supplement προτεταγμένον instead of the usual προκείμενον, cf. **810**.8-9.

16-17. A paragraphus should separate the body of the text from the subscriptions, but it has been placed incorrectly underneath l. 17 instead of underneath l. 16. Such separators also occur in other texts in this archive, cf. **806**.12-13, **807**.22-23, **810**.17-18, **811**.19-20, **813**.18-19, **814**.15-16 and **816**.23-24.

26. For the meaning of ὑποστάσεως for introducing the tax on land, cf. D. Hagedorn - K.A. Worp in *ZPE* 121 (1998) 188, note to l. 10.

The amounts of 337½ (l. 32) + 264 (l. 34) + 102 (l. 36) + 75½ art. (l.

37) for the tax on village-dwellers together make 779 art. This leaves 1,015 - 779 = 236 (σλϛ) artabas unaccounted for; the latter amount (ca 23 % of the total) probably represents the πολιτικά (l. 29), but for some reason the amount was never filled out. The lopsided ratio between the amounts for πολιτικά and κωμητικά may be simply accidental.

31. For Τα(α)μπεμοῦ in the 5th *pagus,* cf. P. Pruneti, *I centri abitati dell' Ossirinchite. Repertorio toponomastico* (Florence 1981; = Pap.Flor. 9), 188f.; A. Benaissa, *Rural Settlements of the Oxyrhynchite Nome. A Papyrological Survey.* (Version 1 [2009] = Trismegistos Online Publications, IV), s.n.

32. A name Αὖσις occurs in *CPR* XIII 6.v.110 (III^{a}), a name Ἄυσις in *P.Harr.* I 80.42 (250^{p}) and in *P.Oxy.* LIV 3769.4 (334^{p}); cf. also the name Αὔσιος in *SB* XVIII 13637.3 (99^{p}). A female of the name Αὖσις occurs in *SB* VI 9572.18 (61/2^{p}).

33. For Ποσομποῦς in the 5th pagus, cf. P. Pruneti, *op.cit.*, 153f.; A. Benaissa, *op.cit.*, s.n.

34. Here the village elders are meant; on these, cf. A. Tomsin, *Étude sur les πρεσβύτεροι dans les villages de la χώρα égyptienne,* Acad.Roy.Belg., Bull.Cl. de Lettres, sér. V^{e}, Tome XXXVIII (Brussels 1952) 95-130, 467-532.

35. For Μοῦχις, cf. P. Pruneti, *op.cit.*, 110f.; A. Benaissa, *op.cit.*, s.n. The information that this village was situated in the 5th pagus (l. 31) seems to be new.

37. The amounts of $36\frac{2}{3}$ (l. 40) + $14\frac{3}{4}$ (l. 42) + $2\frac{1}{4}$ (l. 43) + $21\frac{1}{2}\frac{1}{3}$ art. (l. 45) together make $75\frac{1}{2}$ art. In this case the total is subdivided, since payments are made by 4 different groups of persons (πιττάκια).

For Πινῦρις, cf. P. Pruneti, *op.cit.*, 152; A. Benaissa, *op.cit.*, s.n.; the information that this village was situated in the 5th pagus (l. 31) seems to be new.

39-45. These lines contain information on the payments of tax-grain made by individual persons.

810: UNDERTAKING BY A BOATMAN TO DELIVER WHEAT TO ALEXANDRIA

P.Mich. inv. # 4027.B ?6.xi.372P

H. 27 x W. 34 cm. Margins: at the top 2.5, at the bottom 3.5 (after the signature), at the LH side 4, and at the RH side 2 cm. Verso: blank. Two visible *kolleseis*: one at ca 10 cm from the right of the front and the second at ca 14 cm from the first *kollesis*. Photo: see http://wwwapp.cc.columbia.edu/ldpd/app/apis/item?mode=item&key=michigan.apis.----.

1 Ὑ̣πα̣τ̣είας Φλα̣ουίων Μο̣δέστου τ̣[ο]ῦ̣ λαμπ(ροτάτου) ἐπάρχου τοῦ ἱεροῦ πραιτωρίου κα̣ὶ̣ Ἀ̣ρειν̣θέου̣ [τοῦ λαμπ(ροτάτου) κόμητος καὶ μαγίστρου τῆς] π̣ε̣δ̣ι-κῆς παρατάξε(ως) [Ἁθὺρ ι].

2 Αὐρηλίοις Διοσκόρῳ Εὐλογίο̣υ̣ καὶ Πέτρῳ Ἀ̣γαθίνου καὶ Ἀγαθίνῳ Διδύμου καὶ Σα̣[ραπίωνι Πλουτ-άρχου] κ̣α̣ὶ̣ Ἱ̣έρακι

3 Σερήνου καὶ Τιμαγέ̣ν̣ε̣ι Σερή̣νου τοῖς πᾶσ̣ι βουλευ-ταῖς τῆς Ὀξυρυγχιτῶν πό̣λ̣[εως ἐπιμεληταῖς σίτου Ἀλ]ε̣ξ̣α̣[νδ]ρίας

4 παρὰ Αὐρηλί[ο]υ Ἰακὼβ Ἰάσω̣νος ἀπὸ Πα̣νὸς πόλεως οἰκοῦντος ἐν Βαβυλ̣[ῶνι κυβερνήτο]υ̣

5 δεσ̣ποτικο̣ῦ πολυκώπου ἀ̣π̣ὸ ἀριθμῶ Μ̣έμφεως̣ μετ' ἐγγ̣ύου τῆς τοῦ̣ [γόμου παραδόσεως καὶ τοῦ ἐ]πε-νεγ-

6 κε̣ῖ̣ν ἄπο[χ]α γράμματ[α] (M. 2) Αὐρη̣[λ]ίων Γερο̣ν-

τίου Ποσιδ̣ω̣ν̣ί̣ο̣υ̣ κ̣α̣[ὶ Εὐλο]γ̣ί̣ου Πλου[τίωνος δι᾽ Ἀμμωνίου υἱοῦ] ̣ ἐπαν( ) (M. 1)

7 Ὁμ̣[ολ]ο̣γ̣ῶ̣ ὀ̣μ̣ν̣ύ̣ς̣ τ̣ὸ̣ν̣ σ̣ε̣β̣ά̣σ̣[μι]ο̣ν̣ θ̣ε̣ῖ̣ο̣ν̣ [ὅ]ρ̣κον τ̣ῶ̣[ν] δεσποτῶ̣ν̣ [ἡμ]ῶν Οὐα̣[λ]ε̣ντινια̣ν̣[οῦ καὶ Οὐάλεντος καὶ Γρα]τ̣ιανοῦ

8 τ̣ῶ̣[ν αἰωνί]ων Αὐγο̣ύ̣[στων ἐ]γὼ μὲν ὁ κ̣υ̣βερνήτη̣ς̣ παρειληφ̣[έν]α̣ι καὶ ἐνβεβλ̣ῆ̣σ̣θα̣[ι εἰς τὸ προτε]ταγμέ[νον π]λοῖον ἀπ[ὸ λόγου τ]ῆς πρ̣ώ̣[τ]η̣ς ἰνδικ-

9 τ̣[ί]ονος πυ[ροῦ ν]έ̣ου καθαρ̣οῦ ἀ̣κ̣ρ̣ίθ̣[ου καὶ ἀβρόχου καὶ ἐ]κ̣τὸς

10 πά̣[σης αἰτί]α̣ς καθε̣σ̣[τηκότος] μέτρῳ̣ δημ̣[ο]σίῳ̣ με[τρ]ή̣σι τῇ̣ κελ[ευσθ]ή̣ση̣ ἐπὶ [τὸ αὐτὸ] (ἀ̣ρ̣τ̣ά̣β̣α̣ς̣) [Ἀιε, τὸν δὲ] γ̣ό̣μ̣ο̣ν

11 κατενέγκω̣ ἐπὶ τὴν [λαμπροτ]ά̣την Ἀλ̣ε̣ξ̣άνδρεια[ν κ]αὶ παρ[αδώσ]ω̣μεν εἰ̣ς [τ]ο̣ὺ̣ς ἐ̣κε[ῖσε δημοσίους θησα]υρούς

12 ἀ̣ρ̣ιθμ̣ῷ̣ π̣λήρης κα̣[ὶ τῆς τού]των παραδ̣ό̣σεως̣ ἄ̣π̣οχα γρ̣ά̣[μμα]τ̣α ὑποδέξασθαι ἐπ̣᾽ [ὀνόματος ὑμῶ]ν̣ τῶν

13 ἐπ̣ι̣μελητῶν καὶ ἐ̣[πενεγκεῖ]ν καὶ ἀναδοῦναι ὑμ̣ῖν, ἐγὼ δὲ ὁ [ἐ]γ̣γυητὴς VACAT ἐ̣[κουσί]α̣

14 καὶ̣ α̣ὐ̣θαιρ̣έτῳ̣ γνώ̣[μη̣ ἐγγυ]ᾶσθαι τὸν αὐ̣τὸν κυβ̣ε̣ρνήτ̣ην Ἰ[α]κ̣ὼβ παραδίδουντα τ̣[ὸν γόμον τοῦ σίτο]υ̣

15 ἐ̣κ π̣λήρ̣ου̣ς̣ καὶ ἐπιφ̣[έροντα τ]ὴν ἀποχήν. Εἰ δὲ συμ̣βαίη αὐτὸν ἐν τῇ̣ παραδόσι γενόμ̣[ενον λοιπασθῆ]ν̣α̣ι̣

16 ἐπ[άν]αγκε̣ς̣ ἐμὲ τ[ὸ]ν [ἐγγυητὴ]ν ὑποστῆναι καὶ

π̣λ̣η̣ρῶσαι τὸ ζητούμεν[ο]ν πρὸς αὐτ̣[ὸν μέτρον καὶ
κα]θ̣αρὰν̣
17 τὴν̣ ἀποχὴν ἐπε̣ν̣[εγκεῖν εἰς] τὸ ἐμ μηδενὶ με^{μ}φθῆν̣α̣ι
ἢ̣ ἔ̣ν̣ο̣χος εἴην τῷ̣ θ̣είῳ ὅρκῳ. [(M.3) Αὐρήλιος
Εὐλόγι]ος
)——————
18 Πλ̣ο̣υτίωνο̣ς̣ δι’ ἐ̣μοῦ Ἀμ̣[μωνίου υἱ]οῦ ἐνγυῶμαι ἅμα
Γερον̣τ̣ίου Ποσιδων̣[ίο]υ τὸν προκί[μ]ε̣νον Ἰα κ[ὼβ
πολυκωπίτην] π̣αραδί-
19 δουντα τὸν γόμον τῶν̣ [τοῦ σίτου] ἀρταβῶν χειλίων
δε̣[κ]α̣πέντε ἐκ πλήρους κα[ὶ] ἐπιφέροντ̣α̣ [τὴν
ἀποχὴν] ὡς πρόκιτε.
20 (M. 4) Αὐρήλιος Γερόντιος Πο[σιδωνίου] πολιτευ-
όμενος ἐγγυ[ῶ]μ̣αι ἅμα Εὐ[λο]γίῳ Πλουτίω[ν]ος
δι’ Ἀμμ̣[ωνίου υἱοῦ τὸ]ν προκί-
21 μενον Ἰα κ̣ὼβ̣ πολυκ[ωπίτην π]α̣ραδίδουντ̣α̣ τὸν γό-
μο[ν] τ̣ῶν τοῦ σ[ί]τ̣ου ἀρταβῶν̣ [χ]ε̣ι̣λίων δε̣[κα-
πέντε ἐκ] πλήρους
22 κα̣ὶ ἐπιφέροντα τὴν̣ [ἀποχὴν] ὡ̣ς πρόκιτα̣ι. (M.5)
Αὐρήλι̣ο[ς Ἰ]ακὼβ Ἰά[σ]ωνος παρ̣[έ]λ̣α̣βον κα̣ὶ [ἐν-
εβαλόμ]ην̣ τὰς ^{τ}οῦ
23 πυροῦ ν̣έου καθ[αροῦ ἀ]κρίθου καὶ ἀβρό̣[χ]ο̣υ ἀρ-
τάβας χιλε[ί]ας δεκα[πέντε καὶ] παραδώ-
24 σω ὡς πρόκιτα[ι.]
25 (M. 6) Δι’ [ἐμ]οῦ Ἁρπάλου ἐ[γρ]ά(φη).

1 l. Ἀρινθέου 2 ϊερακι Pap. 3 l. χαίρειν 4 ϊακωβ ϊασωνος Pap.
5 l. ἀριθμοῦ; μετ᾿εγγυου Pap. 8 l. ἐμβεβλῆσθαι 10 l. μετρήσει,

κελευσθείσῃ 11 l. παραδώσομεν 13 ὑ̈μιν Pap. 14/18/21 ϊ̈ακωβ Pap. 14/21 l. παραδίδοντα 15 l. παραδόσει 16 ὑ̈ποστηναι Pap. 17 l. ἐν 18 l. ἐγγυῶμαι, Γεροντίῳ, προκείμενον 19 l. χιλίων, πρόκειται 20-21 l. προκείμενον 21 l. χιλίων 22 l. πρόκειται; Αὐρήλιος: -η- ex αυ corr. 23 l. χιλίας 23-24 παραδ$_{ω}$σω Pap. 24 l. πρόκειται.

For translation and further commentary, see the copy of the text at **809**.

6. We are unable to resolve the abbreviation ἐπαν( ) with certainty; the problem is compounded in that this word appears to be missing in the copy in **809**.6. Maybe this had something to do with the circumstances under which Gerontios and Eulogios became sureties; are we dealing with some form of the participles ἐπαν(αγκασθείς) (= 'having been forced to [this task]' or ἐπαν(αιρεθείς) (= 'having obtained [this task] by lot')?
8. The duplicate in **809**.8 inserts after παρειληφ̣έναι the element παρὰ τῶν ἑξῆς ἐγγεγραμμένων.
8-9. The word division in προτε]τα- | γμέ[νον is exceptional and irregular.
9. This copy leaves out the qualification of the indiction as εὐτυχοῦς which is found in the double **809**.8; for the absence itself, cf. **808**.9n.
13. The final alpha of ἐ̣[κουσί]α̣ is prolonged extraordinarily to the right.
18. Cf. **809**.16-17n.

811: DECLARATION BY A BOATMAN / *KATASTATHS* TO DELIVER WHEAT TO ALEXANDRIA

P.Mich. inv. # 4023 372P

H. 27 x W: 23.6 cm (at the longest surviving section). Margins: at the top 1.5-2.0, at the bottom 1, at the LH side ca 3.5 cm. The RH side is damaged (missing). The verso is blank. One *kollesis* is visible on the verso on the edge of the LH side of the front. *Kollema*: ca 2-3 cm. At ca 10 cm after the *kollesis*, there are visible traces of ancient repair (a large strip of papyrus); this is not a *kollesis*. Photo: see http://wwwapp.cc.columbia.edu/ldpd/app/apis/item?mode=item&key=michigan.apis.4359.

1 Ὑπ ατείας Φλαουίων Μοδέστου καὶ Ἀρινθέου τῶ̣[ν λαμπροτάτων, Month, Day].

2 Αὐρηλίοις Διοσκόρῳ Εὐλογίου καὶ Πέτρῳ Ἀγαθεί[νου καὶ Ἀγαθίνῳ Διδύμου καὶ Σαραπίωνι Πλουτάρχου]

3 καὶ Ἱέ ρακι Σερήνου̣ [καὶ] Τ̣ιμαγένι Σερήνου τοῖς π̣[ᾶσι] β̣ο̣υ̣λ[ευταῖς τῆς Ὀξ υρυγχιτῶν πόλεως ἐπιμεληταῖς σίτου]

4 Ἀλεξανδρείας VACAT

5 παρὰ Αὐρηλίου Ὡρ ίωνος Ἡρ ακλᾶ ἀπὸ κώμης Φ̣ο̣β̣[ώου τοῦ Ὀξ υρυγχίτου νομοῦ κυβερνήτου δημοσίου]

6 πλοίου μετ᾽ ἐγγύου τῆ̣ς [ἐ]π̣ι̣φ̣ε̣ρ̣[ομέ]ν̣ης ἀποχῆς τοῦ σ[ίτου Ἀλεξανδρείας Αὐρηλίου Ἀμμωνίου]

7 υἱοῦ Εὐλογίου Πλουτίωνος πολ(ιτευομένου) τῆς αὐτῆς πόλεω̣[ς. Ὁμολογοῦμεν ὀμνύντες]

8 τὸ̣ν̣ σεβάσμιον θεῖον ὅρκον τῶν δεσποτῶν ἡμῶν [Οὐαλεντινιανοῦ καὶ Οὐάλεντος καὶ Γρ̣ατιανοῦ τῶν αἰωνίων]

9 Αὐγ̣ο̣ύ̣στων ἐπὶ τῷ ἐμὲ τὸν καταστάτην Ὡρίων̣[α

10 δημ̣ο̣σ̣ί̣ο̣υ̣ πολυκώπου ὑπὸ Ἰακὼβ Ἰάσωνος ἀπ[ὸ Πανὸς πόλεως

11 το̣ῦ ἐ̣μ̣βληθέντος αὐτῷ ὑπὸ τοῦ αὐτοῦ κυβερ(νήτου) Ἰακὼ[β ἀρταβῶν]

12 χιλίων δεκαπέντε καὶ τοῦτο καταστῆσαι ἐν τ[

13 ἐπὶ τῆς αὐτῆς Ἀλεξάνδρειαν ἄχρις ἂν τὴν παρά-[δοσιν ποιήσηται ἐν τοῖς ἐκεῖσε δημοσίοις ὁρρίοις]

14 τοῦ προκιμένου μέτρου τοῦ σίτου ἐκ π{ ̣}λήρους κ̣[αὶ ὑποδέξασθαι ἄποχα γράμματα τῆς τούτων παρα-]

15 δόσεως ἐπ᾽ ὀνόματος ὑμῶν τῶν ἐπιμελητ[ῶν καὶ ἐπενεγκεῖν καὶ ἀναδοῦναι ὑμῖν εἰς τὸ]

16 μηδεμίαν μέμψιν περὶ ἐμὲ γένεσθαι, ἐγὼ δὲ ὁ ἐγ[γυητὴς Ἀμμώνιος ἑκουσίᾳ καὶ αὐθερέτῳ γνώμη̣]

17 ἐγγυᾶσθαι τὸν αὐτὸν Ὡρίωνα καταστάτην ἐπιφέ̣[ροντα τὴν ἀποχὴν τοῦ σίτου· ἐὰν δὲ]

18 ἀμέλια τίς ὑπ᾽ αὐτοῦ γένηται ἐμὲ τὸν ἐγγυητὴν ἐ[πάναγκες ὑποστῆναι πάντα τὰ πρὸς αὐτὸν περὶ τούτου]

19 ζ̣ητούμενα εἰς τὸ ἐν μηδενὶ μεμφθῆναι ἢ ἔνοχ[ος εἴην τῷ θείῳ ὅρκῳ.]

20 (M. 2) Αὐρήλιος Ὡρίωνος Ἡρακλᾶ ὤμωσα τὸν τῖον

ὅρκον καὶ κα[ταστήσω -------- εἰς]

21 Νεάπολιν τῆς λαμπροτάτης Ἀλεξαντρίας καὶ παρα-μ̣[ενῶ αὐτῷ ἐπὶ τῆς αὐτῆς Ἀλεξανδρείας ἄχρις ἂν τὴν παράδο-]

22 σιν ποιήσεται ἐν τοῖς ἐκῖσε δημοσίοις ὡρίοις τοῦ προκι̣[μένου μέτρου τοῦ σίτου καὶ τὴν ἀποχὴν καθαρὰν]

23 ἐπενέγκω ὡς πρόκιται καὶ ἐπερωτητὶς ὡμολόγησ[α. N.N. ἔγραψα ὑπὲρ αὐ-]

24 τὸς γ̣ράμματα μὴ εἰδότο̣ς̣. (M.3) Αὐρήλιος Ἀμμώνιος Εὐλογίου ἐ̣[γγυῶμαι τὸν αὐτὸν καταστάτην Ὡρί-ωνα ἐπιφέροντα τὴν ἀποχὴν]

25 τοῦ σ̣ί̣τ̣ου ὡς πρόκιται.

26 (M.4) Δ(ι') ἐμοῦ Ἁρπά̣λου̣ [ἐγράφη.]

1 ϋπατειας Pap. 2 l. Ἀγαθί[νου 3 ϊερακι Pap. (-α- < ι), l. Τιμαγένει 6 εγ'γυου Pap. 7 υϊου Pap. (1st υ corr., ex α?) 9 l. τὸ 10 ϊακωβ ϊασωνος Pap. 11 ϊακωβ 12 l. τοῦτον? See introd. 13 l. Ἀλεξανδρείας 14 l. προκειμένου 16 l. αὐθαιρέτῳ 17 ἐγγυᾶσθαι Pap. 18 l. ἀμέλεια; εγ'γυητην Pap. 20 l. Ὡρίων; ὤμωσα ex ὤμασα corr. (l. ὤμοσα), l. θεῖον 21 l. Ἀλεξανδρείας (2nd α ex ε corr.) 22 l. ποιήσηται, ἐκεῖσε, ὁρρίοις, προκειμένου 23/25 l. πρόκειται 23 l. ἐπερωτηθεὶς 23-24 l. αὐτοῦ

"In the consulate of the Flavii Modestus and Arintheus, *viri clarissimi*, [Month, Day]. To the Aurelii Dioskoros son of Eulogios and Petros son of Agathinos and Agathinos son of Didymos and Sarapion son of Ploutarchos and Hierax son of Serenus and Timagenes son of Serenus, all councillors of the city of the Oxyrhynchites and commissioners of wheat for Alexandria, from Aurelius Horion son of Heraklas, from the village of Phoboou of the Oxyrhynchite nome, boatman of a state ship, with as surety of the receipt that is presented of the wheat transported to Alexandria Aurelius Ammonios son of Eulogios grandson of Ploution, *politeuomenos* of the same city. We acknowledge swearing the august imperial oath of our lords Valentinianus and Valens and Gratianus the eternal Augusti, that I the *katastates* Horion --- of a state ship with many oars under Jacob son of Jason, from Panopolis (and responsible ?) for a cargo of in total one thousand fifteen artabas of new clean and unadulterated wheat put on board by the same pilot Jacob and that I shall deposit this in (Neapolis?) in the most illustrious Alexandria, and that I shall stay with it / him (?) in the same Alexandria until he has performed delivery of the afore-mentioned total of wheat into the local public granaries in full and that he will accept the receipts of delivery thereof in the name of you, the commissioners, and that I shall bring back these and hand over to you so as to incur no blame; I, the surety Ammonios (acknowledge) that I serve of my free will and voluntarily as surety for the same *katastates*, Horion, that he will produce the receipts for the wheat. If he neglects his duties in any respect, I, the surety, shall of necessity fulfill all that is being requested from him on this account so as to incur no blame in any respect, otherwise may I be liable to the imperial oath.

(M. 2) I, Aurelius Horion son of Heraklas, have sworn the imperial oath and shall bring the afore-mentioned --- to Neapolis in the most illustrious Alexandria and I shall stay with

it / him (?) in the same Alexandria until he has made delivery of the aforementioned amount of wheat into the public granaries there and I shall produce the clean receipt as stated above and having been asked the formal question I have assented. I, N.N. have written it for him, since he does not know letters.
(M. 3) I, Aurelius Ammonios son of Eulogios, guarantee that the aforementioned *katastates*, Horion, produces the receipt of the wheat as stated above.
(MK. 4) It has been written through me, Harpalos."

The papyrus is not only difficult to read in some places, but it is also incomplete at the right side and our interpretation of this unique text is somewhat speculative. Although in the present text, which is a declaration to six town councillors of Oxyrhynchus in their capacity of commissioners of wheat for Alexandria (ἐπιμεληταὶ σίτου Ἀλεξανδρείας), a cargo of 1,015 artabas of wheat is to be transported on a ship under the boatman Jacob son of Jason, precisely as in **809 - 810** (also from the year 372p), we are not necessarily dealing with the *same* cargo. Only so much is certain that the ship on which Jacob was a boatman had a capacity to hold at least 1,015 artabas (on the capacity of Nile ships in Graeco-Roman Egypt, cf. I.J. Poll, *Ladefähigkeit und Grösse der Nilschiffe*, Archiv 42 [1996] 127-138).

The author of the text, Aurelius Horion son of Heraklas, is called a καταστάτης (ll. 9, 17) and he agrees to καταστῆσαι (l. 12, cf. l. 20). The verb καθίστημι is frequently used in the papyri and has various different meanings; cf. for the 'liturgical' meaning N. Lewis, *The Compulsory Services of Roman Egypt*[2]

[Florence 1997] 60, for the 'juridical' meaning H. Maehler in *Archiv* 33 [1987] 28). The substantive καταστάτης (listed in *LSJ* with only 2 attestations) occurs in the papyri published to date only in *P.Oslo* III 88.16,35 (cf. *LSJ*, Revised Supplement) and in *SPP* III^2.1 10 (cf. the *Wörterlisten*); cf. also the form κατάστατοι in *Pap.Lugd.Bat.* XXX 2.9 and note *ad loc.* Furthermore, one may compare the form ὑποκαταστάτην (ed.: l. -τον?) in *P.Lips.* I 55.9-10, and the genitive ὑποκαταστάτου in *P.Flor.* III 325.3 and *P.Oxy.* LXVII 4614.2. In the note to the Oslo papyrus, the editors consider the possibility that it may be a Greek translation of the Roman 'stator' (cf. H. Mason, *Greek Terms for Roman Institutions* [Toronto 1974; = *AmStudPap* 13] p. 85b s.v. στάτωρ; Fr. Kayser in *BIFAO* 90 [1990] 241ff.), but this meaning does not really seem applicable here.

Starting out from the meaning of the adjective ὑποκαταστάτος = Lat. 'substitutus' (cf. *P.Oxy.* LXVII 4614.2n.) and the aspect of Greek nouns in -της (these are mostly *nomina agentis*), Horion may, within the context of the whole document, be taken as someone who replaces the boatman Jacob, at a certain place, i.e. in Neapolis in Alexandria, in order to fulfill a certain obligation, i.e. the delivery of 1,015 artabas of tax-grain into the local public granaries. In this reconstruction, Jacob himself may have accepted the original obligation to transport such a cargo, while in fact he would entrust the actual transport from the Oxyrhynchite nome to Alexandria to a substitute. Horion, with as his own surety Aurelius Ammonios son of Eulogios grandson of Ploution (already known from **809** - **810**), now promises under oath that he, after having taken over care and responsibility from Jacob, will fulfill all of Jacob's obligations and that he (Horion) himself will produce the receipt of the delivery in Alexandria to the councillors in Oxyrhynchus (cf. ll. 17, 22-23).

Alternatively, our Horion may have declared in this text that he himself will assist in putting down (cf. the etymology of καταστῆσαι, l. 12) a cargo to the quarter of Neapolis in Alexandria and that he will stay there with it (cf. παραμ̣[ενῶ, l. 21) until Jason has delivered his cargo and has received receipts to the name of the said councillors which he will bring back to them.

Ultimately, one's view on the nature of the document may imply the change of τοῦτο into τοῦτον in l. 12 (then to be related to Jacob the boatman); the neuter τοῦτο can be connected only with the word πολύκωπον (sc. πλοῖον) or words like μέτρον = 'amount' (of cargo) or φορτίον.

1. For this consulate, cf. **807**.1-2n.

2. For these councillors see above, the general introduction, § 2.

5. For the village of Φοβώου, cf. Pruneti, *I centri abitati*, 215f.; A. Benaissa, *Rural Settlements of the Oxyrhynchite Nome. A Papyrological Survey*. (Version 1 [2009] = Trismegistos Online Publications, IV), s.n. After this name one may supplement τοῦ (αὐτοῦ) Ὀξυρυγχίτου (νομοῦ).

A restoration here of Horion's function as καταστάτου rather than κυβερνήτου (?) could be defended by comparing l. 9, ἐμὲ τὸν καταστάτην Ὠρίων̣[α; in the latter passage, the article here seems to have anaphoric value.

6. After τοῦ σ[ίτου one could supplement τοῦ καταχθέντος εἰς Ἀλεξ-άνδρειαν.

7. Is this the same Eulogios πολιτευόμενος as in *P.Oxy*. XLVIII 3393.6 (365P)?

9. The scribe uses an ἐπὶ τῷ + inf. construction instead of ἐγὼ μὲν ὁ καταστάτης κτλ. In l. 16 he continues, however, with the usual ἐγὼ δὲ ὁ ἐγγυήτης κτλ. One may supplement, e.g., Ὠρ ίων̣[α N.N. (gen.) τοῦ N.N. πολυκωπίτην]. Similar ἐπὶ τῷ + inf. constructions are found in **804**.11 and **806**.9

11. Supplement, e.g., Ἰα κὼ[β Ἰά σωνος γόμου σίτου νέου καθαροῦ καὶ ἀδόλου ἐπὶ τὸ αὐτὸ (ἀρταβῶν)].

12. Supplement, e.g., τῇ Νέᾳ Πόλει τῆς λαμπροτάτης Ἀλεξανδρείας καὶ παραμένειν αὐτῷ].

14. μέτρον = '(Tax) amount'; for this meaning, cf. **806**.9n.

20. Supplement, e.g., κα[ταστήσω τὸν προκείμενον N.N. / τὸ προκείμενον μέτρον εἰς].

23. A restoration of Αὐρήλιος Θώνιος Ἀμμωνίου (cf. **807**.25n) would fill the lacuna and there may seem some similarity in the handwriting. It is, however, also true that there is some inconsistency in the writing errors made in each subscription, cf. above, αὐτὸς for αὐτοῦ (correct in **807**.25), and **807**.25, εἰδώτος for εἰδότος (correctly spelled above).

26. For the subscription by the notary Harpalos, see **808**.21n.

812: COPY OF A *HYPOMNEMA* (REPORT OF PROCEEDINGS)

P.Mich. inv. # 4016 + P.Med. inv. 165 17.v.373P
= *SB* XIV 11615 (+ *BL* 9:275, 10:210; photo in *Aegyptus* 56 [1976] 60-64, pl. V)

P.Mich. 4016: H. 27.4 x W. 17.5 cm. Margins: at the top 1.4 cm, at the bottom 8.4 cm. Broken at the LH and RH side. No *kollesis* visible. Verso blank.
The Michigan fragment joins to the RH side of the Milano fragment; the two fragments are separated below by way of | |. Photo: see http://wwwapp.cc.columbia.edu/ldpd/app/apis/item?mode=item&key=michigan.apis.4352.

1 | |Ἀντίγραφον ὑπομνήματο̣ς̣.

2 Ὑπ ατ[είας τῶν δεσ]ποτῶν ἡμῶν Οὐαλεντινιανοῦ καὶ Οὐάλεντος αἰων| |ίων Αὐγούστων τὸ δ//, Παχὼν κ̣β ἐν Πηλουσίῳ·

3 εἰσαχ[θέντος Ψου]τί̣ου Θεόδωρος ῥ(ήτωρ) εἶ(πεν) ὑπὲρ Σερήνου ἀπὸ τῆς Ὀξυρυγχειτ| |ῶν καὶ προσέθηκεν· ἐπὶ τῆς πρώτης ἰνδικτίονος Ψόε̣ις κ̣[υβερνήτης

4 ὁρμ[ώμενος ἀπ]ὸ κώμης [Π]απα τοῦ Ἡρακλεοπολίτου νομοῦ ῥητὸν μέ| |τρον σίτου ὑπεδέξατο ἐ̣ν χιλίαις τετρακοσίαις ἑ̣ξ̣ή̣κοντα δύο ἥμισ[ει ἀρτάβαις εἰς]

5 Ἀλε̣ξ[ανδρείαν ̣]ον τὸν α̣ὐ̣τὸν ἐνεγυήσατο ὁ συνηγο-

ρούμενος κ̣α̣ὶ̣ | | ἀ̣πε̣κόμ̣ισεν, ἀλλὰ Δωρόθεος ὁ
ἐπικίμενος σπεκουλάτωρ εἰσ̣[± 9]
6 .α[. . . . .]α̣ι παρεσκ̣[ε]ύασεν καὶ ταύτης ἕνεκεν τῆς
προφάσεως ὁ μεν | |[. . . . . .]̣υπως τῆς χιρογραφίας
ἕνεκεν μεθοδεύ̣ε̣τ̣[αι αὐτόν· δι᾽ ὅ]
7 παρ̣α̣κ̣α̣λ̣ῶ κ̣ελεῦσέ̣ σου τὴν [ἐ]ξουσίαν ὥσται ἔρεσ-
θαι μὲν τοῦ ψηφιστοῦ τ| |[ὸ μὴ ἐνόχλησιν ἡ]μεῖν
γένεσθαι. VACAT
8 Φλ(άουιος) Εὐμάτιος Παρθένιος ὁ λαμ(πρότατος)
[ἡ]γεμ(ὼν) εἶ(πεν)· Ἀπεστάλη ἀναφορὰ περ[ὶ τ]ῶν
σ̣πε̣| |[κουλατόρων καὶ ---]χ̣[.]σατο μέτρον ἐπὶ τοῦ
ἐν Ἀλεξανδρείᾳ̣. Κλ̣α̣[υδιο̣ Πατρικιο̣
9 τὴν ἀναφορὰν παρὰ το[ῦ] σ[π]εκουλάτορος καὶ ταύ-
την ἐπιδεδώκαμεν τ̣| |[.
Θεόδωρος ῥ̣(ήτωρ) εἶ(πεν)· παρα]κ̣αλῶ τὴν ἐξου-
σίαν τὴν σὴν κελεῦσαι . . . .[
10 παρὰ τῶν ὑποδεκτῶν παρα̣σχεθῆναι ὥσται μηδεμί̣α̣ν
ἐνόχλησ| |[ιν ἡμῖν γενέσθαι] VACAT
11 Φλ(άουιος) Εὐμάτιος Παρθένιος ὁ λαμ(πρότατος)
ἡγεμὼν εἶ(πεν)· Τί παρὼν Ἀθανάσιος π̣ο̣λ̣ι̣-
τ̣(ευόμενος)[| | ---------- ; Ἀθαν]άσιος εἶ(πεν)· Οἱ
καταβε̣[βληκότες ἄποχα (?) γραμ-]
12 ματα ἀναφορ̣ᾶς ἐκομίσ̣α̣ντο παρὰ τῶν ἐπικειμένων
σπεκουλατόρω̣| |[ν· Θεόδωρος ῥ̣(ήτωρ) εἶ(πεν)·
παρακαλῶ]. τ.ς προστᾶξαι σο̣[υ τὴν ἐξου]σ̣ί̣αν
ὥσται διὰ τῶν[μηδὲν]
13 ἀνάλωμα γέ[νη]τ̣α̣ι. VACAT
14 Φλάουιος Εὐμάτιος Παρθένιος ὁ λαμ(πρότατος)

ἡγεμ(ὼν) εἶ(πεν)· Ποίοις ναυκλήροις ὁ Σ| |[ε̣ρῆνος κατα]βέβληκεν τὸν σῖτον; Ἀθ̣ανάσιος εἶ(πεν)· Ἐπὶ τη̣[

15 Φλ(άουιος) Εὐ[μά]τιος Πα[ρ]θένιος ὁ λαμ(πρότατος) ἡγεμὼν εἶ(πεν)· Τίνι; Ἀθανάσιος εἶ(πεν)· Τοῖς να| |[υκλήρο]ι̣ς τοῖς ἐνβαλαμένοις τὰ γενήματα. VACAT

16 [Φλάουιος Εὐμάτιος Παρθένιος ὁ λαμ(πρότατος) ἡγεμ(ὼν) εἶ(πεν)· | |]των ἀνενεχθέντων οἱ διαψηφισταὶ ἰδιω̣τι[κ

17 [καὶ παρασχέτωσαν | |] τοῖς ναυκλήροις ἄποχα γραμμάτια τοῖς συν ̣[

Ed.princ. SB XIV 11615: l. 5 ἑ̣α̣υ̣τὸν 7 παρ' αὐτῷ̣ 11 εἶ(πεν)· . . 13 γε.....[

3 ὕπερ, ἰνδικτιονος Pap., l. Ὀξυρυγχιτῶν, Ψόις 4 l. ἥμισυ 5 l. ἐπικείμενος 6 l. χειρογραφίας 7 l. κελεῦσαι, ἡμῖν 7 (and 10) l. ὥστε 8 (and 11, 14,15) l. Εὐμάθιος 14-15 were written in ekthesis. 15 *SB* prints Πα[ρ]θένιοις; λαμ(πρότατος): in *SB* (and in *ed.princ.*) is an erroneous]-bracket in λ]αμ(πρ.); l. ἐμβαλομένοις

"Copy of a *hypomnema*. In the consulate of our Lords Valentinianus and Valens, eternal Augusti, for the 4th time, Pachon 22 in Pelusium. After Psoutios had been led into the court room, the barrister Theodoros began to speak for Serenus from (the city) of the Oxyrhynchites and he added: At the time of the first indiction the boatman Psoeis, coming from the village of Papa in the Herakleopolite nome received a specified amount of wheat consisting of one thousand four hundred sixty-two and a half artabas for Alexandria ---. My client was surety for him and he brought ---, but Dorotheus the *speculator* in charge of the case prepared --- and on that pretext he in a --- way goes after him because of the contract. And for that reason I ask that your Competence orders to request the accountant that there be no hindrance whatsoever for our party.

Fl. Eumathios Parthenios *vir clarissimus* the *praeses* said: A report was sent concerning the *speculatores* and --- the amount in the presence of the (residing official?) in Alexandria Claudius Patricius --- the report from the *speculator* and we have submitted this to ---. Theodoros the barrister said: I request that your Competence orders --- from the collectors to be given, in order that there be no further hindrance to us.

Fl. Eumathios Parthenios *vir clarissimus* the *praeses* said: What [has] Athanasios the *politeuomenos,* who is present, [to say]?

Athanasios said: "Those who have unloaded got receipts for the report from the *speculatores* in charge. ---

Theodoros the barrister said: I request your Competence to order that through the [*speculatores*?] no extra cost arises.

Fl. Eumathios Parthenios *vir clarissimus* the *praeses* said: To what kind of *naukleroi* has Serenus (or Psois? see l. 14n.) handed over the wheat?

Athanasios said: ---

Fl. Eumathios Parthenios *vir clarissimus* the *praeses* said: To whom?

Athanasios said: To the *naukleroi* who took the crops on board their ships.

Fl. Eumathios Parthenios *vir clarissimus* the *praeses* said: --- of the reported --- the *diapsephistae* private (?) --- and they must provide receipts to the *naukleroi* --- "

This text, labelled 'copy of a hypomnema' (l.1), contains in fact a report of a lawsuit held on 17.v.373 in Pelusium before the *praeses Augustamnicae* Fl. Eumathios Parthenios (cf. ll. 8, 11, 14, 15 and the restoration in 16). Various other parties mentioned in this report are (in order of first appearance):

—A certain Psoutios (l. 3) who is led into the court room, probably as a defendant. What his profession was and what he was accused of remains unclear.

—A lawyer/barrister (ῥ̣(ήτωρ)) Theodoros (l. 3, cf. the restorations in ll. 9 and 12) who speaks on behalf of a certain Serenus from the Oxyrynchite nome. Maybe he was a town councillor of Oxyrhynchus and commissioner of wheat for Alexandria, identical with Serenus son of Eusebios mentioned in **802**.4 (perhaps also in **815**.2 [where the name of the son of Eusebios is not preserved]).

—A boatman (?, note the restoration of κ̣[υβερνήτης) Psois from Papa in the Herakleopolite nome (ll. 3-4, cf. l. 14n.).

—A *speculator* Dorotheos (cf. ll. 5, 9).

—A certain Claudius Patricius (l. 8) who must be the *praefectus annonae Alexandriae*; for him see **816** (374[p]).

—A certain Athanasios, *politeuomenos* (cf. l. 11, reappearing in ll. 14, 15); for him see below at l. 11n. His role is to give certain further information about what had happened in the past on the path leading to this trial.

Due to the mutilated state of the document, some precise details of what the issue of the lawsuit was, escape us. After the date, an indication of he place of the lawsuit and an introduction of the parties, l. 4 mentions a cargo of 1462 ½ art. of wheat that was received by Psoeis the boatman who probably undertook to transport this to Alexandria some time during the first indiction (372/3^{p}), while Serenus acted as his surety. In Alexandria the *speculator* Dorotheus, representing the government administration, seems to have created administrative problems but their precise nature is unclear; it may have to do with what the prefect addresses at the end, ll. 16-17. So much seems certain that the general issue was, as usual, the claim that one of the parties concerned should be no longer hindered by the other party (cf. the term ἐνόχλησιν in ll. 7 and 10) and that any further costs should be avoided (ll. 12-13). At the end of the preserved text, the prefect seems to issue some general regulations on what documents are to be given to shipowners.

2. For the 4th consulate of the emperors Valentinianus and Valens in 373^{p} (already attested on 11.iv in *P.Col.* VII 168.11), cf. *CSBE*^{2}, app. D.

The omission of the article τῶν before αἰωνίων is standard in the consular formula of this year, cf. the general introduction, § 7; cf. also a similar remark made on this subject as regards the oath formulas discussed in the general introd., § 5.

3. The personal name Ψούτιος does not occur frequently. His precise role in this lawsuit remains unclear.

The restoration of κ̣[υβερνήτης is suggested by the general context of this trial report; cf. also introd., § 4.

5. The term συνηγορούμενος indicates a lawyer's client (cf. *P.Oxy*. IV 707ᵛ, col. 2.12, i.e. Serenus who is represented by Theodoros (cf. l. 3).

Instead of α̣ὐ̣τὸν, one may consider reading τ̣ο̣ῦ̣τον, but if we do that, there is reason to separate the preceding article from the demonstrative pronoun and connect τον with the letters preceding these three letters.

For the term *speculator* used for a civil government administrator, cf. *P.Nepheros* p. 96ff. and *P.Oxy*. LIX 4002.5-6n. The term is mentioned rather frequently in the papyri, recently attested in *P.Bodl*. I 166.11,18, *P.Erl.Diosp*. 1.173, *SB* XXII 15311, 15605.3 and H. Cuvigny, *La Route de Myos Hormos* (Cairo 2006) p. 224 n. 62. A *speculator* Dorotheus is also mentioned in *SB* XIV 11701.1 (Hermop., 330-350ᵖ), but it is not likely that he is the same person.

6. Restore here after ὁ μὲν | | [συνηγορούμενος / βοηθούμενος]?

7. As within the context the infinitive ἔρεσθαι seems to come from ἔρομαι = 'to ask' and as this verb normally governs the accusative of the person asked rather than the genitive (cf. *LSJ* s.v.), the assumption that a preposition like παρά has fallen out before τοῦ ψηφιστοῦ seems inescapable.

ψηφιστοῦ = *calculator*, cf. *LSJ* s.v. The term occurs also in *P.Cair.Masp*. III 67309.6,11, *SB* XIV 11616.6, and *P.Herm.Landl*. G.415 (according to the photo, one cannot replace here the reading δι(ὰ) ψηφιστῶ[ν] with διαψηφιστή[ς]); cf. also below, l. 16 διαψηφισταί.

8. --]χ̣[.]σατο μέτρον: or should one print --]χ̣[.]σα τὸ μέτρον?

For the *praeses Augustamnicae* Fl. Eumathios Parthenios, cf. *P.Oxy*. XLVI 3308.7n.

In itself, it seems possible to connect ἐπὶ τοῦ ἐν Ἀλεξανδρείᾳ. with the following Κλα̣[υδιο̣ Πατρικιο̣, i.e., read Κλα̣[υδίου Πατρικίου). It is however possible that Claudius Patricius was one of the persons present at the trial and that he actually spoke the words recorded at the start of l. 9 (i.e. read Κλα̣[ύδιος Πατρίκιος εἶ(πεν)· ἐδεξάμεθα]). In that case, one could connect the *speculator* in l. 9 with the *speculator* mentioned in l. 5.

11. An Athanasios *politeuomenos* is known in Oxyrhynchus as a shipowner

from *P.Oxy*. VII 1048.5 (after 392P; cf. Appendix B # 4); are these men identical? It remains also to be seen whether he is to be identified with the town councillor / shipowner Athanasios mentioned in *P.Harr*. I 94.4 (mid IVP; cf. Appendix B # 3). Cf. also **820**.13, where the Athanasios mentioned there may be only the father of an N.N. *politeuomenos*. It seems most economical to take the name of Athanasios as the subject of εἶ(πεν); this involves the supplement of the letters]άσιος preceding the verb to Ἀθαν]άσιος; this would necessitate the assumption, that the earlier mention of Athanasios in the preceding is part of the question of the *praeses* Fl. Eumathios Parthenios.

Οἱ καταβε̣[βληκότες: for the restoration of this plural participle, cf. l. 14, κατα]βέβληκεν τὸν σῖτον.

11-12. The restoration of ἄποχα γράμ]|ματα is based on the expectation that people who have unloaded their cargo in Alexandria are supposed to get receipts for their delivery. It is however true that the following word ἀναφορ̣ᾶς seems to refer to the document mentioned first by the *praeses* in l. 8.

12. It is conceivable that one should understand / restore ὥσται διὰ τῶν [σπεκουλατόρων μηδὲν]

13. Or should we read γέ[νεσ]θ̣α̣ι (making the infinitive dependent on ὥσται in l. 12)?

14. Or should one read Ψ̣[οεις κατα]βέβληκεν κτλ.?

At line end, restore, e.g., ἐπὶ τῇ[ς πρώτης ἰνδικτίονος (cf. l. 3), or ἐπὶ τῇ[ς Ἀλεξ̣ανδρείας?

16. A διαψηφιστής (= Lat. *rationalis*, cf. *LSJ s.v.*) is a financial comptroller; for other attestations of the term, cf. *P.Ant*. I 33.8, *ChLA* XII 524.4 and *P.Lips*. I 34^{r}.4, ^{v}.2 .

813: UNDERTAKING BY A BOATMAN TO DELIVER BARLEY TO ALEXANDRIA

P.Mich. inv. # 4021 10.vii.373^{p}

H. 27.3 x W. 36.5 cm. Two columns. Margins: at the top 2.4 cm, broken at the LH and RH side. Bottom margin (col. II), 3.5 cm.Verso blank. Photo: see http://wwwapp.cc.columbia.edu/ldpd/app/apis/item?mode=item&key=michigan.apis.4357.

1 [Υ] π̣ατείας τῶν δεσποτῶν ἡμῶν Οὐαλεντινιανοῦ καὶ Οὐάλεντος αἰων̣ί̣ων Αὐγούστων τὸ δ, Ἐπεὶφ ι̣ς̣.

2 [Αὐ]ρ̣[η]λ̣ίοις Οὐρίωνι Πτολεμαίου καὶ Εἰσυχίῳ̣ Εἰουλιανοῦ καὶ Σαραπίωνι Πλουτάρχου

3 [καὶ Ἱέ]ρ̣ακος Σερήνου V A C A T τῶν πάντων βουλευτῶν

4 [τῆς λα]μ̣(πρᾶς) καὶ λαμ(προτάτης) Ὀξ̣υ̣ρ̣υ̣γχιτῶν πόλεως ἐπιμεληταῖς κριθῶν Ἀλεξ̣α̣νδρείας

5 [παρὰ Α]ὐρηλίου Εἰσιδώρου Οὐρίωνος ἀπὸ τοῦ αὐτοῦ Ὀξυρυγχίτου κυβερ(νήτου) π̣λ̣ο̣ί̣ο̣υ̣

6 [Πτολεμ]ίνω Εὐλογίω πολιτευομένου μετ᾽ ἐγγύου τῆς τοῦ κόμου παραδώσεως καὶ τοῦ

7 [ἐπενεγ]κ̣εῖν ἐκ πλήρ̣ο̣υ̣ς ἄποχα γράμματα τοῦ αὐτοῦ καὶ προκιμένου Πτολεμίνω γεούχω

8 [τοῦ αὐτοῦ] π̣λίου. Ὁμολ̣ογοῦ̣μεν ὀμνύντες τὼν σεβάσμιον θεῖον ὅρκον τῶν δεσποτῶν

9 [ἡμῶν] Ο̣ὐαλε̣ντινι̣α̣νοῦ καὶ Οὐάλεντος καὶ Γρατιανοῦ τῶν αἰωνίων Αὐγούστων ἐγὼ μὲν̣

10 [ὁ κυβ]ε̣ρ̣(νήτης) π̣α̣ρ̣ε̣ι̣λ̣ηφέναι καὶ ἐμβεβλῆσθαι εἰς τὸ προκίμενον πλῖον ὑπὲρ γενή̣-

11 [ματος τῆς εὐτυχο]ῦς πρώτης νέας ἰνδικτίονος κριθῆς νέας καθα̣ρ̣ᾶς ἀδόλου καὶ [

12 [. . . . . ἐκτὸς π]άσης ἐτίας καθεστηκοιείοις μέτρῳ̣ δημ̣ω̣σίῳ̣ μετρήσι τῇ̣ κελε̣[υσθεί-]

13 [σῃ̣ ἐπὶ τὸ αὐτὸ (ἀρτάβας) -ι]α, τὸν δὲ γόμ[ον] κατε̣νέγκουμεν ἐπὶ τὴ[ν Ἀλε]ξ̣ά̣ν̣δ̣ρ̣ειαν [καὶ]

14 [παραδώσομεν εἰς τοὺς ἐ]κ̣εῖσε̣ δ̣η̣[μοσίο]υ̣[ς θησα]υ̣ροὺς ἀριθμῷ̣ πλήρης [καὶ τῆς τούτων παρα-]

15 [δόσεως ἄποχα γράμματα ὑποδέξασθαι, ἐγὼ δ]ὲ ὁ ἐνγυητὴς ἑκουσίᾳ̣ καὶ αὐ[θαιρέτῳ γνώμῃ]

16 [ἐγγυᾶσθαι τὸν αὐτὸν κυβερνήτην παρ]α̣δοῦντα τὸν γόμον τούτον τῶν [κριθῶν καὶ ἐπιφέ-]

17 [ροντα τὴν ἀποχὴν ἐπ᾽ ὀνόματος ὑμῶν] τῶν ἐπιμελητῶν εἰς τὸ ἐμ μη̣[δενὶ μέμψιν]

18 [περὶ ἡμᾶς ἐκ τούτου γένεσθαι ἢ] ἔνωχη εἶμεν τῷ̣ θείῳ̣ ὅρκῳ̣.

---

19 (M. 2) [Αὐρ(ήλιος) Πτολεμῖνος Εὐλογίου πο]λιτευόμενος ἐγγυῶμαι τὸν προκείμενον [κυβερνήτην Ἰσίδωρον]

20 [ἐπιφέροντα τὴν ἀποχὴν τοῦ προ]κ̣ειμένου γόμου τῶν κριθῶν ἐκ πλήρους [ὡς πρόκειται.]

21 (M. 3) [Αὐρήλιος Ἰσ ίδωρος Ὡρ ίωνος παρ]έλαβε καὶ ἐνεβάλομαι τὰς τῶν κριθ̣[ῶν καθαρὰς ἀρτάβας]

22 [---κοσίας ἕνδεκ]α καὶ παρ̣αδώσω πλήρες ὡς πρόκιτα[ι.

23 Δι' ἐ(μοῦ) Ἰακὼβ ....( ).

Col. II:

24 ἔστι δ̣έ̣·

25 κριθῶν ὑποστάσεως ἐπ̣ὶ τὸ αὐτοῦ·

26 οὕτως·

27 αS ἰνδικ(τίωνος)

28 πολ(ιτικῶν) Θεόδωρος Δημητρίου καὶ Πελ̣[αῖος/-ἅγιος καὶ]

29 Παν̣αροῦς (ἀ̣ρ̣τ̣ά̣β̣α̣ι̣) β̣

2 l. Ὡρίωνι, Ἡσυχίῳ (-ω ex -ο corr.) Ἰουλιανοῦ 3 l. Ἱέρακι, τοῖς πᾶσι βουλευταῖς 4 l. Ἰσιδώρου Ὡρίωνος 6 l. Πτολεμίνου Εὐλογίου, γόμου παραδόσεως 7 l. προκειμένου Πτολεμίνου γεούχου 8 l. πλοίου, τὸν 10 l. προκείμενον πλοῖον 12 l. αἰτίας, καθεστηκυίας; δημ̣ω̣σίῳ: -μ̣ω̣- ex corr. (l. δημοσίῳ); l. μετρήσει 13 l. κατενέγκομεν 15 l. ἐγγυήτης 16 l. παραδόντα, τούτων 17 l. ἐν 18 l. ἔνοχοι εἴημεν 21 l. παρέλαβον, ἐνεβαλόμην 22 l. πρόκειται 23 ϊακωβ Pap. 25 l. αὐτό

"In the consulate of our lords Valentinianus and Valens the eternal Augusti, consuls for the 4th time, Epeiph 16. To the Aurelii Horion son of Ptolemaios and Hesychios son of Julianus and Sarapion son of Ploutarchos and Hierax son of Serenus (vacat), all town councillors of the illustrious and most illustrious city of the Oxyrhynchites and commissioners of barley for Alexandria, from Aurelius Isidoros son of Horion, from the same Oxyrhynchite nome, boatman of a ship of Ptoleminos son of Eulogios, *politeuomenos*, with as surety of delivery of the cargo and the complete production of the certificates of delivery the same and already mentioned Ptoleminos (land)owner of the same ship. We acknowledge, swearing the august imperial oath of our lords Valentinianus and Valens and Gratianus, the eternal Augusti, that I the boatman have received and loaded into the aforementioned ship from the produce of the fortunate first new indiction [-]11 artabas in total of new, pure, unadulterated barley, free of any fault and measured with the public measure according to the ordered measurement and we shall transport the cargo to Alexandria and shall deliver it to the public granaries there in full and that I shall receive certificates of delivery of these and that I, the surety, serve on my own free will as surety for the same boatman, that he delivers the cargo of this barley and that he produces the receipt in the name of you, the commissioners, so as to incur no blame whatsoever in this matter, or else may I be liable to the imperial oath.

(M.2) I, Aurelius Ptoleminos son of Eulogios, *politeuomenos*, serve as a surety for the aforementioned boatman Isidoros that he produces the receipt of the aforementioned cargo of barley in full as stated above.

(M. 3) I, Aurelius Isidoros son of Horion, have received and loaded the *n*-hundred eleven artabas of barley and I shall deliver them in full as stated above.

(Written) through me, Jacob -."

This text is a duplicate of **814** written by a different scribe who does not know his Greek so well.

1.For the 4th consulate of the emperors Valentinianus and Valens in 373^{p} (already attested on 11.iv in *P.Col.* VII 168.11), cf. *CSBE*^{2}, app. D. *s.a.* 373.

The omission of the article τῶν before αἰωνίων is standard in the consular formula of this year, cf. the general introduction, § 7; cf. also a similar remark made on this subject as regards the oath formulas discussed in the general introd., § 5 and fn. 34.

2. Aurelius Horion son of Ptolemaios and Aurelius Hesychios son of Julianus occur not only in the duplicate **814**.2, but also in **816**.5-6. In the latter text they are called neither Αὐρήλιοι nor βουλευταί, but only ἐπιμεληταί without specification of the kind of ἐπιμέλεια (i.c. κριθῶν or σίτου; sometimes, the same Oxyrhynchite councillor can be *epimeletes* of both products, cf. the table in *P.Oxy.* LXVII, p. 206). From **813** and **814** on the one hand and **816** on the other hand it follows that ἐπιμεληταὶ σίτου were town councillors, even if they were not so styled; cf. N. Lewis, *The Compulsory Public Services of Roman Egypt*^{2} (Florence 1997) 25-26, stating sub 3 that ἐπιμεληταί belonged to the bouleutic class.

3. The scribe left here (and in **814.**2-3) space open, to be used for inserting an extra name.

6. For the *politeuomenos* (Fl.) Ptoleminos son of Eulogios, see K.A. Worp in *ZPE* 115 (1997) 208. He occurs also in *P.Michael.* 33.1,17 (for its date [367/8^{p}] see *BL* 10:122).

7-8. In accordance with its etymology, the meaning of γεοῦχος is 'landowner'. Unless one wishes to assume the omission of an element <καὶ τοῦ κεκτημένου> vel sim. here *and* in **814**.6 one has to consider whether in the present context γεοῦχος [τοῦ αὐτοῦ] π̣λ<ο>ίου really can mean 'owner of the same ship' (maybe the phrase is some form of contracted expression of: 'landowner [and owner] of the same ship'). In *PSI* VIII 948 one finds reference made to a γεουχικὸν πλοῖον, i.e. a ship owned by a landowner.

10-11. ὑπὲρ γενήματος occurs here instead of the slightly more usual ἀπὸ γενήματος (for this, cf. not only the copy in **814**.8, but also **800**.11 and **815**.8; in **805**.10, the preposition is restored as ἀπὸ).

11-12. Should one read καὶ [ἀβρόχου] | (12) [........ καὶ ἐκτὸς π]άσης or καὶ | (12) [ἀβρόχου καὶ ἐκτὸς π]άσης? For the formula expected here, cf. *P.Oxy.* LXVII 4608.7-8, 4610.9, 4612.8 (cf. *App. A*, ## 2, 4, 6).

13. κατενέγκουμεν (l. κατενέγκομεν; for the form, cf. **808**.10n.): the singular is expected instead of the plural (cf. εἶμεν in l. 18); the plural is however defensible in view of the phrasing ὁμολογοῦμεν ὀμνύντες (i.e. the boatman and the surety together).

14. For the phrasing εἰς τοὺς ἐκεῖσε δημοσίους θησαυρούς, cf. **808**.11, **814**.11 and the restorations in **801**.16, **809**.11 and **810**.11.

16. παραδούντα: this form is also found in **804**.13/14. For the transfer of athematic participles to their thematic counterparts, cf. B.G. Mandilaras, *The Verb in the Greek Non-Literary Papyri*, § 872. Here the aorist participle has a future meaning (cf. S.G. Kapsomenakis, *Voruntersuchungen zu einer Grammatik der Papyri der nachchristlichen Zeit* [München 1938] 29). On the other hand, in **808**.14,17, **809**.14,20, **810**.14,18/19,21 and **815**.12, one finds the participle written in the form παραδίδουντα, in **809**.17 and **815**.15/16 the regular spelling παραδίδοντα.

17-18. The formula εἰς τὸ ἐμ μη[δενὶ μέμψιν] / [περὶ ἡμᾶς ἐκ τούτου γένεσθαι, restored here after the parallel in **814**.14 (though this is not complete, as **814** has μηδεμίαν μέμψιν for ἐμ μηδενὶ μέμψιν), is slightly unusual. More usual is a phrasing εἰς τὸ ἐμ μηδενὶ μεμφθῆναι, cf. **802**.11, **803**.18, **807**.21-22, **809**.16, **811**.19 and **819**.8.

21. The formula παρέλαβον καὶ ἐνεβαλόμην is a standard element in receipts issued by boatmen; cf. (e.g.), *P.Cair.Isid.* 50.6,22,38; *P.Charite* 21.2; *P.NYU* II 48.4 and *P.Oxy.* X 1260.6.

23. The same notary Jacob occurs also in **814**.20. What follows after his name is all but certain; was it a verb like ἐγράφη, or did he add his personal signature in a form of scrawl?

29. Underneath l. 29 approx. 4 cm have been left blank. If our interpretation is correct, only one small tax payment of 2 artabas of barley was made by 2 persons. After the empty space one or more entries should have followed. The delivery of 2 artabas by Theodoros son of Demetrios and Pel[aias / Pel[agios together with Panarous is only a fraction of the amount of barley mentioned in l. 13, i.e. [-]11 artabas.

814: UNDERTAKING BY A BOATMAN TO DELIVER BARLEY TO ALEXANDRIA

P.Mich. inv. # 4018 10.vii.373^{p}

H. 28 x W. 30 cm. Written parallel with the fibers. Margins: at the LH side 2.6, at the top 1.8 and at the bottom (in which the notarial signature) 9.5 cm. At the LH border there is a *kollesis*. The back is blank. Photo: see http://wwwapp.cc.columbia.edu/ldpd/app/apis/item?mode=item&key=michigan.apis.4354.

1 Ὑπατις$^{\text{(M.. 2)}}$ τείᾳ (M. 1) τῶν δεσποτῶν ἡμῶν Οὐαλεντινιανοῦ καὶ Οὐάλεν̣τ̣ο̣ς̣ αἰων̣ί̣ων Αὐγούστων τὸ δ/ Ἐπεὶφ ις.

2 Αὐρ[ηλίο]ις Ὡρίωνι Πτολεμαίου καὶ Ἡσυχίῳ Ἰουλιανοῦ καὶ Σαραπίωνι Πλουτάρχου καὶ Ἱέρακι Σερή̣νου VACAT

3 VACAT βουλ(ευταῖς) τῆς λαμπ(ρᾶς) καὶ λαμπ(ροτάτης) Ὀξυρυγχειτῶν πόλεως ἐπιμεληταῖς κριθ̣(ῶν) Ἀλεξανδρεί[ας]

4 παρ[ὰ Αὐρηλίο]υ Ἰσιδώρου Ὡρίωνος ἀπὸ τοῦ αὐτοῦ Ὀξυρυγχείτου κυβερ(νήτου) πλοίου Πτολεμίνου Εὐλογίου πολι[τευ(ομένου)]

5 μετ᾿ ἐγ[γύου τῆς το]ῦ γόμου παραδόσεως καὶ τοῦ ἐπενεγκεῖν ἐκ πλήρους ἄποχα γράμματα τοῦ α̣ὐτοῦ καὶ [προκει-]

6 μένο[υ Πτολεμίν]ου γεούχου τοῦ αὐτοῦ πλοίου. Ὁμολογοῦμεν ὀμνύντες τὸν̣ σεβ[ά]σ̣μι̣ον̣ θεῖ̣ον̣

ὅ̣ρ̣κ̣ο̣ν̣ [τῶν]

7 δεσποτ̣[ῶν ἡμῶν Οὐαλ]εντινιανοῦ καὶ Οὐάλεντος καὶ Γρατιανο̣ῦ τῶν αἰωνίων Αὐγο̣ύ[σ]των ἐγὼ μὲ̣ν ὁ̣ [κυβερνή-]

8 της π̣[αρειληφέναι καὶ] ἐ̣μβεβλῆσθαι εἰς τὸ προκίμενον πλοῖον ἀπὸ γενήματος τῆς εὐτυχο̣ῦ̣[ς πρώτης]

9 νέας ἰ̣[νδικτίονος κρι]θ̣ῆς νέας καθαρᾶς ἀδόλου καὶ ἐκτὸς πάσης αἰτία̣ς̣ κ̣α̣θ̣εστηκυείης μ[έτρῳ̣ δημοσίῳ̣]

10 μετρήσ̣[ει τῇ̣ κελευσθείσῃ̣ ἐπὶ] τ̣ὸ̣ αὐτὸ (ἀρτάβας) VACAT, τ[ὸν δὲ γό]μ̣ον κατενέγκω̣ ἐπὶ τ̣ὴ̣ν̣ [Ἀλεξάνδρειαν]

11 καὶ παρα[δώσω εἰς τοὺς ἐκε]ῖ̣σε δημοσίους θησαυροὺ[ς ἀριθμ]ῷ̣ πλήρης καὶ τῆς τούτων π[αραδόσεως]

12 ἄποχα γ̣ράμμ̣[ατα ὑποδέξασ]θ̣α̣ι̣, ἐγὼ δ]ὲ ὁ ἐγγυητὴ̣[ς ἑκουσίᾳ̣ κ]α̣ὶ αὐθερέτῳ̣ γνώμῃ̣ ἐ̣γ̣γ̣[υᾶσθαι τὸν αὐ-]

13 τὸν κυβερνήτ[ην παραδίδον]τα τὸν γόμον τοῦτον τῶν̣ [κριθῶν καὶ] ἐπιφέ̣ροντα τὴν ἀποχὴν [ἐπ' ὀνόματος]

14 ἡμῶν τῶν ἐπ̣[ιμελητῶν] εἰς τὸ μηδεμίαν μέμψ[ιν περὶ ἡμᾶ]ς̣ ἐκ τούτου γένεσθαι ἢ ἔνοχοι [εἴημεν]

15 τῷ̣ θείῳ̣ ὅρκῳ̣.

---

16 (M. 2) Αὐρήλιος Πτολεμῖνος Εὐλ[ογίου πολ(ιτευόμενος) ἐγγυῶμαι τὸ]ν προκείμενο[ν κυβερνήτη]ν

Ἰσίδωρον ἐπι̣[φέροντα τὴν ἀποχὴν]
17 τοῦ προκε̣ιμένου γόμου [τῶν κριθῶν ἐ]κ πλήρους ὡς π[ρόκειται.]
18 (M.3) Αὐρήλιος Ἰσ ίδωρος Ὡρ ίω[νος παρέλαβ]ε̣ καὶ ἐνεβάλομα̣[ι τὰς τῶν κρι]θ̣ῶν καθαρὰς ἀ̣ρ̣[τάβας ---κοσίας]
19 ἕνδεκα καὶ παραδώ[σω ἐκ πλή]ρ̣ους ὡς πρόκιτ[αι.]
20 Δι' ἐ(μοῦ) Ἰα̣κ̣ὼ̣β̣ [. . . .]

1 ὕπα- Pap.; Ὑπατείᾳ corr. from Ὑπατις 2 1st καί: κ ex η corr., ϊουλιανου ϊερακι Pap. 3 l. Ὀξυρυγχιτῶν, Ἀλεξανδρεί[ας: perhaps abbreviated after -εί (which seems to be written in superposition)? 4 ϊσιδωρου (first ι ex corr.?), l. Ὀξυρυγχίτου 5 μετ' εγ[; γόμου: 2nd -ο- ex corr.; επενεγ'κειν Pap. 8 l. προκείμενον; γενήματος: first abbreviated to γενή(ματος), then written out in full as yet 9 l. καθεστηκυίας 12 εγ'γυητη[ς Pap. (i.e. there is a small dash coming down from 'inside' the initial epsilon on top of the 1st γ); -γγυη- written over, εγ'γ[Pap., l. αὐθαιρέτῳ 13 τούτων 14 l. ὑμῶν 16 ϊσιδωρον Pap. 18 l. παρέλαβον καὶ ἐνεβαλόμην 19 l. πρόκειτ[αι]

"In the consulate of our lords Valentinianus and Valens the eternal Augusti, consuls for the 4th time, Epeiph 16. To the Aurelii Horion son of Ptolemaios and Hesychios son of Julianus and Sarapion son of Ploutarchos and Hierax son of Serenus (vacat), town councillors of the illustrious and most illustrious city of the Oxyrhynchites and commissioners of barley for Alexandria, from Aurelius Isidoros son of Horion, from the same Oxyrhynchite nome, boatman of a ship of Ptoleminos son of Eulogios, *politeuomenos*, with as surety of delivery of the

cargo and the full production of the certificates of delivery, the same and already mentioned Ptoleminos (land) owner of the same ship. We acknowledge, swearing the august imperial oath of our lords Valentinianus and Valens and Gratianus, the eternal Augusti, that I the boatman have received and loaded into the aforementioned ship from the produce of the fortunate first new indiction < > artabas in total of new, pure, unadulterated barley, free of any fault and measured with the public measure according to the ordered measurement and I shall transport the cargo to Alexandria and shall deliver it to the public granaries there in full and that I shall receive certificates of delivery of these and that I, the surety, serve on my own free will as surety for the same boatman, that he delivers the cargo of this barley in full and that he produces the receipt in the name of you the commissioners so as to incur no blame whatsoever in this matter, or else may I be liable to the imperial oath.
(M. 2) I, Aurelius Ptoleminos son of Eulogios, serve as a surety for the aforementioned boatman Isidoros that he will bring back the receipt of the aforementioned cargo of barley in full as stated above.
(M. 3) I, Aurelius Isidoros son of Horion, have received and loaded the *n*-hundred eleven artabas of barley and I shall deliver them to the granaries as stated above.
(Written) through me, Jacob -."

This text is a duplicate of **813**, written by a different scribe who made fewer spelling mistakes. The hands of the surety (ll. 16-17), the boatman (ll. 18-19), and of the notary Jacob

(l. 26) are the same as in the previous text. For various copies concerning the same transport, cf. the general introduction, § 1 n. 14. **814** lacks the second column of **813**, but one cannot be certain that each individual copy featured such a second column.

10,11. κατενέγκω: the duplicate **813**.13,14 features the plurals κατενέγκομεν, παραδώσομεν.
13. It seems methodically preferable to restore here in the lacuna the regular form of the participle rather than a misspelling παραδίδουν]τα; cf. also **815**.12 and, in general, **813**.16n.
14. There is a slight varIation between the wording here, μηδεμίαν μέμψ[ιν, and the wording in **813**.17-18, ἐμ μη[δενὶ μέμψιν.
19. There is a slight variation between the text written here, ἐκ πλή]ρους, and the text written in **813**.22, πλήρες.

815: UNDERTAKING BY A BOATMAN TO DELIVER WHEAT TO ALEXANDRIA

P.Mich. inv. # 422 (= *P.Mich*. XV 724; cf. *BL* 8:219, 10:127) 365[P]

H. 24.5 x W. 15 cm. Medium-brown papyrus, broken off at the top. Margins: at the LH side 4, at the bottom 6 cm. Three vertical folds are still visible; a horizontal fold runs parallel to the direction of the writing at 14.5 cm. from the bottom. The back is blank. Photo: see http://wwwapp.cc.columbia.edu/ldpd/app/apis/item?mode=item&key=michigan.apis.2162.

---

1 Traces of 1 line

2 Ε̣ὐ̣σ̣εβίου καὶ Σαραπίωνος Πλο[υτάρχου καὶ Ἱέρακι Σερήνου βουλ(ευταῖς) τῆς Ὀξυρυγχιτῶν πόλεως ἐπιμελ(ηταῖς) σίτου Ἀλεξανδρείας]

3 παρὰ Αὐρηλίου Παήσι̣ο̣ς Ὥρου ἀπὸ το[ῦ αὐτοῦ Ὀξυρυγχίτου, κυβερνήτου πλοίου Διογένους Διογένους ἀπὸ]

4 λογιστῶν, μετ᾽ ἐγγύου τῆς τοῦ γόμου π[α]ρ[αδόσεως καὶ τοῦ ἐπενεγκεῖν ἄποχα γράμματα Αὐρηλίου Διογένους]

5 Διογέν[ου]ς τοῦ προκε[ι]μένου <καὶ> αὐτο[ῦ γεούχου τοῦ αὐτοῦ πλοίου. Ὁμολογοῦμεν ὀμνύντες]

6 τὸν σεβάσμιον θεῖον ὅρκο̣ν̣ τῶν δεσποτ[ῶν ἡμῶν Οὐαλεντινιανοῦ καὶ Οὐάλεντος αἰωνίων Αὐγούστων]

7 ἐγὼ μὲν ὁ κυβερ(νήτης) παρειλη[φ]έ̣ναι παρὰ τῶν [ἑξῆς ἐγγεγραμμένων καὶ ἐμβεβλῆσθαι εἰς τὸ προκείμενον πλοῖον]

8 ἀπὸ γεννήματος τῆς εὐτυχοῦς θS´´ νέας [ἰνδικτίωνος σίτου νέου καθαροῦ ἀδόλου καὶ ἐκτὸς πάσης]

9 αἰτίας καθεστηκότος μέτρῳ δημοσίῳ μετ̣[ρήσει τῇ κελευσθείσῃ ἐπὶ τὸ αὐτὸ (ἀρτάβας) χιη, τὸν δὲ γόμον κατενέγ-]

10 κω ἐπὶ τὴν λαμ(προτάτην) Ἀλεξάνδριαν καὶ παραδώσω [εἰς τοὺς ἐκεῖσε δημοσίους θησαυροὺς ἀριθμῷ πλήρης καὶ τῆς]

11 τούτων παραδόσεως [ἄποχ]α γράμματα ἐπ[ενεγκεῖν,

ἐγὼ δὲ ὁ ἐγγυητὴς ἑκουσίᾳ καὶ αὐθαιρέτῳ γνώμ̣η̣]
12 ἐγγυᾶσθαι τὸν αὐ[τὸ]ν κυβερ(νήτην) παραδίδουντα τ̣[ὸν γόμον τοῦτον τοῦ σίτου καὶ ἐπιφέροντα τὴν ἀποχὴν ἐπ᾽ ὀνόματος]
13 ὑμῶν τῶν ἐπιμελητῶν ἢ ἐμὲ τὸν ἐγγ[υητὴν ἐπάναγκες ὑποστῆναι πάντα τὰ πρὸς αὐτὸ ζη]-
14 τούμενα περὶ τ̣ο̣ύ̣του τοῦ γόμου εἰς τὸ ἐμ̣ [μηδενὶ μεμφθῆναι ἢ ἔνοχος εἴην τῷ θείῳ ὅρκῳ.]
15 (M. 2) Αὐρήλιος Διογένης Διογένους ἐ[γγυῶμαι τὸν προκείμενον κυβερνήτην Παῆσιν πα-]
16 ραδίδοντα τὸν γόμον τοῦ σίτου καὶ [ἐπιφέροντα τὴν ἀποχὴν ὡς πρόκειται.]
17 (M. 3) Αὐρήλιος [Πα]ῆ̣σις Ὥρ ου ὑπεδε[ξ]άμην καὶ ἐνεβ[αλόμην τὸν γόμον σίτου καθαροῦ ἀρτάβας ἑξακοσίας δεκα-]
18 οκτώ, (γίν.) (ἀρτ.) χιη´´ καὶ παραδώσω ὡς πρό(κειται). Αὐρή[λιος N.N. ἔγραψα ὑπὲρ αὐτοῦ γράμματα μὴ εἰδότος.]
?19? [Δι᾽ ἐμοῦ N.N. ἐγράφη.]

2 l. Σαραπίωνι 8 l. γενήματος 9-10 l. κατενεγκεῖν 10 l. Ἀλεξάνδρειαν 12 l. παραδίδοντα 14 l. ἐν 17 ὑπεδε[χ]όμην ed.princ.

"[- - -] son of Eusebios, and Sarapion son of Ploutarchos, and Hierax son of Serenus, all councillors of the city of the Oxyrhynchites (and) commissioners of wheat for Alexandria, from Aurelius Paësis son of Horos, from the same Oxyrhynchite (nome), boatman of a ship belonging to Diogenes son of Diogenes, ex-*curator*, with the aforementioned Aurelius Diogenes son of Diogenes, himself owner of the aforesaid boat, as surety for the delivery of the cargo and the production of the receipt. We acknowledge, swearing the august imperial oath by our lords Valentinianus and Valens, the eternal emperors, that I, the boatman, have received from the persons mentioned herein below and have put on board the aforesaid boat, from the harvest of the fortunate new 9th indiction a total of 618 art. of wheat, new, pure, free of barley and unadulterated, measured with the public measure and the prescribed way of measuring; I shall transport this cargo to the most illustrious Alexandria and deliver it safe and undamaged to the local granaries in full number, and I shall produce certificates of delivery for these issued to the name of you, the commissioners, and that I, the surety, serve voluntarily and out of my free will as surety for the aforementioned boatman that he delivers the artabai of wheat and that he produces receipts issued to the name of you, the commissioners, or that I, the surety, am necessarily responsible for everything that may be requested from him concerning this cargo so as to incur no blame in any respect, otherwise may I be liable to the divine oath.

(M. 2) I, Aurelius Diogenes son of Diogenes, am surety for the aforementioned Paesis, boatman, that he delivers the cargo of wheat and that he produces the receipt, as stated above.

(M. 3) I, Aurelius Paësis, son of Horos, have received and put on board the cargo of six hundred eighteen artabai of clean wheat, total 618 art., and I shall deliver, as stated above. I, Aurelius N.N., have written on his behalf as he is illiterate."

For commentary to this text, see the *ed.princ.*, where in the introduction *SB* XIV 11548 should be added to the list of sureties (see *CPR* XXIV, p. 13 fn. 8; the text *P.Laur.* IV 162 mentioned there = **800** in this edition). For sureties in general, see K.A. Worp, "P.Leid.Inv. I 425: eine Gestellungsbürgschaftsurkunde aus Memphis", in: S. Janeras (ed.), *Miscellanea Papyrologica Ramon Roca-Puig en el seu vuitantè aniversari* (Barcelona 1987) 337-40;. B. Palme, "Pflichten und Risiken des Bürgen in byzantinischen Gestellungsbürgschaften", in: G. Thür - Fr. J. Fernández Nieto (edd.), *Symposion 1999. Vorträge zur griechischen und hellenistischen Rechtsgeschichte* (Pazo de Mariñán, La Coruña, 6.-9. September 1999), (Köln - Weimar - Wien 2003) 531-55 (= *Akten der Gesellschaft für griechische und hellenistische Rechtsgeschichte,* 14).

For the date of the present document (*ed.princ.*: IV)) see now N. Gonis in *ZPE* 143 (2003) 165 n. 8: "a dating [of P.Mich. XV 724] to 365/6 is suggested in the APIS entry on the WWW [by P(aul) H(eilporn)]; comparison with PWash.Univ.II 82 (367) and now POxy. LXVII 4598, 4600, 4606 (all three of 361), etc., suggests that the date should be narrowed to 365". As all other dating elements are lacking, any more precise dating depends, of course, on the reading of the numeral of the indiction in l. 8. The first editor read this as a theta (= 9) but later apparently changed it implicitly into an alpha (= 1). For this change of mind compare his remark in *CdE* 69 [1994] 134 fn. 6, where *P.Mich.* XV 724 is dated '373?'. Within the chronological parameters of the archive, indiction 1 = either 372/3 or 357/8. The photo shows, however, that the reading of a theta = 9 is indeed correct and this reading is confirmed *per epistulam* by A. Verhoogt; the 9th indiction is 365/6p and its harvest in Oxyrhynchus fell in the summer of 365 (for the harvest in Oxyrhynchus in relation to the indiction, cf. *CSBE*[2] 32). All of this has, of course, consequences for the restoration of the imperial oath in l. 6 which should *not* mention the emperor Gratianus before the year 367; therefore, the entry for this text in *CSBE*[2] p. 278 should be adapted and moved to p. 277.

Several lacunose passages in the *ed.princ.* (especially ll. 1-6) can now be supplemented on the basis of parallel documents in this archive; hence, e.g., our restoration of the term (in itself unlikely) γεούχου in l. 5, for which see **813**.7n.

2 For these commissioners of wheat, cf. the general introd., § 2. The Eusebios mentioned here may have been the same man as the father of a certain Theon mentioned below in **820**.7.
3. For the boatman mentioned here, cf. the general introd., § 4.
9. The gender of the participle καθεστηκότος proves that in the preceding text σῖτος / πυρός rather than κριθή needs to be restored.
12. The proposal to read ἐμ[ὸ]ν for the first editor's αὐ[τὸ]ν (cf. *BL* 8:219) should not be taken over, cf. the corresponding passages in other such contracts.

816: LETTER OF THE *PRAEFECTUS ANNONAE*

P.Mich. inv. # 4022 = *P.Turner* 45 after 10.iv.374[p]

H. 25.7 x W. 34.8 cm. Margins: at the top 2.1, at the LH side 3, at the RH side 0.2, at the bottom 4.8 cm. There is a *kollesis* at 15.4 cm from the LH edge. The RH side is broken at a *kollesis* at 18.8 cm from the first *kollesis*. Verso: one line along the fibres and two texts, separated by blank space, across the fibers. Photo: see http://wwwapp.cc.columbia.edu/ldpd/app/apis/item?mode=item&key=michigan.apis.2136.

1 Ἀ(ντίτυπον)

2 Φλαούιος Κ[λ]αύδιος Πατρίκιος ὁ λαμπρότατος ἔπαρχος ἀννώνῃ̣ς̣ Ἀλεξανδρείας {εξ}

3 [ἐ]ξ̣άκτορ[ι] Ὀξυρυγχείτου χαίρειν.

4 κατὰ τὴν ἀ[π]οσταλῖσ[α]ν παρὰ σοῦ πρὸς τὴν τάξιν ἀναφορὰν γίγνωσκε εἰσκαικομίσθαι τοῖς

5 κατὰ Ἀλεξάνδ̣ρειαν θείοις θησαυροῖς ἐκ τοῦ ὑπὸ σαὶ νομοῦ δι(ὰ) Ὡρίωνος Πτολεμαίου καὶ Ἡσυ-

6 χίο̣υ̣ Ἰουλιαν[ο]ῦ καὶ κοινων<ῶν> ἐπιμελητῶν διὰ τῶν ἑξῆς πολυκωπιτῶν ὑπὲρ β´´ ἰνδικ(τίωνος) σίτου

7 ἀρτάβας χιλίας ἐννακοσίας τεσσεράκοντα τρῖς, τῇ μὲν πρὸ μιᾶς Νωνῶν Ἀπριλίων ἀρτάβας ὀκτα-

8 κοσίας ἐννενήκοντα ἥμισυ, καὶ τῇ πρὸ τεσσάρων Εἰδῶν τῶν αὐτῶν ἀρτάβας χιλίας πεντή-

9 κοντα δύο ἥμ̣ι̣σ̣υ ὑπατίας τοῦ δεσπότου ἡμῶν Γρατιανοῦ αἰωνίου Αὐγούστου τὸ γ καὶ Φλ(αουίου)

10 Ἐκ̣ουτίου τοῦ λαμ(προτάτου) κόμιτος καὶ ἀναφέρεσθαι τοῖς λόγοις ἐξ ὑποσημιώσεως Ἀγαθοῦ Δαίμονο(ς)

11 καὶ Μεγετίου καὶ Νεμεσίωνος καὶ Ἀσκλᾶ ἀπὸ στρατιᾶς ὑποδεκτῶν καὶ ἐξ ἀναφορᾶς ἰδίῳ

12 κινδύνῳ Ἀρίου καὶ Ἰσιδώρου τῶν ταβουλαρίων τῆς τάξεως καὶ Ἐπιμάχου καὶ Προεχίου

13 οἰκονόμων καὶ Διον̣υ̣σίου βοηθοῦ διακεντήσεως ἧς τὸ ἀντίτυπον ὑποτέτακται ἡ ἐμὴ

14 καθοσιώσεως μεμάθηκεν, ὅπερ τῆς καταβολῆς ἕνεκεν ἀντιγραφῆναί σ̣οι προσέταξα. ἔρρωσο.

15 ἔστι δέ·

16 δι(ὰ) Παωμ[ίο]υ (ἀρτ.) ωϙL, δι(ὰ) Παaβεῦς (ἀρτ.) ͵ΑνβL΄.

17 Φλ(αούιος) Ἰσίδωρος ταβουλάριος συμφωνῖ τὸ προκίμενον μέτρον τοῦ σίτου ἐν ἀρτάβαις

18 χιλίαις ἐννακοσίαις τεσσεράκοντα {τρῖς} τρισὶν ὡς πρόκιται.

19 Φλ(αούιος) Νεμεσί[ω]ν ὑποδ(έκτης) ἐσημιωσάμην τὴ<ν> ἀποχὴ<ν> τοῦ σίτου ἐν ἀρτάβαις χιλίαις ἐννακοσίαις

20 τεσσεράκοντα τρισὶν μόναις.

21 Φλ(αούιος) Ἐπίμαχος οἰκονόμος συμφωνῖ τὸ προκίμενον μέτρον τοῦ σίτου ἐν ἀρτάβαις

22 χιλίαις ἐννακοσίαις τεσσεράκοντα τρισὶν μόναις.

23 Φλ(αούιος) Ἀμμώνιος βοηθ̣(ὸς) συμφωνῖ ἐν ἀρτάβαις χιλίαις ἐνναkοσίαις τεσσεράκοντα τρισὶν μόν(αις).

24 (M. 2) Αὐρήλιος Σεραπίων ἐπιμελητὴς ἔσχον ἅμα τοῖς κοι(νωνοῖς) τὴν ἐπενχθῖσαν ὑπὸ σοῦ αὐθεντικὴν ἀποχὴν τοῦδε τοῦ ἀντιτύπου

25 τούτου ὡς πρόκειται.

4 l. ἀποσταλεῖσαν, εἰσκεκομίσθαι 5 l. σὲ 7 l. τρεῖς 10 l. ὑποσημειώσεως 16 l. Παaβεῦτος 17/21 l. συμφωνεῖ, προκείμενον 18 l. πρόκειται 19 l. ἐσημειωσάμην 23 l. συμφωνεῖ 24 l. ἐπενεχθεῖσαν

Verso

(perpendicular to the writing on the recto):

26 (M. 3?) Παυμίου σί(του) (ἀρτ.) ωϘS´ καὶ Παaβεῦτος σί(του) (ἀρτ.) ͵ΑνβS´ πολυκωπιτ(ῶν)

27 τ̣ῆ̣ς̣ β ἰνδικ(τίωνος)

(parallel to the text on the recto):

28 λόγος κρ̣[ι]θ̣[ῆ]ς TRACES ̣π̣εδεξα Κοπρέως ἐπὶ τῆς πέ⟦ ̣ ̣⟧μπτης ἰνδικτίωνος

29 ο̣ὔ̣τ̣[ω]ς̣·

30 παρὰ Κο̣π[ρέ]ω̣ς καὶ τ[ῶν] ἀδελφῶν ἀπὸ λόγου φόρου (ἀρτ.) λαʃ%, ἀπὸ λόγου ἐχθέσεως (ἀρτ.) ζ, διαφόρου (ἀρτ.) β γ´, ὁμοῦ (ἀρτ.) μʃ%γ.

31 παρὰ Πα[̣ ̣] φ[ό]ρ̣[ου] (ἀρτ.) λα β), ἐχθέσεως (ἀρτ.) ε, διαφόρου (ἀρτ.) α β), ὁμοῦ (ἀρτ.) ληϛ´.

32 παρὰ Π̣λ[̣ ̣]τ̣ι καὶ Διδ̣[ ] α̣π̣ὸ λο̣γου ἐχθέσεως (ἀρτ.) ιε, διαφόρου (ἀρτ.) ε, ὁμοῦ (ἀρτ.) κ

33 παρὰ Το[..]υ̣ ἀπὸ Πέτν[η λό]γ(ου) κ̣ε̣φαλαίου (ἀρτ.) κβ, διαφόρου (ἀρτ.) ζ γ´, ὁμοῦ (ἀρτ.) κθ γ́.

34 παρὰ [Πα]τ̣α̣εῖς ἀ̣π̣ὸ̣ ἐ̣π̣ο̣ι̣κ̣ί̣ο̣υ̣ Μελαντίου κεφαλαίου (ἀρτ.) ιζ, διαφόρου (ἀρτ.) ε β), ὁμοῦ (ἀρτ.) κβ β).

35 παρὰ Ν̣[..].κ Παύλ̣ο̣υ̣ . λ̣λ̣ω̣[.] καὶ Κοπρι (ἀρτ.) ϛ διαφόρου (ἀρτ.) β, ὁμοῦ (ἀρτ.) η.

VACAT (6 cm)

36 τούτω̣ν ἀνηνέχ̣θ̣η διὰ Κοπρέως εἰς τὴν πόλιν εἰς Μεσορὴ κε (ἀρτ.) ιγ

37 κ̣α̣ὶ ἀ̣[νη]νέχθη εἰ̣ς̣ τ̣ὴν πόλιν διὰ τοῦ μικροῦ χιμαυ Ἀγάθωνος (ἀρτ.) ιε

38 καὶ ε̣[ἰ]ς̣ ἕτερον π̣λῖον διὰ Ἠλ ίας ἀπὸ ἐποικίου Ψάμμιδος (ἀρτ.) ιϛ

39 Παυμ̣[ίω̣] π̣οταμίτη̣ (ἀρτ.) α

40 Παπ̣[ ]ν̣ουθίου ἀπὸ .[ ]εννω μέτρα τέσσαρες

41 Μαρ[τυ]ρίω̣ ἀμπελ̣[ο]υ̣ργῷ μέτρα πέν̣ται, τῷ ὄνῳ μέτρω̣ν α

42 και ἀνενέχθη δι' ἐ̣μ̣οῦ εἰς τὴν πόλιν (ἀρτ.) α.

31,32 ἐκθέσεως Μελανθίου 38 πλοῖον 41 πέντε, μέτρον 42 ἀνηνέχθη

"Copy. Flavius Claudius Patricius, *vir clarissimus, praefectus annonae Alexandriae*, to the *exactor* of the Oxyrhynchite nome, greeting. Know that in accordance with the report which you sent to my office one thousand nine hundred and forty-three artabas of wheat for the 2nd indiction have been brought to the imperial granaries in Alexandria from the nome under your administration through Horion son of Ptolemaios and Hesychios son of Julianus and their associate commissioners, through the boatmen named below: on the day before the nones of April eight hundred and ninety and a half artabas, and on the fourth day before the ides of the same month one thousand and fifty-two and a half artabas, in the consulate of our lord Gratianus, eternal Augustus, for the 3rd time and of count Fl. Equitius, *vir clarissimus*; and (know further) that these are being entered into the accounts with a subscription by Agathos Daimon, Megethios, Nemesion, and Asklas, receivers in the civil service. My devotion has been informed by a report (made) at their own risk by Arios and Isidoros, *tabularii* of the office, Epimachos and Proechios, *oeconomi*, and Dionysios, auditing (?) assistant, of which a copy is appended, and I have ordered that these facts be written in reply to you in consideration of the payment. Farewell.

'To wit: through Paomios, 890 ½ art.; through Paabeus, 1052 ½ art.'

'Fl. Isidoros, *tabularius*: the stated quantity of wheat, amounting to one thousand nine hundred and forty-three artabas, is accurate as stated.'

'I, Flavius Nemesion, receiver, have signed the receipt for the wheat amounting to one thousand nine hundred and forty-three artabas exactly.'

'Fl. Epimachos, *oeconomus*: the stated quantity of wheat, amounting to one thousand nine hundred and forty-three artabas, is accurate.'

'Fl. Ammonios, assistant: it is accurate, amounting to

one thousand nine hundred and forty-three artabas of wheat exactly.'

(M. 2) 'I, Aurelius Sarapion, commissioner, have received together with my associates the original receipt of which you presented this copy, as stated.'

(Back, M. 3?) 'Paymios 890 ½ art. wheat and Paabeus 1052 ½ art., boatmen, for the 2nd indiction.'

Back, ll. 28-42:

28 Account of barley --- of/through Kopreus for the 5th indiction,

29 as follows:

30 From Kopreus and his brothers/ associates, on account of rent, 31 art(abas); on account of arrears, 7 art.; on account of interest, 2 ⅓ art., together makes 40 ⅓ art.

31 From Pa---, for rent 31 ⅔ art., for arrears 5 art., for interest 1 ⅔ art., together makes 38 ⅙ art.

32 From Pl--- and Did--- on account of arrears 15 art., on account of interest 5 art., together makes 20 art.

33 From To-- from Petnê on account of capital 22 art., for interest 7 ⅓ art., together makes 29 ⅓ art.

34 From Pataeis from the hamlet of Melanthiou, for capital 17 art., for interest 5 ⅔ art., together makes 22 ⅔ art.

35 From --- and Kopreus (?) (for capital ?) art. 6, for interest 2 art., together makes 8 art.

36 Of these (amounts) were transported to the city on Mesore 25: 13 art.;

37 and to the city through the small *chimau* of Agathon: 15 art.;

38 and to another boat through Elias from the hamlet of Psammis: 16 art.;
39 to the boatman Paümios: 1 art.;
40 to Papnouthios from --ennô: four *metra*;
41 to Martyrios vinedresser: five *metra*, for the donkey 1 *metron*;
42 and transported through me to the city: 1 art.

For a detailed commentary on the recto of this text see its first edition (by J.C. Shelton) in *P.Turner* 45. For a thorough further discussion of this type of document (for which cf. also *P.Oxy*. XXIV 2408 [397p], *P.Ryl*. IV 652 = *SB* XXIV 16262 [before 374p?], and perhaps *SB* XVI 12580 = *C.Epist.Lat*. I 235 = *ChLA* XII 519 [late IVp]), see F.A.J. Hoogendijk in *ZPE* 112 (1996) 165-177 (the text published there is now *SB* XXIV 16261) and the supplementary remarks made by B. Palme in *CPR* XXIV 2, introd. (esp. p. 13; in fn. 8, *P.Mich*. XV 724 = now **815** in this edition)

11. Supplementary to Shelton's comments on the name Μεγέτιος, compare the name Μεγέθιος in *P.Petra* I 5.8 (where see the note ad loc.). Interchange between -τ-/-θ- is common enough in the papyri (see F. Th. Gignac, *Grammar*, I 87, compare in this text l. 34 and the spelling of the name of the *praeses* Fl. Eumathios Parthenios in **812**.8,11,14,15, i.e. Εὐμάτιος for Εὐμάθιος).

The verso of the text was mostly disregarded in the first edition which only presented a transcript of ll. 26-27, 30, and 36.

The 5th indiction is presumed by Shelton to relate to the year 376/7p. The text offers an account of various categories of payments, viz. for rent (φόρος, ll. 30, 31), arrears (ἔχθεσις, ll. 30, 31, 32), interest (διάφορον, ll. 30-35) and capital of a loan (κεφαλαῖον, ll. 33, 34). In l. 35 a category indication for the first payment of 6 artabai is lacking; most likely this, too, was 'for capital'. In ll. 30-35, the interest was apparently consistently 1/3rd (= 33.333 %) of the preceding entry ('arrears' or 'capital'). The total amount in ll. 30 - 35 is (40 1/3 + 38 1/3 + 20 + 29 1/3 + 22 2/3 + 8 =) 158 2/3 art.; the total amount in ll. 36 - 42 = 46 art. + 10 *metra* (= 1 art.?).

28. π̣εδεξα seems to come from an aorist form of ὑποδέχομαι, ' to receive', i.e. ὑ̣πεδεξά(μην). A sign of abbreviation, however, is lacking and the precise construction of the following genitive Κοπρέως is unclear. Something like 'Account of barley which I received through Kopreus' vel sim. may have been intended. On the name Kopreus, see S.B. Pomeroy, "Copronyms and the Exposure of Infants in Egypt", in: R.S. Bagnall & W.V. Harris, *Studies in Roman Law in Memory of A. Arthur Schiller* (Leiden, 1986) 147-162, in particular 158 ("The form Κοπρεύς tends to appear in Oxyrhynchus") .

30. The addition is correct: 31 + 2 + 7 ⅓ = 40 ⅓.

31. The scribe made an error in his addition: 31 ⅔ + 5 + 1 ⅔ = 38 ⅓ rather than 38 ⅙.

32. The addition is correct: 15 + 5 = 20.

33. For the Oxyrhynchite village Πέτνη in the Middle toparchy, see P. Pruneti, *I Centri abitati*, 148-49; A. Benaissa, *Rural Settlements of the Oxyrhynchite Nome. A Papyrological Survey*. (Version 1 [2009] = Trismegistos Online Publications, IV), s.n.

The addition is correct: 22 + 7 ⅓ = 29 ⅓ .

34. An Egyptian personal name [Πα]τα̣εῖς (here undeclined) is not yet known, but cf. *PSI* VIII 954.58 κλ]ήρου καλουμένου Παταειτ[where we are obviously dealing with an Oxyrhynchite *kleros*-name.

For an Oxyrhynchite village Μελανθίου in the Middle toparchy, see P. Pruneti, *op.cit.*, 102; A. Benaissa, *op.cit.*, s.n.

The addition is correct: 17 + 5 2/3 = 22 2/3.

35. The addition is correct: 6 + 2 = 8.

37-38. The text of the entries in l. 37, κ̣α̣ὶ ἀ̣[νη]νέχθη ε̣ἰ̣ς τ̣ὴν πόλιν διὰ τοῦ μικροῦ χιμαυ Ἀγάθωνος (ἀρτ.) ιε, and l. 38, καὶ ε̣[ἰ]ς̣ ἕτερον π̣λῖον (l. πλοῖον) διὰ Ἡλ ίας ἀπὸ ἐποικίου Ψάμμιδος (ἀρτ.) ις, yields the information that in l. 38 'another boat' is referred to, while in the preceding lines the word πλοῖον is not encountered. Therefore, one wonders whether in l. 37 the term χιμαυ (not yet attested as an Egyptian [rather than Greek] personal name) is perhaps an (equally unattested) Egyptian word for a boat. In that case, the small boat of Agathon conveyed 15 artabas to the city (= probably Oxyrhynchus), while 16 artabas went (in)to another boat through Elias from the hamlet of Psammis? For Egyptian loan words in Greek papyri in general, cf. S. Torallas Tovar, "Egyptian Lexical Interference in the Greek of Byzantine and Early Islamic Egypt", in P.M. Sijpesteijn - L. Sundelin (eds.), *Papyrology and the History of Early Islamic Egypt*, Leiden, 2004 (= *Islamic History and Civilization. Studies and Texts*, 55) 163-198, esp. the appendix (pp. 178-198).

38. For the toponym Ψάμμιδος, cf. P. Pruneti, *op cit.*, 221 and A. Benaissa, *op.cit.*, both *s.v.*Ψεμμ( ) attested only in *SB* I 1945.32; are we dealing with various forms of the same name?

39: Is this the same boatman Paümios as in l. 26 (cf. also l. 16)?

40. Or read Πατ̣[ερ]μ̣ουθίου? In any case the genitive seems to be an error for the dative. It is also difficult to decide whether hereafter the Oxyrhynchite village name should be Π̣[ε]εννω or Μ̣εννω (with a broad my); the first option seems slightly more likely.

41. It is unclear how τῷ ὄνῳ should be taken: with the preceding or with the following? Was the entry added as an afterthought and was there not sufficient space between ll. 41 and 42 for writing it on a fresh line?

817: LIST OF ORIGINS OF TRANSPORTED GRAIN

P.Mich. inv. # 4028.B ca 357/8 or 372/3^{p}?

H. 6.5 x W. 15.2 cm. Broken on all sides except the RH side, where there is a margin of 5.4 cm. There is a *kollesis* at 4.2 cm from LH edge. Photo: see http://wwwapp.cc.columbia.edu/ldpd/app/apis/item?mode=item&key=michigan.apis.4364.

[ἔστι δέ·]	
[σίτου] ὑποστάσεως	[(ἀρτ.)] Ἀρ̣[
οὕτως·	
α̣ ἰνδικ(τίωνος)	
Σαραπόδωρος Τιμοθέου	(ἀρτ.) ν
Ἀρσινόη θυ(γάτηρ) Ἡραίσκου	(ἀρτ.) β
Traces of 1 line	

"---; That means: of the total of wheat 1,100 + art(abas) as follows: of the 1st indiction, Sarapodoros son of Timotheos, 50 art.; Arsinoë daughter of Heraiskos, 2 art.; ---"

This fragment contains part of a survey of grain loaded; for parallels see **809** col. ii and **813** col. ii. Originally this piece was attached (probably also as a second column) to a document like **800**, **803**, **808**, **809**, **810**, **813**, **814** or **815**; that document however, may not have been preserved. In view of the amount of grain partly preserved in l. 2 this list must have been originally much longer, since the two preserved entries in ll. 5 and 6 amount to only 52 artabas.

2. For the meaning of ὑποστάσεως, cf. **809**.26n.
4. In view of the chronological parameters of the whole dossier, the first indiction may be related to 357/8 or 372/3P.

818: SUBSTITUTION OF A LITURGY ?

P.Mich.inv. # 4028.C 356, 357 or 360P

H. 8 x W. 5.3 cm. Margins: at the top 1.8, at the LH side 1.5 cm. The fragment is broken on the RH and the bottom side. Photo: see http://wwwapp.cc.columbia.edu/ldpd/app/apis/item?mode=item&key=michigan.apis.10549.

1 ὑπατείας τ[ῶν δεσποτῶν ἡμῶν Κωνσταντίνου Αὐγούστου τὸ ̣´]
2 καὶ Ἰο υλι[ανοῦ τοῦ ἐπιφανεστάτου Καίσαρος τὸ ̣´, Month, Day]
3 Αὐρήλιος Δι[όσκορος βουλευτὴς τῆς λαμ(πρᾶς) καὶ λαμ(προτάτης) Ὀξυρυγχιτῶν]
4 πόλεως ἐπ[ιμελητὴς σίτου / κριθῶν Ἀλεξανδρείας
5 Αὐρήλιοις Σα[son of N.N. καὶ N.N. son of N.N. καὶ N.N. son of N.N. τοῖς πᾶσι]
6 βουλευταῖς τ[ῆς αὐτῆς πόλεως ὑπὲρ τῆς]

7 διαδοχῆς Καλ[

8 ὑπ̣ο̣δ̣ο̣χὴν τ̣ῆ[ς

---

2 ϊουλι[-- Pap. 8 ϋπ̣ο̣δ̣ο̣χην Pap.

Not enough of this text has been preserved to establish with certainty what kind of document these scanty remains belong to. διαδοχή (l. 7) means 'succession' and διάδοχος means, as well as 'heir', also 'successor in a function'. If this is correct, one might be dealing with the succession in a liturgy or office of a certain Kal- (of course, any name in Καλ- may be restored) by another person. Unfortunately, it can no longer be established with certainty, which function is being taken over, but it seems conceivable that the office of ὑποδέκτης = '(tax) collector' was concerned, compare l. 8, ὑποδοχήν.

1-2. Constantius Augustus and Julianus Caesar held the consulate jointly in 356p (Constantius VIII & Julianus Caesar I), 357p (Constantius IX & Caesar Julianus II) and 360p (Constantius X & Julianus Caesar III); cf. *CSBE*[2] App. D, *s.aa.* 356, 357, 360.

3. An Aurelius Dioskoros son of Eulogios appears as councillor of Oxyrhynchus and commissioner responsible for the transport of tax-grain to Alexandria also in **807**.3, **808**.2, **809**.2, **810**.2, **811**.2 (all from 372p), cf. also the general introd., § 2; for that reason we have restored his name here. Even so, it cannot be ruled out that one should restore the name as that of Αὐρ. Δι[ογένης Διογένους] (cf. **800**.3, from 354p), or that of Αὐρ. Δι[ονύσιος son of N.N.] (cf. **805**.4, from 367p).

5. An Aurelius Sarapion son of Ploutarchos is frequently attested in this archive as councillor of Oxyrhynchus and as responsible for matters concerning the transport of tax-grain to Alexandria; cf. the general introd.,

§ 2; hence, one may consider restoring his name here, too. On the other hand, a town councillor Aurelius Sarapion son of Herm[occurs in *P.Oxy.* LXVII 4607.2 (= *App. A*, # 2).
6. After πόλεως one may continue as elsewhere, with ἐπιμεληταῖς σίτου / κριθῶν Ἀλεξανδρείας.

819: DECLARATION TO CLEAN WHEAT

P.Mich. inv. # 4028.D 365 - 367^{p} (bef. 24.viii)

H. 18.7 x W. 9.8 cm. Margin at the bottom: 7.5 cm. Writing parallel with the fibers. The fragment is only complete at part of the bottom and on the RH side. Photo: see http://wwwapp.cc.columbia.edu/ldpd/app/apis/item?mode=item&key=michigan.apis.10550.

----

1 [ ] Traces of 1 line
2 [Ὁμολογῶ ὀμνὺς τὸν σεβάσμιον θεῖον ὅρ]κ̣ον τ̣ῶ̣ν̣ [δε]σ̣ποτῶν ἡμῶν
3 [Οὐαλεντινιανοῦ καὶ Οὐάλεντος αἰων]ίων Α̣ὐ̣-[γούστ]ων ὑποδε-
4 [δέχθαι μὲ τὴν κριθολογίαν παρὰ τῶν] ἐμ-β[αλομένω]ν κτητόρων
5 [πρὸς τό, εἰ συμβαίη —ὃ μὴ εἴοιτο— κίνησίν] τινα̣ [γένεσ]θ̣αι ἢ ἄλλης
6 [τινὸς ῥυπαρίας ὑπὸ τῆς μείζονος ἐξο]υσίας̣ <κριθο-λογίας> ἕ̣[νε]κ̣εν ἐπάν̣α̣γ̣-

7 [κες ἐμὲ τὸν κυβερνήτην ὑποστῆναι] καὶ πληρῶσαι τὸ περὶ τού̣του̣
8 [ἀποβησόμενον εἰς τὸ ἐν μηδενὶ μεμ]φθῆναι ἢ ἔνοχος εἴην
9 [τῷ θείῳ ὅρκῳ̣.]
10 (M. 2) [Αὐρήλιος N.N. ὤμοσα τὸν θεῖον ὅρ]κ̣ον καὶ ἔσχον τὴν κριθολογία̣[ν]
11 [ὡς πρόκειται. Αὐρήλιος N.N. ἔγρ]αψα ὑπὲρ αὐτοῦ γράμματα
12 [μὴ εἰδότος.]

7 πληρῶσαι: -ω- ex -ια-.

"--. I acknowledge, swearing the august imperial oath of our lords Valentinianus and Valens, the eternal augusti, that I have accepted the *krithologia* (= picking of barley) from the landowners, who have loaded (the cargo), so that if from a higher authority any legal action arises (may this not happen!) because of <barley picking> or of any other dirt, I, the boatman, shall take upon me and fulfill of necessity the resulting obligation, so that no blame attaches to me in any respect, otherwise may I be liable to the imperial oath. I, Aurelius N.N. son of N.N. have sworn the imperial oath and have accepted the picking of barley, as written above. I, Aurelius N.N. son of N.N. have written from him, since he is illiterate."

This small fragment is all that remains of a declaration by an unknown Aurelius to have accepted the κριθολογία, for which compare **803** and **807**. There are certain divergences between the texts of **819**.6-8 and **807**.19-21, i.e.:

819.6 --------------ἐξουσίας <κριθολογίας> ἔ̣[νε]κ̣εν ἐπάναγ-
7 [κες ἐμὲ τὸν κυβερνήτην ὑποστῆναι] καὶ πληρῶσαι
τὸ περὶ τούτου | (8) [ἀποβησόμενον ------, versus
807.19 ----------------ἐξουσίας προφάσι κριθολογία<ς> τοῦ
20 αὐτοῦ γό̣μου ἐ̣μὲ τὸν κυβερ(νήτην) ὑποστῆναι τὸ
21 περὶ τούτου ἀπο̣βησόμενον ------

This seems to preclude that **819** is only part of a copy of **807** (compare, however, a similar situation in two copies of the same text, **809**.6 and **810**.6 + note ad loc.).

Without doubt this declaration was directed to a group of town councillors of Oxyrhynchus who were in charge of the collection of wheat destined for Alexandria or Pelusium.The text probably started as usual with a (post-)consular date, a month and a day. After the address followed a description of the author of this document (who also transported the cargo from Oxyrhynchus to Alexandria / Pelusium).

1-2. There is no room in the lacuna at the beginning of l. 2 to include Gratianus' name in the oath formula (cf. general introduction, § 5). This implies that the text must be dated before 24.viii.367.
5. ἢ ἄλλης: see **807**.18n. for the omission of some words expected before ἤ.
10-11. The lacunas at the beginning of these lines are large enough to have contained the names of the κυβερνήτης, and that of the scribe, maybe also their father's names.

820: LIST OF SHIPMENTS OF GRAIN

P.Mich. inv. # 4028.E ca 355-375P

H. 27.6 x W. 10.5 cm. The fragment is broken on all sides. Photo: see http://wwwapp.cc.columbia.edu/ldpd/app/apis/item?mode=item&key=michigan.apis.10551.

1] ̣ Ὀξυρυγχίτου [
2] τοῦ ἀποσταλέντος μέτρ[ου
3 εἰς τὰ κατὰ Π]η̣λούσιον ὅρια εἰς λόγον το[ῦ γενήματος (?)
4 τῆς εὐτυχοῦς] ̣ ς νέας ἰνδικτίονος· VACAT
5 εἰς τὴ]ν λαμπροτάτην Ἀλεξ-άν[δρειαν διὰ
6]ενος Θέωνος Εὐσε-β[ίου
7] καὶ Διονυσίου Θε̣-ω̣[νος ἀρτάβαι *n*]
8 παρειλημ(μέναι) κα]ὶ ἐμβληθ(εῖσαι) εἰς τ̣[ὰ ὑποτε-ταγμένα πλοῖα
9] υ̣ἱ̣ο̣ῦ Λιμενίου ἀπὸ πρι[μιπιλαρίου
10]λ̣ου̣ Εὐδαίμονος Ἀετί[ου
11 ο]υ Πτολεμίνου πολ(ιτευομένου) ὑ̣[πὸ N.N.
12] οὕτω[ς·

13] ̣ ̣υ̣ Ἀθανασίου πολ(ιτευομένου) ὑπὸ Μουσ[

14] Ἰουλιανοῦ πολ(ιτευομένου) ὑπὸ Ἀγαθ[

15 Ἀ]ε̣τίου πολ(ιτευομένου) ὑπὸ Παυῆν Τιμοθέου κ[

16] ̣ίου Ἀπολλωνίου ὑπ̣[ὸ] Κ̣[

17 Π]τολεμίνου πολ(ιτευομένου) ὑ[πὸ N.N.

18] ̣ι̣ο̣υ̣ ἀπὸ πριμικ̣ηρ[ίου ὑπὸ N.N.

---

3 l. ὅρρια 14 ϊουλιανου Pap.

"-- of the Oxyrhynchite --- of the dispatched measure --- to the granaries in Pelusium on account of the harvest of the fortunate *n*th new indiction --- to the most illustrious Alexandria through --- son of Theon son of Eusebios --- and Dionysios son Theon *n* artabas --- received and put on board of the following ships: --- of the son of Limenius *ex-primipilarius,* --- son of Eudaimon son of Aetius --- of Ptoleminus the *politeuomenos* under the command of N.N. --- as follows: --- of Athanios the *politeuomenos* under the command of Mous]---]of Julianus the *politeuomenos* under the command of Agath[---] of Aetius the *politeuomenos* under the command of Paues son of Timotheos (boatman?) --- son of Apollonios under the command of --- of Ptoleminus the *politeuomenos* under the command of N.N. --- ios *ex- primicerius* under the command of N.N. ---"

This text, mutilated at all sides, contains a list of ships

with their owners, boatmen and cargoes. Similar texts are found below in *App. B*, in particular texts # 1 = *P.Oxy*. XLII 3079, # 3 = *P.Harr*. I 94, # 4 = *P.Oxy*. VII 1048 and # 5 = *P.Heid*. IV 313; see also the discussion of them by N. Gonis in *ZPE* 143 [2003] 163-65.

At the LH side of ll. 9 -11 and 13 - 18, the word πλ(οῖον) (cf. *P.Oxy*. VII 1048; *P.Heid*. IV 313) or πλοῖον (cf. *P.Oxy*. XLII 3079) rather than διὰ πλοίου (*P.Heid*. IV 315) has to be supplemented. This was followed apparently by the name of the shipowner and that of his father (cf. l. 10n.). As far as the text is preserved, these names were, with the exception of l. 16, followed by the indication of a (former) function. The preposition ὑπὸ introduces the ship's boatman, probably also followed by his father's name (cf. l. 15 and *P.Heid*. IV 313 = *App. B* # 5) and the mention of the word κυβερνήτην (cf. *App.B* # 1 = *P.Oxy*. XLII 3079; *App. B* # 3 = *P.Harr*. I 94). At the right side the cargo, rather than the ship's capacity, is missing. None of the shipowners or boatmen mentioned in the present text can be certainly identified with such persons mentioned in the parallel texts. We do not, however, exclude the possibility that several of them (in particular, cf. *App. B* # 1 = *P.Oxy*. XLII 3079; *App. B* # 4 = *P.Oxy*. VII 1048 + *BL* 8:240; *P.Heid*. IV 313 = *App. B* # 5, cf. the councillor Ἱέραξ in l. 3) belong to the archive published here.

1. This may have been the original first line of this text, containing the addressee of the text, i.e. the exactor of the Oxyrhynchite nome (cf. *P.Heid*. IV 313, introd.): ἐξάκτορ]ι̣ Ὀχ υρυγχίτου, or the strategus of this nome (cf. **802**, **805**), στρατηγῶ]ι̣ Ὀχ υρυγχίτου (the same use of iota adscript in the

form στρατηγῶι is found in *P.Ammon* I 3.6 [348^{p}]. After a space of approximately 1 cm this may have been followed by the contents of the present text. Only '*exempli gratia*' one could think of something like βρεούιον (or γνῶσις, λόγος) τοῦ ἀποσταλέντος μέτρου σίτου εἰς τὰ κατὰ Πηλούσιον ὅρρια εἰς τὸν λόγον τοῦ γενήματος τῆς εὐτυχοῦς *n* νέας ἰνδικτίωνος· ὁμοίως εἰς τὴν λαμπροτάτην Ἀλεξάνδρειαν. This in turn was, e.g., followed by γίνονται *n* ἀρτάβαι ὑπὸ + an unknown number of persons βουλευτῶν καὶ ἐπιμελητῶν σίτου?) παρειλημ(μέναι) καὶ ἐμβληθεῖσαι εἰς τὰ ὑποκείμενα πλοῖα.

3. ὅρια: l. ὅρρια. For this term (= granary), cf. S. Daris, *Il Lessico latino*, 79; cf. also **811**.22.

4. Read δευτέρ]ạς, ἑβδόμ]ῃς, ὀγδό]ῃς or ---τ]ῃς? Unfortunately, we have too little evidence for assigning the indiction mentioned here to any particular year in our calendar. Given the chronological perimeters of the archive a year between ca 355 -375^{p} seems most likely. For the concept of 'new' indiction, cf. *CSBE*^{2}, Chapt. 5.

6-7. At least 3 persons are involved in this transaction. Most likely, these persons are *politeuomenoi* ('*curiales*') of Oxyrhynchus and commissioners of wheat to be transported to Alexandria or Pelusium. They seem to be mentioned with their own names, their father's names and their grandfather's names (cf. l. 6; cf. **801**.4). It cannot be excluded that in *P.Wash.Univ.* II 82 (= **805**).4 the correct reading is Διονυσίου Θ̣[έωνος. An Εὐσέβιος occurs as the father of an unknown βουλευτής / ἐπιμελητής in **815**.2.

8. Perhaps read ἑξῆς (cf. *App. B* # 5 = *P.Heid*. IV 313.4) instead of ὑποκείμενα.

8-9. Between these lines (as between ll. 11-12) approximately 3 cm have been left free. It seems likely that in the lacuna at the right in this space the word οὕτως has been lost (cf. l. 12). At the LH side a supplement like εἰς Πηλούσιον (c.q. Ἀλεξάνδρειαν) may be fitted in and between ll. 11-12 εἰς Ἀλεξάνδρειαν (c.q. Πηλούσιον). One should reckon with the possibility that there are in fact two 'lists', ll. 9-11, 'for Pelusium' and ll. 12-18, 'for Alexandria'.

9.] υ̣ἱ̣ο̣ῦ Λιμενίου ἀπὸ πρι[μιπιλαρίου: cf. **808**.4-5n.
10. It is impossible to read πλο]ί̣ου̣. Unless one reads at the beginning of this line Αὐρη]λ̣<ί>ου̣, in (only?) this case the ship's owner seems mentioned by his own name, that of his father *and* that of his grandfather. The name 'Aetios' also occurs in l. 15 (q.v.).
11. Is this the same man as in l. 17, in **813**.6,7,19, **814**.4,6,16, and in *P.Michael.* 33.2,17 (cf. **813**.6n.)?
13. Is this the same man as the Athanasios προπολιτευόμενος in *P.Oxy.* XLVIII 3394.16 (364-367^{P})? or —in view of the date perhaps less likely— the shipowner Athanasios πολιτευόμενος in *P.Oxy.* VII 1048.7 (cf. Appendix B # 4; post 392^{P}) ? For these Oxyrhynchite *(pro)politeuomenoi*, cf. K.A. Worp in *ZPE* 115 (1997) 218.
14. Is this Julianus the same man as the shipowner Julianus mentioned in *P.Oxy.* XLII 3078.3?
15. Is this Aetios the same man as the shipowner Aetios πολιτευόμενος in *P.Oxy.* VII 1048.6?

ὑπὸ Παυῆν Τιμοθέου κ[: it seems better to restore κ[υβερνήτην (in such a context, ὑπὸ governs the accusative) than to assume that there were two boatmen on one ship (restoring κ[αὶ N.N. κυβερνήτας).
16. Maybe one should print ὑπ̣[ὸ] κ̣[υβερνήτην, followed by a personal name, cf. *P.Wash.Univ.* II 83.2n.
17. Cf. above, l. 11n.
18. For the office of an (ex-)*primicerius*, cf. S. Daris, *op.cit.*, 94; *P.Oxy.* LIX 3986.9-10n.

821: LIST OF TAX GRAIN

P.Mich. inv. # 4028.F ca 355-375P

H. 15.5 x W. 7.5 cm. LH margin: 2.0 cm. Broken on all other sides. Photo: see
http://wwwapp.cc.columbia.edu/ldpd/app/apis/item?mode=item&key=michigan.apis.10552.

[̣ ̣ ̣]λ[ ] (ἀρτ.) ι̣ [
Ἡρᾶς Π ̣[̣ ̣ ̣]τ̣ος (ἀρτ.) ι [
Ἀπφοῦς Ἀπφοῦτος [(ἀρτ.)
Φαβουρῖνος Ἀπφοῦτος [(ἀρτ.)
Χωοῦς Πανεχώτου κ[αὶ
κοι(νωνοὶ) σιτ̣ολόγ(οι) [(ἀρτ.)
Φαβουρῖν[ο]ς̣ Ἀπφοῦτος [(ἀρτ.)
α[ἱ] π(ροκείμεναι).
Ἀκούτου δ[ι]' Εὐλογίου καὶ [
ο]υ κ[αὶ Κο]λλούθου καὶ ̣[

Ερ̣[ ] ̣ πραιπ(οσιτ--)
 ̣[ ] η̣Ḷ αἱ π(ροκείμεναι)
ὑπατ[είας τῆς πρ]οκ(ειμένης), Θὼθ δ.

This fragment contains part of a survey of amounts of tax grain loaded in several villages of the Oxyrhynchite nome by various persons like Heras son of N.N. (l. 2), Apfous son of Apfous (l. 3), Favorinus son of Apfous (ll. 4, 7), Choous son of Panechotes and associate *sitologi* (ll. 5-6), (cf. **809**, col. ii). It is complete only at the LH side and possibly at the bottom. For similar texts, see **822-826**.

4. The same person is mentioned in l. 7. The name Φαβουρῖνος (Lat. Favorinus) is rare, cf. *SB* III 7243 = VI 9746.25 and the *ed.princ.* of *SB* XXII 15264, note to line 1.
8. This line (cf. also the end of l. 12) points back to the total given at the beginning of an account (cf. H.C. Youtie, *Scriptiunculae* II [Amsterdam 1973] 817, 819, 837 n.72)
9. For the village Ἀκούτου, see P. Pruneti, *I centri abitati*, 26, A. Benaissa, *Rural Settlements of the Oxyrhynchite Nome. A Papyrological Survey.* (Version 1 [2009] = Trismegistos Online Publications, IV), *s.v.*, and cf. also A. Calderini - S. Daris, *Dizionario geografico, Supplemento* II 10. If, however, the form Ἀκούτου would represent the personal name Ἀκοῦς, the genitive should be corrected into a nominative.

Is Eulogios the same person as in **809**. 33 (cf. there also the notes to ll. 5-6, 34)?
11. This and the following lines are separated from the preceding ones by a free space of approximately 2 cm. It is very likely that ll. 11-13 form the conclusion of this document. In l.11, at the beginning one may consider a restoration of the name of Hermias followed by a preposition ἀπό, cf. the ex-*praepositus* of the same name in **806**.5. For the function of a *praepositus*, cf. **806**.5n.
12. Here probably a total was given; it is possible that this line started with (γ̣ί̣ν̣ο̣ν̣τ̣α̣ι̣) [(πυροῦ) (ἀρτάβαι) *n*.
13. Unfortunately, we do not know precisely which aforementioned consulate was meant. Thoth 4 = Sept. 1 or 2 (in a leap year). Given the chronological parameters of the archive, a year between ca 355 -375^{p} seems most likely.

822: LIST OF TAX GRAIN

P.Mich. inv. # 4028.G ca 355-375P

H. 19.4 x W. 7.4 cm. Margin at the top 4.9, at the right 1 cm. The papyrus is broken at the LH side. Photo: see http://wwwapp.cc.columbia.edu/ldpd/app/apis/item?mode=item&key=michigan.apis.10553.

]η̣ς̣ Χαιρήμονος (ἀρτ.) σνθ γʹʹ
οὕτω]ς·
ἀ]μ̣μ(ωνος) (ἀρτ.) σιδ γʹʹ
]εῖτος (ἀρτ.) με
] ̣
οὕτω]ς· (ἀρτ.) νθL ι̣ο
ἀ]μμωνος (ἀρτ.) ιβS´
Ἡ]ρ̣ακλάμμωνος (ἀρτ.) η Ld
καὶ] Πατερμουθίου σιτολ(όγων) (ἀρτ.) λη γʹʹ
]φο̣υ̣ καὶ Θεοδώρο̣[υ] κ̣[α]ὶ̣
σιτολό]γ(ων) (ἀρτ.) ρκβ̣

This text is similar to the preceding one. Amounts range from 8 ¾ (l. 8) to 259 ⅓ (l. 1) artabas.

1-4. 214 ⅓ (l. 3) + 45 (l. 4) make a total of 259 ⅓ art. (l. 1).
6-9. 12 ½ (l. 7) + 8¾ (l. 8) + 38 ⅓ (l. 9) make a total of 59 ½ 1/12 (l. 6) art.
11. Before σιτολόγ(ων) one may supplement κοινωνῶν. If the 122 artabas mentioned in this line were split up (cf. the preceding notes), another column (starting with οὕτως) should have followed the preserved column.

823: LIST OF TAX GRAIN

P.Mich. inv. # 4028.H ca 355-375P

H. 7 x W. 2.3 cm. On both sides the text runs parallel to the fibers. On the first side, there is a free space of 2.5 cm in between ll. 1-2. Photo: see http://wwwapp.cc.columbia.edu/ldpd/app/apis/item?mode=item&key=michigan.apis.10554.

Side I:

---

1 (ἀ̣ρ̣τ̣.) S′
2 (ἀρτ.) ϛ dκο
3 (ἀρτ.) θ γ̣[

Side II:

---

1 ο]υ Πατερμουθίου ἀπὸ τῆς α(ὐτῆς)

This text is similar to that of **821** - **822** and **824** - **826**. It is incomplete at all sides. Exceptionally, this fragment has writing on both sides, but it is impossible to decide which side was written as the 'recto', and which as the 'verso'. On side 'II' presumably 'ἀπὸ τῆς α(ὐτῆς) κώμης' was meant.

824: LIST OF TAX GRAIN

P.Mich. inv. # 4028.I ca 355-375P

H. 11 x W. 5.2 cm. The text runs along the fibers. There is a bottom margin of 4 cm. Photo: see http://wwwapp.cc.columbia.edu/ldpd/app/apis/item?mode=item&key=michigan.apis.10555.

The fragment (complete at the bottom and partly so at the right) features a series of endings of proper names (all lost, but probably ending in -ο]υ or -ο]ς) followed by:

(ἀρτ.)] γ̣[
]̣ (ἀρτ.) δ[
]̣ (ἀρτ.) ι ̣[
]̣ (ἀρτ.) α ̣[
] (ἀρτ.) ς ̣[
]̣ (ἀρτ.) ς ϊ̣[ο
]̣ (ἀρτ.) γ
]̣ (ἀρτ.) ι κδ´´
] (ἀρτ.) η ς´´

This text is similar to that of **821** - **823** and **825** - **826**; the amounts range from 1+? (l. 4) to 10 1/24 (l. 8) artabas.

825: LIST OF TAX GRAIN

P.Mich. inv. # 4028.J ca 355-375P

H. 7.7 x W. 5 cm. The text runs along with the fibers. The other side is blank. The fragment is broken on all sides. Photo: see http://wwwapp.cc.columbia.edu/ldpd/app/apis/item?mode=item&key=michigan.apis. 10556.

] (ἀρτ.) κε
] (ἀρτ.) δ
]σιτολογ( ) (ἀρτ.) νη γ´
] (ἀρτ.) αL
] (ἀρτ.) γL

This text is similar to that of **821** - **824** and **826**. It is complete only at the right. In the lacuna in front of σιτολογ( ) in l. 3 one should perhaps supplement a form of κοινωνοί. Amounts range from 1.5 (l. 4) to 58 1/3 (l. 3) artabas.

826: LIST OF TAX GRAIN

P.Mich. inv. # 4028.K ca 355-375P

H. 27.5 x W. 13.5 cm. Margins: on all sides damaged, but perhaps a margin of ca. 2.7 cm at the bottom. A *kollesis* is visible on the front at ca. 6 cm from the LH side. Verso: blank. Photo: see http://wwwapp.cc.columbia.edu/ldpd/app/apis/item?mode=item&key=michigan.apis.10557.

Col. I

	]Endings of (at least) three lines	
4	]ς Ἀφοῦτος	(ἀρτ.) αS//
5	] ̣ ̣ Ἡρακλείου	(ἀρτ.) Traces
6	Ἡρ]άκλειος Πλέειν	(ἀρτ.) Traces
7	Ἀπ]φ̣ους καὶ Πάρακε	(ἀρτ.) ζ γ̣ʹ
8	]νοῦτις Ἀπολλῶτος	(ἀρτ.) μ ̣
9	]ώνιος Ἀμόιτος	(ἀρτ.) μδ
10	]αρίων Σευήρου	(ἀρτ.) ζ β>
11	] ̣τας Δημητρίου	(ἀρτ.) ι̣ε̣ γ̅ι̅ο̅
12	] ̣νοῦτις Πούλιτος	(ἀρτ.) β κ̅ο̅
13	]ν̣ Ἡρᾶτος	(ἀρτ.) ϛ κ̅ο̅
14	] ̣ Πατερμουθίο̣υ	(ἀρτ.) ι ̣ ″
15	Ἡράκ]λειος Ναρώουτος	(ἀρτ.) ϛ̣ β>
16-17	] Traces of at least two lines	[(ἀρτ.) *n.*
18	]ν̣ πρεσβύ̣τ̣[ε]ρ̣[ος]	(ἀρτ.) ϛ κ̅ο̅
19	ἄ]μμων Ψεναμ[ουν]	(ἀρτ.) γ Ld
20	]ς Σερήνου [	(ἀρτ.) κζ Lη
21-22	] Two (?) lines lost [	
23	]θιο[	
24	] Τ̣ιμόθεος ὀπτίων [	
25	] ̣άμμων Ἡρακλ[	
26	] ̣ου ἐλαιουργο[	
27	]τ̣ι̣ς̣ Καμῆτος [	

Col. II:

28 ζ πάγου Τεξεί [

29 Πρωτᾶς πρεσβύτερ[ος

30 Ἑ̣λ̣ικ(ῶνος) δ πάγου [

31 οὕτω[ς

32 Ἰ̣σ̣ίδ[ω]ρος Συ̣[

33 Ἀνοῦφις Ἀμμων̣[

34 Παπνοῦθι[ς

35 Ἀδαίο[υ

36 κ̣[αὶ

The text on this fragment is similar to that of **821 - 825**. The amounts referred to range from 1½ (l. 4) to 44 (l. 9) artabas (cf. also l. 8: 40+? art.).

6. Read Πλέιν, cf. *P.Wash.Univ.* I 54.3 (IV/V); cf. also the dative Πλειντι in *P.Harr.* I 93.i.2, ii.12 (III^{p}) and the τόπος Πλειν in *P.Lond.* IV 1421.12 (VIII^{p}).
7. The name Πάρακε is not yet listed in the usual papyrological onomastica. Is the name Παρακλῆ / Φαρακλε (cf. *Tyche* 1 [1986] 110) intended?
8. Consulting D. Hagedorn's *Konträrindex zu den Wörterlisten* one finds that possible restorations include Ἀ]νοῦτις, Τι]νοῦτις, Παπ]νοῦτις and Ψενπ]νοῦτις.
24. For literature on the ὀπτίων (= lat. '*optio*'; for earlier attestations, cf. S. Daris, *Il Lessico latino*^{2}, 78) cf. *P.Oxy*. LXIV 4434.2n.; the *DDBDP* now lists some 150 attestations of the term.

28. Τεξεί: cf. P. Pruneti, *I centri abitati*, 200 and A. Benaissa, *Rural Settlements of the Oxyrhynchite Nome. A Papyrological Survey*. (Version 1 [2009] = Trismegistos Online Publications, IV), s.v. The information that this village, situated in the μέση τοπαρχία, belonged to the 7th pagus confirms the view expressed in *P.Oxy.* LV 3795.12n.
29. It is impossible to tell whether in the case of the πρεσβύτερος Protas one is dealing with a Christian priest (there are many attestations among the 4th century papyri) or with the headman of village (cf. **809**.34).
30. Ἐλ ικ(ῶνος): cf. P. Pruneti, *op.cit.*, 46; A. Benaissa, *op.cit.*, *s.v.* The information that this village belonged to the 4th pagus is new.
35. For the village of Ἀδαίου, cf. P. Pruneti, *op.cit.*, 23f.; A. Benaissa, *op.cit.*, *s.v.*

Appendix A: Undertakings by Oxyrhynchite Town Councillors to Deliver Wheat or Barley to Pelusium / Alexandria from the Oxyrhynchus Papyri

For counterparts of these documents kept in New York City (Columbia University) and in St. Louis (Washington University), see above **802** and **805**.

(1) *P.Oxy*. LXVII 4606
(361P)

1 [Ὑπατείας Φλαουίων Ταύρου καὶ Φλωρ]ε̣ν̣τ̣ίου τῶν λαμ̣(προτάτων), Θὼθ ̣ ̣

2 [Σεπτιμίῳ Ἀπολλωνίῳ] στρατηγῷ [Ὀξυρυγχίτου]

3 [παρὰ Αὐρηλίων Διοσκουρίδου τοῦ καὶ ?]Ἰ̣ο̣[υλι]ανοῦ Ἰουλιανοῦ <τοῦ καὶ> Διοσκουρίδου καὶ Ἰου̣[λιανοῦ (?)

4 [c. 29] ̣ ̣ ̣ ̣ κ̣[α]ὶ̣ Σαραπίωνος Πλουτάρχου τῶν πάντ[ων βουλευτῶν]

5 [τῆς λαμ(πρᾶς) καὶ λαμ(προτάτης) ?Ὀξυρυγχι]τῶν πόλεως ἐπιμελητῶν σίτου Πηλουσ̣ί̣ο̣υ̣. [Ὁμολογοῦμεν]

6 [ὀμνύντες τὸν σεβάσμιον θεῖον ὅρκο]ν̣ τ̣[ῶ]ν̣ δ̣ε̣σ̣π̣οτῶν̣ ἡμ̣ῶν Κωνσταντίου αἰω̣ν̣ίου Αὐγ[ούστου καὶ]

7 [Ἰουλιανοῦ τοῦ ἐπιφανεστάτου Καίσ]α̣ρ̣ο̣ς̣ παριλη-

φέναι καὶ ἐμβεβλῆσθαι εἰς̣ τ̣ὸ̣ ἑξῆς̣ [ὑποτεταγ-μένον]

8 [πλοῖον ἀπὸ γενήματος τῆς εὐ]τ̣υ̣[χοῦς] ε̣S// ν̣έ̣ας̣ ἰ̣νδικτίονος π̣υ̣ρ̣ο̣ῦ̣ ν̣έ̣ο̣υ̣ καθ̣αρο̣[ῦ ἀκρίθου καὶ ἀβρόχου]

9 [καὶ ἐκτὸς πάσης αἰτίας καθεστηκότος μέτρ]ω̣ δημοσίῳ μετρήσι τῇ κελευ[σ]θ̣ίσῃ ἐ̣π̣[ὶ τὸ αὐτὸ ἀρτάβας ὀκτακοσίας]

10 [c. 27]. . κ̣ε̣νωθεσ̣ίαν ε. . [.]. . ου μέρος κ̣ε̣ κοσκ(ινευμένον) . . . [

11 [c. 27]. . . καθὼς ὁ ζυγοστάτης ὑπέβαλεν ἰδι̣. [

12 [c. 25 κα]τ̣ε̣ν̣ε̣ν̣κῶμεν ἐπὶ τῇ λαμ(προτάτῃ) Πηλουσ̣ιωτῶν̣ [μητροπόλει

13 [c. 29]. . . θησ̣α̣υ̣ρ̣[ ]. . . [. . . . .] ἀριθ̣μῷ π̣[λήρης

14 [c. 29]. . . ε̣ἰ̣ς̣ τ̣ὸ̣ ἐ̣ν̣ μηδενὶ μεμφθῆναι ἢ ἔν̣[οχοι εἴημεν τῷ]

15 [θείῳ ὅρκῳ up to c. 20]. VACAT

16 [εἰς πλοῖον ἰδιωτικὸν . . . . . . β]ε̣ν̣ε̣φικιαρίου [τά]ξεως τ̣[ο]ῦ λαμ(προτάτου) δουκὸς . . [

17 [c. 16 ἀπὸ τοῦ Ὀξ υ]ρ̣[υ]γ̣χ̣ί̣του α̣ἱ̣ [π(ροκείμεναι)] τ̣ο̣[ῦ] σ̣ί̣τ̣[ο]υ̣ ἀ̣(ρτάβαι) ω″, οὗ ἐ[γ](γυητὴς) [

18 [c. 28].[. . .]. . .[. . . .]. (vac.?)

19 (M. 2) [Αὐρήλιος Σαραπίων Π]λ̣ο̣υ̣τ̣ά̣ρ̣χ̣[ου] π̣αρίλ̣η̣φ<α> τὰς̣ τ̣οῦ σίτ̣ου ἀ̣ρτάβας ὠκτακοσί̣α̣ς̣ [

20 [Αὐρήλιος c. 8 σ]υ[μπ]αρίληφα ἅ̣μ̣α̣ τ̣ο̣ῖ̣ς̣ κο̣ι̣(νωνοῖς) καὶ συνπ̣α̣ρ̣α̣δ̣ώ̣[σω

7 l. παρειληφέναι 9 l. μετρήσει, κελευσθείσῃ 12 l. κατενεγ-

κοῦμεν 19 l. παρείληφα, ὀκτακοσίας 20 l. συμπαρείληφα, συμπαραδώσω

(2) *P.Oxy.* LXVII 4608
(362[P])

1 [Ὑπ ατείας Κλαυδίο]υ Μαμερτίνου καὶ Φλαουίου Νεβιέτ̣[τ]α̣ [τῶν λαμπροτάτων.]

2 [Γαίῳ̣ Ἰο υλί]ῳ̣ Λευκαδίῳ̣ στρατηγῷ̣ [Ὀξυ-ρυγχίτου]

3 [παρὰ Αὐρηλίων] Πέ̣τρου Ἀγαθίνου καὶ Ἀμμωνίου Ἀπίωνος [καὶ N.N. s. N.N.]

4 [καὶ Σαραπίω]ν̣ο̣ς Πλουτάρχου καὶ Δωροθέου Ἀ̣ρ̣σι-ν̣ό̣ου τῶν [πάντων βουλευτῶν τῆς Ὀξυρυγχιτῶν πόλεως]

5 [ἐπιμελητῶν κρι]θ̣ῆ̣ς̣ Ἀ̣λ̣εξ̣α̣νδρίας. Ὁ̣μ̣ο̣λ̣ο̣γο̣ῦ̣μ̣εν ὀ̣[μνύντες τὸν σεβάσμιον θεῖον ὅρκον τοῦ]

6 [δεσπότου ἡμῶν Ἰο]υλια[ν]οῦ αἰων̣ί̣ο̣υ Αὐγούστου παριληφέν̣[αι καὶ ἐμβεβλῆσθαι εἰς τὸ ὑπο-]

7 [τεταγμένον πλοῖον ἀπὸ] γ̣ε̣νή̣μ̣ατο̣ς̣ τ̣ῆ̣ς̣ ϛS´´ ἰ̣ν̣δ̣ι̣κ̣-τ̣[ίον]ο̣ς κ̣ρ̣[ιθῆ]ς̣ [νέας καθαρᾶς ἀδόλου καὶ]

8 [ἀβρόχου καὶ ἐκτὸς πάση]ς αἰτίας κατεσκη̣κ̣υ̣ί̣α̣ς̣ μέ̣τρο̣ δ̣η̣μοσ̣[ίῳ μετρήσει τῇ κελευσθείσῃ]

9 [ἐπὶ τὸ αὐτὸ (ἀρτάβας) ψα, τὸν δὲ γόμο]ν̣ κατ-ενιγ̣κοῦμεν ἐπὶ τὴν λαμ(προτάτην) Ἀλ̣ε̣ξ̣[άν-δρειαν?

10 [c. 20]. κ̣α̣ὶ̣ τῆς παραδώσεως ἄποχα

γράμ(ματα) [ἐπενεγκεῖν εἰς τὸ ἐν μηδενὶ μεμ-
φθῆναι]
11 [ἢ ἔνοχοι εἴημεν τῷ θε]ίῳ ὅρκῳ.
12 (M. 2) [εἰς πλοῖ]ο̣ν̣ ἰδ̣ι̣ωτικὸν̣ . . . . [
13 [ ]ν̣ . [.] . . . . . κυβ̣ε̣ρ(νήτου) τοῦ αὐτοῦ . . . . [
14 [αἱ π(ροκείμεναι) τῆς κρ]ι̣θ̣(ῆς) (ἀρτάβαι) ψ̣α̣
ο̣ὗ ἐ̣γ(γυητὴς) . . . . [
15 (M. 3) [Αὐρήλιο]ς̣ Σαραπίων Πλουτάρχου
σ̣υ̣ν̣[παρείληφα
16 [. . . . .] ἑ̣π̣τ̣α̣κοσίας μίαν κ̣α̣ὶ̣ [?]

Verso

1 (M. 4) (ἀρτάβαι) ψα
2 ὧν πολ(ιτῶν) (ἀρτάβη) α
3 κωμ(ητῶν) (ἀρτάβαι) ψ

5 l. Ἀλεξανδρείας 6 l. παρειληφέναι 8 l. καθεστηκυίας μέτρῳ 9 l. κατενεγκοῦμεν 10 l. παραδόσεως 15 l. συμπαρείληφα

(3) *P.Oxy.* LXVII 4609
(362[p])

1 Ὑπ ατείας Κλαυδίου Μαμε̣ρ̣τ̣[ίνου καὶ Φλαουίου
Νεβιέττα τῶν λαμπροτάτων.]
2 Γ̣α̣ΐ̣ῳ Ἰ̣[ο]υ̣λ̣ί̣ῳ Λε̣[υκαδίῳ στρατηγῷ Ὀξυρυγ-
χίτου]
3 παρὰ Αὐρηλίων Π̣έ̣τρου Ἀγαθ̣ί̣[νου καὶ N.N. s. N.N.
καὶ N.N. s. N.N. καὶ Σαραπίω-]

4 νος Πλουτάρχου καὶ Δω̣ροθ̣[έου Ἀρσινόου τῶν πάν-
των βουλευτῶν τῆς Ὀξυρυγχιτῶν πόλεως ἐπιμε-
λητῶν]

5 σίτου Ἀλεξα̣ν̣δρίας. Ὁ̣μ̣[ο]λ̣[ογοῦμεν

6 αἰωνίου Ἀγούστου παριλη̣[φέναι ἀπὸ
γενήματος τῆς]

7 ε̣ὐ̣τυχοῦς ϛʹ ʹ ναίας ἰνδικτί[ονος σίτου καθε-]

8 σ̣τ̣ηκότας μέτρῳ̣ δημ̣ο̣σ̣[ίῳ
κατενεγκοῦ-]

9 με̣ν ἐπὶ τὴν λαμ(προτάτην) Ἀλεξα̣[νδρ-

10 π̣λ̣ήρης καὶ τῆς παρα̣δ̣ό̣[σεως ἄποχα γράμματα ἐπε-
νεγκεῖν εἰς τὸ ἐν μηδενὶ μεμφθῆναι ἢ ἔνοχοι]

11 ε̣ἴη^με^ν τῷ̣ θείον̣ ὅρκῳ̣. [

---

12 (M.2?) εἰς πλ(οῖον) ἰδιωτικ̣ὸ̣ν̣ [

13 ἀπὸ τοῦ [Ὀ]ξυρυγ̣[χίτου

14 οὗ ἐγγυητὴ̣ς̣ [

15 (M.3) Α̣ὐ̣[ρήλ]ι̣ο̣ς̣ . . . . .[

16] . . . .[

Verso

1 (M.4) (Ἀρτάβαι) ʹΤ[

2 ὧν

3 π̣ο̣λ(ιτῶν) (ἀρτάβαι) ιθ . .

4 κωμ(ητῶν) (ἀρτάβαι) ʹΓσν̣β . . .

5 τ̣α̣μ̣(ιακῶν) (ἀρτάβαι) ξζSʹ

4 νος from corr. (over initial iota and other traces unrecognizable) 5 l. Ἀλεξανδρείας. 6 l. Αὐγούστου παρειληφέναι 7 l. νέας 7-8 l. καθεστηκότος 11 θείῳ

(4) *P.Oxy.* LXVII 4610
(363^{P})

1 [Ὑπατείας τοῦ δεσπότου ἡμῶν Ἰουλιανοῦ] αἰωνίου Αὐγούστου τὸ δ̣[´ καὶ Φλαουίου Σαλλουστίου τοῦ]
2 [λαμπροτάτου ἐπάρχου τοῦ ἱεροῦ πραι]τωρίου, Παῦνι ι̅θ̣̅.
3 [Γαΐῳ Ἰουλίῳ Λ]ε̣υ̣καδίῳ στρατηγῷ [Ὀξυρυγχίτου]
4 [παρὰ Αὐρηλίων Γενναδ]ί̣[ου] υἱοῦ Ἰουλιανοῦ ἀπὸ λογιστ[ῶ]ν̣ [
5 [καὶ ?Ἱέ]ρ̣α̣κ̣ο̣ς ἀ̣δ̣ε̣λ̣φοῦ καὶ Σερήνου Εὐσεβίου καὶ Α̣.[
6 [τῶν πάν]των βουλ(ευτῶν) τῆς Ὀξυρυγχιτῶν πόλεως ἐπιμελητ̣ῶν [κριθῶν Ἀλεξανδρείας (?). Ὁμολογοῦμεν ὀμνύντες]
7 [τὸν σεβάσ]μιον θῖον ὅρκον τοῦ δεσπότου ἡμῶν Ἰουλ̣ι̣α̣ν̣ο̣ῦ̣ [αἰωνίου Αὐγούστου παρειληφέναι παρὰ]
8 [τῶν ἑξῆς ἐγγεγρα]μ̣μ̣ένων καὶ ἐνβεβλῆσθαι εἰς τὸ ὑποτεταγ̣μ̣[ένον πλοῖον ἀπὸ γενήματος τῆς *η* ἰνδικτίονος]
9 [κριθῆς νέ]α̣ς̣ κ̣α̣θ̣α̣ρ̣ᾶ̣ς ἀδόλου καὶ ἀβρόχου καὶ ἐκτὸς πάσ̣η̣ς̣ [αἰτίας καθεστηκυίας μέτρῳ δημοσίῳ]
10 [μετρήσει τῇ κελ]ευθ̣ί̣σοι ἐπὶ τὸ αὐτὸ (ἀρτάβας) ͵Γ̣τ´ τὸν δὲ γόμον κατεν̣[εγκοῦμεν ἐπὶ]
11 [?καὶ παραδώσ]ο̣μεν εἰς τοὺς ἐκεῖσαι δημοσίους

θησαυροὺς ἀριθμῷ π̣λὴ̣[ρης καὶ τῆς παραδόσεως ἄποχα]

12 [γράμματ]α̣ ἐπενεγκεῖν εἰς τὸ ἐν μηδενὶ μεμφθῆναι ἢ ἔνοχοι̣ [εἴημεν τῷ θείῳ ὅρκῳ.]

---

13 (M. 2) [εἰς πλοῖον ἰδι]ω̣τ̣ικὸν . . [. .] . . [.] . ους̣ ἐπιτρόπου Ἑπτανο[μίας

14 [ἀπὸ τοῦ Ὀξυρ]υ̣γχί̣του αἱ π(ροκείμεναι) τῶν κριθ(ῶν) (ἀρτάβαι) ͵Γ̣τʹ οὗ ἐγ(γυητὴς) [

[ ] VACAT

16 (M. 3) [Αὐρήλιος Γεν]νά̣[διος ?] Ἰουλε̣ι̣ανοῦ παρείληφα ἅμα τοῖς κ̣ο̣[ινωνοῖς

17 [. . . . .]. ια . . . . . ς καὶ παραδ̣ώ̣σω̣ ὡς πρόκειται [

18 (M. 4) [. . . . . . παρ]α̣δώσω ὡς πρόκειται.

7 l. θεῖον 8 l. ἐμβεβλῆσθαι 10 l. κελ]ευσθείσῃ 11 l. ἐκεῖσε 15 l. Ἰουλιανοῦ

(5) *P.Oxy.* LXVII 4611

(363p)

Col. i

----

1 [ ]ου
2 [ἐπιμε]λ̣ητῶν
3 [τοῦ δεσπότου ἡμῶν Ἰουλιανοῦ] α̣ἰωνίου
4 [Αὐγούστου ε]ὐτυχοῦς
5 [*n* ἰνδικτίονος]ω̣
6 [λ]αμ( )
7 [παρα]δώσεως
8 [ ]
9 VACAT
10 [ ].

----

7 l. παραδόσεως

Col. ii

1 (M. 2) ἔστι δέ·
2 σίτου ὑ̈ποστάσεως ἐπὶ τὸ αὐτὸ ἀ(ρτάβαι) ʹΓ̣χνʹ
3 οὕτως·
4 ζSʹʹ ἰνδικτίονος
5 πολ(ιτῶν)
6 Γερόντιος Παιανίου
(ἀρτάβαι) φλα
7 Διονύσιος ἀπὸ β(ενε)φ(ικιαρίων)
(ἀρτάβαι) γ

8 Πτολεμαῖος Κολλούθου

(ἀρτάβη) α

9 θησ(αυροῦ) Κευώθ(εως) Σ̣ευήρου Τούρβωνος απ ̣ ̣ ( )

10 δι(ὰ) Φιλονίκου Ζωΐλου

ἀ(ρτάβαι) ζ

11 κωμητ(ῶν)

12 ζ′ πάγου Σεφὼ

13] ̣ ̣ ̣ δι(ὰ) Παύλου Ἀμάειτος

(ἀρτάβαι) Γ̣ρ̣[η]

14 ϛS′′ ἰνδικ(τίονος)

15 πολ(ιτῶν) Γερόντιος Παϊανίου

ἀ(ρτάβαι) ρ

16 (γίνονται) ὁ̣μοῦ χιρ(ιστικῷ̣)

αἱ π(ροκείμεναι)

17 Ὑπατίας τῆς προκ(ειμένης), Μεσορὴ ̣ ̣.

└────

9 Σεουῆρος 13 Ἀμάϊτος 17 χειρ(ιστικῷ̣) 17 Ὑπατείας

Verso

1 (M.3) κω̣μ̣(ητῶν) (ἀρτάβαι) ͵Γψν

2 (M.2) Ἰωσήπου Τιμοθέου

2 alternate reading: Ἰωσῆ τοῦ

(6) *P.Oxy.* LXVII 4612

(363p)

1 [c. 7] Traces; c. 26 [c. 11] Φ̣λ̣α̣ο̣υ̣ίω Σαλ[λουστίου τ]ο̣ῦ

λ̣αμ̣[(προτάτου)] ἐπάρχου

2 [τ]ọῦ̣ ị[ε]ρọῦ̣ π̣ραιτωρίο[υ.]

3 [Γ]α̣ί̣ῳ Ἰ̣ο̣υλί̣ῳ Λ̣ε̣υ̣κ̣α̣δ̣ί̣ῳ [στρ]α̣τ̣η[γ]ῷ̣ [Ὀ]ξ̣[υ]ρ̣υ̣γχ̣[ί]τ̣ου

4 [παρ]ὰ̣ Α̣ὐ̣ρηλίων ....[...]................[...] κ̣α̣ὶ Σ̣.[...]ι̣.[..
?Σε]ρ̣ή̣ν̣ου καὶ Σερήν[ο]υ Εὐσεβίου κ̣α̣ὶ̣

5 [Ἀμμω]ν̣ίου Ἀπί̣ω̣ν̣ο̣ς [κα]ὶ̣ Σ̣[α]ρ̣α̣π̣ίω̣ν̣[ος] Πλουτάρχ[ο]υ τῷ̣[ν] π̣ά̣[ντ]ων βουλ(ευτῶν) τῆς Ὀξυρυ̣γ(χιτῶν) πόλεως ἐ̣π̣ιμ̣ε̣λ̣[ητῶν]

6 [σ]ί̣[τ]ο̣[υ Ἀλε]ξανδρίας. Ὁ̣μ̣ο̣λ̣ο̣γ[οῦμεν] ὀ̣μν[ύντες] τὸν σεβάσμι[ο]ν θῖον ὅ̣ρ̣κ̣ον [τ]οῦ [δε]σπότου ἡμῶν Ἰουλια[νο]ῦ̣ [α]ἰ̣[ωνίου]

7 Αὐγούσ̣του παριληφέ̣ν̣[αι κα]ὶ̣ ἐ̣μ̣β̣ε̣β̣λ̣ῆσθαι εἰς τὸ ἑξῆς ὑποτ̣ε̣τ̣α̣[γ]μ̣ένον πλοίων ἀπὸ γενήμ̣α̣τ̣ο̣ς

8 τῆς εὐτυχοῦς ζS νέα[ς ἰνδικτ]ί̣[ον]ο̣ς σ̣ί̣τ̣ο̣υ̣ νέου καθαροῦ ἀκρίθου καὶ ἀβρόχου καὶ ἐκτὸς πάσ[η]ς αἰτί̣ας καθεστηκ̣ό̣τ̣ο̣ς

9 μ̣έ̣τ̣ρ̣ῳ̣ δ̣η̣μοσίῳ̣ μ̣[ε]τ̣ρ̣ή̣[σει τ]ῇ̣ κ̣ελευσ̣θί̣[σ]η̣ ἐπὶ τὸ αὐτὸ ἀ(ρτάβας) ʹΓψνʹ[ʹ]· τ̣ὸ̣ν̣ δὲ γόμον κατενενκοῦμεν ἐπὶ̣ τ̣ῆ̣[ς]

10 [λ]α̣μ̣(προτάτης) Ἀ̣λ̣ε̣ξ̣α̣ν̣δ̣ρ̣[έ]ω̣[ν] μ̣[η]τ̣ρ̣ο̣π̣ό̣λ̣[ε]ως ε̣ἰ̣ς̣ [το]ὺ̣ς ἐκεῖσαι δημοσίου̣ς θησα̣υ̣ρ̣ο̣ὺ̣ς ἀριθμῷ̣ πλή̣ρης κ̣α̣ὶ̣ [τ]ῆ̣[ς]

11 [πα]ρ̣α̣δ̣[όσε]ως ..[.........]τ̣α̣ ἐ̣π̣ε̣ν̣ε̣γκ̣[εῖν] εἰς τὸ ἐν̣ μηδενὶ με̣μ̣φ̣θ̣ῆ̣ν̣α̣ι̣ ἢ ἔνοχο̣ι̣ ε̣ἴ̣ημεν̣ [τ]ῷ̣

12 [θείῳ ὅ]ρκῳ̣. Ἔ̣[στι δ]έ̣:

13 (M. 2) ε̣ἰ̣ς πλοῖον ἰδ[ιω]τ̣ι̣κὸν Θέωνος ἀ̣ν̣νου̣μέρος τάξεως τοῦ κυρίω μ̣ο̣υ̣ τ̣[ο]ῦ̣

14 λ̣α̣μ̣(προτάτου) δουκὸ̣ς [οὗ] κ̣υ̣β̣ε̣ρ̣(νήτης) Ὧρ ος [.].

.ιος ἀπὸ Διοκλητια̣νοῦ̣ πόλε̣ως τῆς Θηβαΐδ̣ο̣ς

15 α̣ἱ̣ π̣(ροκείμεναι) τοῦ σίτου ἀ(ρτάβαι) ʹΓ̣ψ̣ν´´ ο[ὗ ἐ]γγυητὴ̣ς Μου[σ]ῆς....[.].ιου ἀπὸ τῆς .[...].

16 πόλεως .[....]. Ἀ̣γ̣γ̣ια̣νοῦ τ̣[ρ]ιβούνου.

17 (M.3) Αὐρήλιος Σαρ[απίων Πλου]τ̣ά̣[ρ]χ̣ο̣[υ] συνπαρείληφα ἅμα τοῖς κοι(νωνοῖς) τὰς τοῦ σίτου καθαρο̣ῦ̣

18 ἀρτάβας τ̣[ρισ]χ̣[ιλίας ἑ]π̣τ̣α̣κο[σία]ς πεντήκοντα μόνα̣[ς] καὶ συμ̣παραδώσω ὡς πρ(όκειται).

19 (M.4) Αὐρήλιος Τιμ̣α̣[γ]ἐ̣ν̣η̣ς̣ συν̣παρ-[εί]ληφα ἅμα τοῖς κοι(νωνοῖς) καὶ συ̣ν̣παραδώσω ὡς πρ(όκειται).

1 l. Φλαουίου 6 l. Ἀλεξανδρείας, ὀμνύντες τὸν, θεῖον ὅρκον 7 l. παρειληφέναι, πλοῖον 9 l. κελευσθείσῃ, κατενεγκοῦμεν 10 l. ἐκεῖσε 11 supralinear traces above παραδόσεως 12 l. ἀννουμέρου, κυρίου 17/19 l. συμπαρείληφα 19 l. συμπαραδώσω

Col. ii:

1 (M.5) Ἔ̣σ̣τ̣ι̣ δ̣έ̣·

2 σίτο̣υ̣ ὑ̣π̣ο̣σ̣τ̣ά̣σ̣εως [ἐπὶ τὸ αὐτὸ ἀ(ρτάβαι) ʹΓψν]

3 οὕτως·

4 ζṢ´´ ἰ̣ν̣δ̣ι̣κ̣τ̣ί̣ο̣ν̣ο̣ς̣

5 κωμητ̣ῶ̣ν̣

6 η´´ πάγου Παλώσεως δι(ὰ)

7 Θέωνος κ̣α̣ὶ του . ν̣κ . ι

8 κ . ι̣[.]. .[.]ω̣ν̣ [(ἀ̣ρτάβαι)] ʹΓ̣ψ̣[ν]

9 (γίνονται) αἱ π(ροκείμεναι).

10 Ὑπατίας τῆς π̣ρ̣ο̣κ̣(ειμένης), [Μ]ε̣σ̣ορὴ . .

10 l. Ὑπατείας

(7) *P.Oxy.* LXVII 4613

(364P)

1 Ὑπ̣ α̣τ̣ε̣ί̣α̣ς τοῦ δεσπότου ἡμῶν Ἰουλιανοῦ αἰ̣ωνίου Α̣ὐ̣γ̣ο̣ύ̣σ̣τ̣ο̣υ̣ [

2 Γαΐ̣ῳ Ἰουλίῳ Λευκαδίῳ στρατηγῷ Ὀ̣ξ̣υ̣ρ̣υ̣γ̣χ̣ί̣τ̣ο̣υ̣

3 παρ̣ὰ Αὐρηλίων Γενναδίω Ἰουλιανοῦ κα̣ὶ̣ Σ̣ε̣ρ̣ή̣ν̣[ου] Ε̣[ὐσ]ε̣β̣ί̣ο̣υ̣ κ̣[αὶ N.N. s.]

4 [.] . . . . ς̣ καὶ Σαραπίωνος Πλουτάρχου κ̣α̣ὶ̣ Τιμαγένης Σ̣ε̣ρ̣ή̣[νου τῶν πάντων βουλευτῶν τῆς]

5 Ὀ̣[ξ]υρ[υγ]χιτῶν πόλεως ἐπιμελ̣η̣τ̣ῶν κριθ̣ῶ̣ν Ἀλ[ε]ξ̣- α̣ν̣[δρείας. Ὁμολογοῦμεν ὀμνύντες]

6 τ̣ὸ̣ν̣ σ̣εβάσμιον θῖον ὅρκον τ̣[ο]ῦ̣ δ̣ε̣σ̣π̣ό̣τ̣ο̣υ̣ ἡ̣μ̣ῶ̣ν̣ Ἰου̣- λ̣[ιανοῦ αἰωνίου Αὐγούστου παρειληφέναι]

7 [πα]ρ̣ὰ τ̣ῶ̣ν̣ ἐ̣ξ̣ῆς ἐνγεγραμμένον κ̣α̣ὶ̣ ἐ̣μ̣β̣ε̣β̣λ̣ῆ̣σ̣θ̣αι εἰ̣ς̣ τ̣ὸ̣ [ὑποτεταγμένον πλοῖον ἀπὸ]

8 γ̣ε̣ν̣ή̣μ̣α̣τ̣ο̣ς̣ τῆς εὐτυχοῦς ζ´´ ἰνδικτίωνος . . . . [

9 .[. . . πα]ραδοτίσας τοῖς κατὰ Αλ̣ε̣ξ̣άνδριαν . . . . .[.] . . .[

10 .[.] . . κ̣[αὶ] μ̣[η]δὲν διεψεῦσθαι ἢ ἔνοχοι εἴημεν τ̣ῷ̣ θ[εί̣ῳ̣ ὅρκ̣ῳ̣.

11 (M.2) ε̣ἰ̣ς̣ π̣λ̣(οῖον) ἰ̣δ̣ιωτικὸν Θέωνος Ε̣ὐ̣σ̣ε̣β̣[ίου βουλ(ευτοῦ)

12 . . . . ἀπὸ τοῦ Ὀξ(υρυγχίτου) αἱ π(ροκείμεναι) τῶν κρι[θῶν ἀρτάβαι ? οὗ ἐγγυητὴς ὁ προ-]

13 κ̣[εί]μενος Θέων Ε[ὐ]σεβίου βουλ(ευτής) [

14 (M. 3) [Αὐ]ρήλιος Σερῆνος Εὐσεβίου παρείλ̣ηφα .[.].[

15 . . α̣κ̣οσίας πεντήκοντα μόνας καὶ παρα̣δ̣ώ̣[σω

16 (M. 4) [Α]ὐ̣ρ̣ήλιος Σαραπίων συνπαρείληφ̣α̣ [

17 ὡς πρόκειται.

Verso

18 (M. 5) κριθ(ῶν) ζ′ ἰ̣ν̣δ̣ι̣κτ̣ί̣ο̣ν̣ο̣ς̣

1 Ἰουλιανοῦ, -ν- corr. 3 l. Γενναδίου 4 l. Τιμαγένους 6 l. θεῖον 7 l. ἐγγεγραμμένων 9 l. παραδοθείσας, Ἀλεξάνδρειαν 16 l. συμπαρ-είληφ̣α̣

Appendix B:
Early Byzantine Oxyrhynchite texts concerning Transportation by Ship

(1) *P.Oxy.* XLII 3079
(Early IV[p])

For the date of the text, cf. N. Gonis in *ZPE* 143 (2003) 163-65.

Traces of at least 3 lines

1 πλοῖον Λι . . . . [. . . . . . . κ]υ̣β̣ε̣ρ̣(νήτην)

2 VACAT [. . . .] . [.] .

3 πλοῖον Ἰουλιανοῦ Ἀμμ[ων . . . ὑ]π̣ὸ Ἀπφοῦν

4 κυβερνήτην [(ἀρτ.)] ψμζ

5 πλοῖον Λευκαδίου ὑπὸ Σάλβι̣[ο]ν κυβερ(νήτην)
(ἀρτ.) ʹΓσ̣ιβ

6 πλοῖον Σαραπίωνος σπεκουλάτορος ὑπὸ Ἡράκλειον

7 κυβερ(νήτην) (ἀρτ.) τιη

8 πλοῖον Εὐλογίου Ματρίνου ὑπὸ Ἀπφοῦν

9 κυβερνήτ⟦ου⟧ην (ἀρτ.) ωλ

10 Traces

---

(2) *P.Oxy.* XXIV 2415

(IV[p])

For the date of this text and for alternative readings in ll. 9, 29-30, 34 (incorporated below), see *BL* 11:162. On this text in general, see the remarks made by I.J. Poll in *Archiv* 42 (1996) 133-35 and by N. Gonis in *ZPE* 143 (2003) 165.

Col. i

ἀγ(ωγῆς) (ἀρτ.)] Γ̇ρ, ῷ̣ παρ(άσημον)	
[N.N.]	(ἀρτ.) Γ̇υι
ἀγ(ωγῆς) (ἀρτ.) *n.*,] ῷ̣ παρ(άσημον)	
[N.N.	(ἀρτ.)] Δ̇ρϙη
ἀπὸ το]ῦ Ὀξυρυγχ(ίτου)	
]	(ἀρτ.) Ἀκ
ἀγ(ωγῆς) (ἀρτ.)] Γ̇φ, ῷ̣ παρ(άσημον)	
[N.N.]	(ἀρτ.) Γ̇ωο
ἀπὸ τοῦ Ἄνω Κ]υ̣νοπολίτου	(ἀρτ.) φπ̣ε (ἥμισυ)
]κλ. . . .	(ἀρτ.) φιε
]ίτου	(ἀρτ.) Ἀφκβ
ἀγ(ωγῆς) (ἀρτ.)] Γ̇ρ, ῷ̣ παρ(άσημον)	
[N.N.]	(ἀρτ.) Γ̇υι

14-21 Eight lines lost, l. 21 ends in παρ(άσημον)

Col. ii

22 [Διοσκό]υ̣ροι (ἀρτ.) υλβ

23 [ἄλλο ὑπ]ὸ Θεοκλῆν καὶ Ἡρᾶν ἀπὸ τοῦ Ὑψηλίτου
24 ἀγ(ωγῆς) (ἀρτ.) Γ̓ρ, παρ(άσημον) Ἄμμων (ἀρτ.) Γ̓υϙ

25 [ὑπὸ Σιλ]βανὸν Βησᾶ ἀπὸ τοῦ Λυκοπολ(ίτου)
ἀγ(ωγῆς) (ἀρτ.) Β̓χ, ὧ̣ παρ(άσημον)
26 Ἀπόλλων (ἀρτ.) Β̓ωξ

27 ὑπὸ Ἀμμώνιον καὶ Ἡρακ<λ>ᾶν ἀπὸ τοῦ Μεγάλου
28 Χ̣ω̣ρ̣ί̣ο̣υ ἀγ(ωγῆς) (ἀρτ.) Β̓ψ, παρ(άσημον) Ἑρμῆς
(ἀρτ.) Γ̓α

29 ὑ̣π̣ὸ̣ . . ινον ἀπὸ τοῦ Ἄνω Κυ̣ν̣οπολ(ίτου)
30 [ἀγ(ωγῆς)] (ἀ̣ρ̣τ̣.) Γ̓τ, ὧ̣ παρ(άσημον) Διόνυσος
(ἀρτ.) Γ̓χλ

31 χ̣ο̣ρ̣τ̣η̣γὸν ὑπὸ Παρίονα Σερήνου ἀπὸ τοῦ
32 Ὀξυρυγχίτου ἀγωγῆς (ἀρτ.) Ἀ (ἀρτ.) Ἀκβ̣

33 π̣[λοῖ(ον)] δ̣η̣μ̣ό̣σιον ὑπὸ̣ Σύρον ἀπὸ τοῦ Μετη-
34 λείτου ἀγ(ωγῆς) (ἀρτ.) Ἀω, παρ(άσημον) Ἄμμων
(ἀρτ.) Ἀ𐅵πη

35 ὑπὸ Παῆσιν Ἀτρῆτος ἀπὸ τοῦ Ὀξυρυγχίτου(ἀρτ.) Ἀφ

36 ὑπὸ Ἀπόλλωνα καὶ Παρίονα ἀπὸ τοῦ
37 Λ̣υ̣κ̣οπολίτ(ου) ἀγ(ωγῆς) (ἀρτ.) Ἀυ, παρ(άσημον) Πύθιος (ἀρτ.) Ἀφνϛ

38 ἄ̣[λλο] ὑ̣π̣ὸ̣ Ἁρποκρατίωνα ἀπὸ τοῦ Λεοντοπολ(ίτου),
39 παρ(άσημον) Χρησμ[ὸ]ς, ἀγ(ωγῆς) (ἀρτ.) Ḃσ (ἀρτ.) Ḃυμζ

40 πλοῖ(ον) δ[η]μ(όσιον) ὑπὸ Πύθωνα Δωροθέου ἀπὸ τοῦ
41 Λ̣υ̣κ̣ο̣πολ(ίτου) (ἀρτ.) Ἀφν, παρ(άσημον) Πύθιος (ἀρτ.) Ἀψε

42 ὑ̣π̣ὸ Κολλοῦθον ἀπὸ τοῦ Προσωπίτου

Col.iii

43 ἀγ(ωγῆς) (ἀρτ.) ων, παρ(άσημον) Π[ό]ντος (ἀρτ.) ϡμε

44 πλοῖ(ον) ζευγματικὸν ὑπὸ Ἀγαθος Δαίμονα Πατιήσιος
45 ἀπὸ τῆς Ἑλεαρχία̣[ς] (ἀρτ.) φε

46 πολύκωπον ὑπὸ Νε̣μ[ε]σιανὸν Διονυσίου ἀπὸ τοῦ
47 Ἡρακλεοπολίτ[ο]υ (ἀρτ.) φε

48 ἄλλο ὑπὸ Ἱέρακα Σι[λ]βανοῦ ἀ̣π̣ὸ̣ τ̣ο̣ῦ̣ Ἀπολλωνοπολ(ίτου)

49 ναυκ(λήρου) ἀγ(ωγῆς) (ἀρτ.) Ἀρ, παρ(άσημον) Ἀφρο-
δίτη καὶ Ἀπόλλωṿ (ἀ̣ρ̣τ̣.) Ἀρι̣

50 ἄλλο ὑπὸ Δίδυμοṿ ἀπ̣ὸ̣ τ̣ο̣ῦ̣ Ἀρσ̣ιṿο̣ί̣τ̣ο̣ṳ χορτηγὸν
51 (ἀρτ.) Ἀιε

52 πολύκ(ωπον) ὑπὸ Πεκῦσιν Δ̣ιοṿ(υσίου?) ἀ̣π̣ὸ̣ τοῦ
Ὀξυρυγχ(ίτου)
53 ἀγ(ωγῆς) (ἀρτ.) Ἀ (ἀρτ.) Ἀρ

54 ἄλλο ὑπὸ Θώνιον Ἀγαθοῦ ἀπὸ τοῦ Ὀξυρυγχ(ίτου)
55 ἀγ(ωγῆς) (ἀρτ.) Ἀ (ἀρτ.) Ἀρλζ

56 ζευγματικὸν ὑπὸ Βελλῆ Κορνηλίου ἀπὸ τοῦ
57 Φθενότου (ἀρτ.) υβ

58 ἄλλο ὑπὸ Κοπρῆ Πάσ̣εως ἀπὸ τοῦ Διοσπολ(ίτου)
59 Κάτω (ἀρτ.) φβ

60 χορτηγὸν ὑπὸ Παρίον[α Σ]ερ̣ήνου ἀπὸ το[ῦ]
61 Ὀξυρυγχ(ίτου) ἀγ(ωγῆς) (ἀρτ.) Ἀ̣ ὅ̣λ̣α̣ι̣ (ἀρτ.) Ἀις

62 ὑπὸ Ἡράκλειο[ν κα]ὶ̣ Ἀμβρόσιον ἀπὸ τοῦ
Ὀξυρυγ[χ(ίτου)]
63 ἀγ(ωγῆς) (ἀρτ.) Ἀ (ἀρτ.) Ἀις

64 ὑπὸ Εὐφράντιον ἀπὸ τῆς Ἑλεαρχία̣ς (ἀρτ.) φ
65 ὑπὸ Παχὸ Κρονίου ἀπὸ τῆς Ἑλεαρχ(ίας) (ἀρτ.) χ

Col. iv

66 [. . .] ̣ντι μέρος δημοσίου ὑ[πὸ N.N.]
67 [ἀπὸ τοῦ] Προσωπίτου [(ἀρτ.) *n*.]

68 [ἄλλο] ὑ̣πὸ Ἰσίδωρον Θεοδώρου [ἀπὸ (ἀρτ.) *n*.]

69 [ἄλλο] ὑ̣π̣ὸ̣ Ὀ̣ν̣ν̣ώφριν Ἀλεξάνδρου ἀπὸ [(ἀρτ.) *n*.]

70 ἄλλο [ὑπ]ὸ Κόμωνα ἀπὸ τοῦ Ἄνω [(ἀρτ.) *n*.]

71 ἄλλο ὑπὸ Ἀμβρόσιον Θέωνος [ἀπὸ (ἀρτ.) *n*.]

72 [ἄλλο] ὑπὸ Ἰσίδω̣ρ̣ον Σώζοντ[ος ἀπὸ (ἀρτ.) *n*.]

73 ἄλλο ὑπὸ Κρόν̣[ιο]ν Ἀρίστωνος [ἀπὸ (ἀρτ.) *n*.]

74 ἄλλο ὑπὸ Δωρόθεον Γεμέλλου ἀ[πὸ (ἀρτ.) *n*.]

75 ἄ̣λ̣λ̣ο̣ ὑπὸ Ἰσίδω[ρ]ον Κολλούθου [ἀπὸ (ἀρτ.) *n*.]

76 ἄλλο ὑπὸ Σύρον ἀπὸ τοῦ Μετηλε[ίτου (ἀρτ.) *n*.]

77 ὑ̣πὸ Διογένην Σαραπίωνος ἀπὸ [(ἀρτ.) *n*.]

78 ὑπὸ Πετοβάσ̣τιν ἀπὸ τῆς Ἐλεα[ρχίας (ἀρτ.) *n*.]

79 ὑπὸ Παυῆ Ἀνικήτου ἀπὸ τοῦ Ὀξυ[ρυγχ(ίτου)
(ἀρτ.) *n*.]

80 ὑ̣π̣ὸ̣ Δωρ̣ό̣θ̣ε̣ο̣ν καὶ Πύθωνα̣ [ἀπὸ (ἀρτ.) *n*.]

81 ἄλλο ὑπὸ Κρονίωνα ἀπὸ Ἑρμο[ῦ πόλ(εως)]

82 ἀγ(ωγῆς) (ἀρτ.) ʹΒ, παρ(άσημον) Ἰσάριν [(ἀρτ.) *n*.]

83 ἄλλο ὑπὸ Οὔλπιον Ἀπολλώνιον [.]̣[ἀπὸ]

84 ἀγ(ωγῆς) (ἀρτ.) Ἀρν, παρ(άσημον) Ἄμμων[(ἀρτ.) *n*.]

85 ἄλλο ὑπὸ Σαλούστιον ἀ[πὸ] τοῦ Νειλ[οπολ(ίτου)
(ἀρτ.) *n*.]

86 ἄλλο ὑπὸ Ἀνουβίωνα Σιλβανοῦ ἀ[πὸ]

87 ἀγ(ωγῆς) (ἀρτ.) Ἀφν, παρ(άσημον) Ἰσ̣ά̣ριν [(ἀρτ.) *n*.]

Notes supplementary to the *ed.princ.*:

25 The run of the text in general suggests understanding an extra supplement ἄλλο, but it is not necessary to supply it in the lacuna, cf. l. 27.

29-30: For the same ship apparently, see *SB* XXIV 16270.2 (341[p]).

48. Better supply the accusative ναυκ(ληροκυβερνήτην), linking this to the name of Ἱέρακα in l. 47.

70. Probably restore ἀπὸ τοῦ Ἄνω [Κυνοπολ(ίτου) (ἀρτ.) *n*.], cf. ll. 9 and 29; within the general context of the text the alternative nome names with an element Ἄνω found in *P.Wisc.* I 10.5, Ἄνω Θεοδοσιουπολίτης, and in *P.Thmouis* I col. 92.7-8, Ἄνω Σεβεννύτης, are far less likely.

81. As there is no article τοῦ, supply Ἑρμοῦ πόλ(εως) rather than the editor's Ἑρμο[πολ(ίτου)].

(3) *P.Harr.* I 94
(Mid IV^{p})

For the date of the text, cf. N. Gonis in *ZPE* 143 (2003) 164ff. A photo is not (yet) available on the internet; the reading of line 1 appears doubtful.

1 ν λόγ(ος) ἐνη(νεγμένων?)
2 πλ(οῖον) Ἀπφοῦς Σκυβάλου
3 λ(ίτρα) α (οὐγκίαι) γ γρ(άμματα) ιε
4 πλ(οῖον) Ἀθανασίου βουλ(ευτοῦ) ὑπὸ
5 Πεκῦσιν Ἀμμωνίου κυβερ(νήτην)
6 λ(ίτρα) α (οὐγκίαι) γ γρ(άμματα) ιε
7 πλ(οῖον) Εὐδέμονος ἀκομ-
8 εντανησίου τοῦ δουκὸς ὑπὸ
9 Ἡράκλιον κυβερ(νήτην) λ(ίτρα) α (οὐγκίαι) γ γρ(άμματα) ιγ
10 πλ(οῖον) Ἀσκληπιάδου Ἀχιλλέως
11 ὑπὸ Παῦλον κυβερ(νήτην) λ(ίτρα) α (οὐγκίαι) γ γρ(άμματα) ιδ
12 πλ(οῖον) Ἀπολλωνίου υἱοῦ Διονυ-
13 σίου ἐπισκόπου ὑπὸ Ἀμμώ-
14 νιον κυβερ(νήτην) λ(ίτρα) α (οὐγκίαι) γ γρ(άμματα) ιε
15 πλ(οῖον) Γεσσίου καὶ Ῥωμανᾶ
16 ὑπὸ Θεόδωρον κυβερ(νήτην) λ(ίτρα) α (οὐγκίαι) γ γρ(άμματα) ιδ
17 πλ(οῖον) Ἄμμωνος πρεσβυτέρου

18 ναυκληροκυβερ(νήτου) λ(ίτρα) α (οὐγκίαι) γ
γρ(άμματα) ιδ

1 l. ἐνενηγμένων 2 l. Ἀπφοῦτος 7-8 l. Ευδαίμονος ἀκομενταρησίου

(4) *P.Oxy*. VII 1048

(After 392^{p})

NB: the marginalia are not copied here; the date is 'after 392^{p}', cf. the date of the text on the recto, *P.Oxy*. VII 1033. *BL* 8:240 refers for the general format of this text to *P.Col*. VII, p. 103. A photo is not available on the internet.

1 Βρ(εούιον)
2 / λουσωρ(ία) Πακίου πολ(ιτευομένου) ὑπὸ Θεόδωρον Παρὶτ (ἀρτ.) ωκγ
3 / πλ(οῖον) τοῦ αὐτοῦ ὑπὸ Εὐδαίμονα Σαραπᾶ (ἀρτ.) υιεL
4 / πλ(οῖον) Ἀετίου πολ(ιτευομένου) ὑπὸ Τιμόθεον Κιχῦτος (ἀρτ.) ͵Βχκ
5 / πλ(οῖον) Ἀθανασίου πο̣λ̣(ιτευομένου) ὑπὸ Πλούταρχον Πανίω(νος?) (ἀρτ.) ͵Γχλ
6 / πλ(οῖον) τοῦ αὐτοῦ ὑπὸ Ἀλέξανδρον Κοπρέως (ἀρτ.) ͵δυιζ
7 / λουσωρ(ία) Σατορνίλου λαμ(προτάτου?) ὑπὸ Νεμεσίωνα δ̣ι̣(ὰ) Π̣α̣ῶ̣τος (ἀρτ.) ͵Βυξε

8 (M. 2?) πλ(οῖον) Σατορνίλου λαμ(προτάτου) ὑπὸ
Ἀλέξα ̣ρον Διδ̣ύ̣μου (ἀρτ.) ψοζL
9 κριθῶν (ἀρτ.) ͵Αψνβ
10 πλ(οῖον) Οὐαλερίου πολ(ιτευομένου) ὑπ<ὸ Π>α̣ῦ̣λον
Σαραπίωνος (ἀρτ.) ͵Βρνζ
11 Μακροβίου πλ(οῖον) ὑπὸ Θέ<ω>να Ἀγάθου
(ἀρτ.) ψηL
12 καὶ πέμπτης (ἀρτ.) ωβL
13 ἄλλαι τῆς ι̣( ) εS ̣ην (ἀρτ.) λβ
14 Μακροβίου πλ(οῖον) ὑπὸ Δίδυμον Πλᾶ
(ἀρτ.) ͵Ατλϛ
15 Λευκαδίου πλ(οῖον) ὑπὸ Ἀπφοῦς Εὐδαίμονος
(ἀρτ.) τηL

8 l. Ἀλέξανδρον, δυ of διδυμου corr. 15 l. Ἀπφοῦν

(5) *P.Heid.* IV 313
(Early V[p])

A photo is available on the internet via the website www.papyri.info

---

1 [
λα]μπροτατ̣[
2 [ ] ̣ κ̣αὶ Ἡρακλ̣[
3 [ ] Ἱ̣έρακος βουλευτῶν ̣ ̣[
4 [ ] ̣[̣] ̣[̣] ̣ς εἰς τὰ ἑξῆς <π>λοῖα

5 [ ] ̣ ̣ ̣ ̣[

6 [ ] ̣ω

7 [ ] ̣ οὕτως Δ ̣ ̣ ̣[

8 [π]λ(οῖον) ̣[̣ ̣ ̣ ̣ ̣ ̣] ̣ ὑπὸ Ἠλίαν Ἀνικήτου (ἀρτ.) /Βυκ̣[

9 πλ(οῖον) ̣[̣ ̣ ̣ ̣ ̣ πο]λ(ιτευομένου) ὑπὸ Φοιβάμμωνα
Ὀννωφ̣ρίου (ἀρτ.) χ̣ ̣[

10 πλ(οῖον) Ἡσυχίου ναυάρχου ὑπὸ Ἰωάννην Μακαρίου
(ἀρτ.) φξε̣[

11 [πλ](οῖον) Ἀετίου ναυάρχου ὑπὸ Παῆσιν Μιυσίου
(ἀρτ.) ωοδ[

12 [πλ](οῖον) Πτολεμίνου ἐξάκτορ(ος) ὑπὸ Μαξέντιον
Παμουτίου (ἀρτ.) /Γ⁊ ̣[

13 [πλ](οῖον) Σατορνίλου λα(μπροτάτου) ὑπὸ Ἀνουβί-
ωνα Ἑρμῆτος (ἀρτ.) /Βχν̣[

14 [πλ](οῖον) Δ̣ι̣οσκουρίδου πολ(ιτευομένου) ὑπὸ Θέωνα
Ἀγάθου (ἀρτ.) /ΒριβL´[

15 [πλ](οῖον) Θεοφίλου λαμ(προτάτου) ὑπὸ Θέωνα
Ἀγάθου (ἀρτ.) /Β⁊μθ[

16 πλ(οῖον) Διοσκουρίδου πολ(ιτευομένου) ὑπὸ Ἄριον
Παύλου (ἀρτ.) /Βτκδ[

17 πλ(οῖον) Τατιανοῦ πολ(ιτευομένου) ὑπὸ Παῦλον
Σαραπίωνος (ἀρτ.) /Βωοζ

18 πλ(οῖον) Εὐηθίου ἐξάκτορ(ος) ὑπὸ Ἀρεώτην
Πανχαρίου (ἀρτ.) ωπς

(6) *P.Heid.* IV 314
(Early V^p^)

For this text, cf. now *BL* 9:103-104. A photo is available on the internet via the website www.papyri.info.

1] ̣ ̣
2 Εὐήθιος πολ(ιτευόμενος) ̣[
3 Ἱερ[α]κίων πολ(ιτευόμενος) ̣[
4 Πτολ[ε]μ̣ε̂νος σί(του) κ[αθαροῦ ἀρτάβας]
5 ἑκατὸ̣ν εὐδεύκο̣τα, γί(ν.) σίτου [καθ(αροῦ (ἀρτ.) ρπ]
6 Στρατήγιος πολ(ιτευόμενος) ̣ ̣[̣ ̣] ̣ ̣[
7 Τατιανὸς πολ(ιτευόμενος) ̣ ̣[

(7) *P.Wisc.* II 65: a Re-edition
(V^p^)

Line 11 of the *ed.princ.* was already corrected in *BL* 7:282. The reconstruction and interpretation of this text from Oxyrhynchus can be improved further on the basis of some of the texts published earlier in this volume. They suggest the following newly restored version of the text (a photo of this is available on the internet via the website www.papyri.info):

---

1 ἀπὸ τῆς μεγάλης [Ἑρμοῦ πόλεως κυβερνήτης πλοίου τῆς]
2 κυρίας Αὐρηλίῳ [........................ ἀπὸ τῆς]
3 Ὀ̣ξ̣υ̣ρ̣υγχιτῶν [πόλεως χαίρειν. ὁμολογῶ παρειλη-]

4 φ̣έναι παρὰ σοῦ καὶ ἐ̣[μβεβλῆσθαι εἰς τὸ προκεί-
μενον πλοῖον]
5 ἐν ὅρμῳ̣ τῆς Ὀξ̣υρυ̣[γχιτῶν πόλεως σίτου? ἀρτάβας
χιλίας?]
6 δεκαπέντε ναύλου αὐτῶν χρυ̣[σοῦ νομισμάτια *n*,]
7 ἐπὶ τῷ̣ με τὸν γόμον ἀποκομίσε̣ [εἰς τὴν λαμπρο-
τάτην Ἀλεξάν]-
8 δρειαν καὶ παραδοῦναί σοι ἄδολ[ον καθαρὸν ἀκα-
κούργητον]
9 ἀπὸ πάσης ναυτικῆς κακουργίας .[.................. καὶ]
10 ἅμα τῇ̣ ἀπογομώσι λαβῖν με παρ[ὰ σοῦ τὰ προ-
κ(είμενα) νομισμάτια. Κυρία]
11 ἡ ναυλωτικὴ κ[αὶ] ἐπερωτηθε[ὶς ὡμολόγησα].
12 Αὐρήλιος Κολλοῦθος Πάτος [c 20]
13 [.]....ιπ..κα[c 30]

---

7 l. ἀποκομίσαι 10 l. ἀπογομώσει, λαβεῖν

"--- from the great Hermopolis, boatman of a ship of the Lady, to Aurelius N.N. from the city of the Oxyrhynchites, greetings. I acknowledge having received from you and having put on board the aforesaid ship in the harbour of the city of the Oxyrhynchites one thousand(?) fifteen artabas of wheat (?), the freight thereof being [n] golden *solidi*, on condition that I will transport the cargo to the most illustrious (city of) Alexandria and will deliver it to you unadulterated, pure and undamaged by any nautical damage --- and that I receive at the moment of the unloading from you the aforementioned *solidi*. The contract is authoritative and in answer to the formal question I have given my consent. I, Aurelius Kollouthos, son of Pas, ----"

In this reconstruction, a contract is drawn up in Oxyrhynchus between
(1) a boatman originating from Hermopolis who is captain of a boat of 'the Lady' (ll. 1-2) and
(2) a local inhabitant of Oxyrhynchus whose precise name and status are lost but who may have been a town councillor and curator of wheat / barley for Alexandria (ll. 2-3). The contract concerns the transport of a cargo (precise amount unknown, cf. below at l. 5) from the harbour of Oxyrhynchus (l. 5) to Alexandria (ll. 7-8), for a fee expressed in terms of an unknown number of gold solidi (l. 6; cf. also l. 11n.). It is remarkable that ll. 8-9 contain a clause concerning fraud that is not found also in the Michigan texts. This phenomenon may be explicable in terms of a later development (cf. the date of the Wisconsin text). For similar receipts, see, e.g., *P.Oxy.* LXII 4346; *SB* XXIV 16270-16271 (all from the 4th century C.E.).

1. In indications of a person's origin, the qualification μεγάλης seems especially applicable to Hermopolis, though it is true that in *CPR* X 39.6 one finds a person originating ἀ̣π̣[ὸ τ]ῆς μεγά̣λ̣ης πόλεως Ἀλεξ[ανδρείας].

Given the entire context of the document one expects after the provenance of the contracting person a qualification of this person as a boatman (κυβερνήτης), followed by an indication of the ship (πλοίου) on which he served, and its owner.

1-2. A ship 'of the lady' seems unattested elsewhere, but for the proposed restoration there does not seem to be much of an alternative.

2. The lacuna held the name of the second contracting party and his office or profession. One may restore, e.g. βουλευτῇ (or an abbreviation) τῆς].

4. For the restoration of προκείμενον, cf. **808**.8, **813**.10 (and restored in its copy **814**.8; the same participle is also restored in **800**.10, **804**.9, and **815**.7); the alternative, slightly longer restoration is προτεταγμένον, cf. **809**.8 and its copy **810**.8-9. Of course, in order to fit the size of the lacuna (ca. 30 letters in total), the latter term may have been written in abbreviation.

5. The cargo may have been a number of artabas of barley (κριθή) rather than of wheat (σῖτος). Furthermore, in view of the available space a restoration of the numeral at the end of the line as a form of -κοσίας rather than χιλίας seems less likely. For precisely such an amount of 1,015 artabas mentioned in a similar, but much earlier contract, cf. **809** and its copy **810**.

7. For the ἐπὶ τῷ με + inf. construction, cf. **804**.11, **806**.9, and **811**.9.

The first editor read ἀποκομίσ̣ε̣[σθαι εἰς τὴν λαμπρ(οτάτην) Ἀλεξάν-], but in such contracts the use of the active, rather than the middle is normal. In order to fill the lacuna one may expand the abbreviated λαμπρ(οτάτην) into λαμπροτάτην.

8. In order to fit into the general context, σοι (apparently referring to the inhabitant of Oxyrhynchus) can be taken as a *dativus commodi*. After all, this παραδοῦναι-clause concerns the delivery of the cargo to the officials at Alexandria and it seems unlikely that the Oxyrhynchite man ordering the transport of this cargo was waiting there for the cargo to arrive. It may be, however, that one is dealing here with the product of a confused writer and that σοι should simply be cancelled, i.e. placed between { }.

9. It is at least conceivable that after ἀπὸ πάσης ναυτικῆς κακουργίας the lacuna should be further filled by a restoration of χωρὶς θεοῦ βίας; for the same combination of provisions, cf. *T.Varie* 3.9.

12. Probably Kollouthos was the name of the boatman who concluded the contract and subscribes here.

INDICES

1. Consulates and Postconsulates

2. Months and Days

3. Indictions

4. Emperors, Imperial Oaths

5. Personal names

6. Geographical names

Τεξεί (κώμη)	**826**.28
Φοβώου κώμη	**811**.5
Ψάμμιδος ἐποίκιον	**816**.38
.[ ]εννω	**816**.40 (see note ad loc.)
[N.N. π]όλις	**804**.4
δ πάγος	**826**.30
ε πάγος	**809**.31
ζ πάγος	**826**.28

7. Government officials, soldiers

ἀννουμέρις (for -νούμερος?)	**807**.8
ἀπὸ λογιστῶν	**802**.4, **815**.3/4
ἀπὸ πραιποσίτων	**806**.5
ἀπὸ πριμικηρίου	**820**.18
ἀπὸ πριμιπιλαρίου	**808**.5, **820**.9
βενεφικιάριος	**802**.14n.
βοηθός	**816**.23
βοηθὸς διακεντήσεως	**816**.13
βοηθὸς ἐξακτορίας	**806**.3
βουλευτής	**800**.4,8, **801**.2, **802**.5, **803**.4, **805**.5, **807**.6, **808**.3, **809**.3, **810**.3, **811**.3, **813**.3, **814**.3, **815**.2, **818**.3, 6
διαψηφιστής	**812**.16
δοῦξ	**807**.9
ἔναρχος πρύτανις	**800**.8

8. Professions, Clergy

11. Nomina & verba defectiva